MACKENZIE KING

CITIZENSHIP AND COMMUNITY

Rt. Hon. W.L. Mackenzie King, photographed in Ottawa by Yousuf Karsh in 1941. (Photo by Karsh/National Archives of Canada PA-164304)

Mackenzie King

CITIZENSHIP AND COMMUNITY

Essays Marking the 125th Anniversary
of the Birth of William Lyon Mackenzie King

Edited by John English, Kenneth McLaughlin
and P. Whitney Lackenbauer

ROBIN BRASS STUDIO
Toronto

Published 2002 by
Robin Brass Studio Inc.,
10 Blantyre Avenue, Toronto, Ontario M1N 2R4, Canada
Fax: 416-698-2120 • www.rbstudiobooks.com

Printed and bound in Canada by AGMV-Marquis, Cap-Saint-Ignace, Quebec

The publisher is grateful to Colin Glassco for permission to reprint drawings by Ivan Glassco from *Bigwigs: Canadians Wise and Otherwise* by R.T.L. (Charles Vining), Toronto, Macmillan, 1935.

National Library of Canada Cataloguing in Publication

Mackenzie King : citizenship and community : essays marking the 125th anniversary of the birth of William Lyon Mackenzie King / edited by John English, Kenneth McLaughlin and P. Whitney Lackenbauer.

Includes bibliographical references and index.
ISBN 1-896941-29-X

1. King, William Lyon Mackenzie, 1874-1950. 2. Prime ministers – Canada – Biography. 3. Canada – Politics and government – 1935-1948. I. English, John, 1945- II. McLaughlin, Kenneth, 1943- III. Lackenbauer, P. Whitney IV. Title.

FC581.K5M245 2002   971.062'2'092   C2002-904489-8
F1033.K53M245 2002

*Publication of this book has been supported by a grant
from the Millennium Bureau of Canada.*

Contents

Preface

John English, Kenneth McLaughlin and P. Whitney Lackenbauer

In 1999 the Department of History at the University of Waterloo sponsored a conference on the occasion of the 125th anniversary of the birth of William Lyon Mackenzie King, a three-time prime minister of Canada. King was born on December 17, 1874, in Berlin, Ontario, a town that was unusual in Victorian Ontario: its population was largely German in origin and mixed in religion. His father, John King, was a lawyer with strong political interests; his mother, Isabel, was the daughter of William Lyon Mackenzie, the leader of the 1837 rebellion in Upper Canada.

After being educated in local public schools, Mackenzie King attended the universities of Toronto, Chicago, and Harvard. He entered Canadian politics in 1908 as the member of Parliament for North Waterloo, the constituency where he was born. In 1911, however, he was defeated. In later elections, he chose other constituencies, although he kept personal ties with many of his old friends in Waterloo County.

This book reflects its origins: a community event in Waterloo Region that involved the University of Waterloo, the region's secondary schools, the Waterloo Historical Society, the Kitchener-Waterloo Multicultural Council, scholars across the country, and Woodside, the national historic site that honours King's early years in Waterloo County. The schools King attended, Suddaby school and the Berlin (now the Kitchener) Collegiate Institute, still educate Waterloo Region's youth. His church, St. Andrew's, endures. The streets where he walked and played retain their Victorian names: King, Queen, Victoria, and Wellington. A sense of King's community enlivens and pervades this book; yet so much has changed. Those changes in community and citizenship, and King's perceptions of and influence upon them, are the subject of this book.

The opening paper by National Archivist Ian Wilson discusses what King thought about the past and its records. In a lively paper that introduces fascinating material on

Mr. Wilson's distinguished predecessor Arthur Doughty, Wilson reveals King's at‐
tention to the archives and its collections. Wilson points out that even though
King's sense of mission and history was well developed, he wanted to destroy large
parts of his diary and papers. That destruction did not occur, and the King Papers
are a remarkable collection, one of the finest of any head of state of any nation.

Ulrich Frisse studied for his doctorate at Philipps-University in Marburg, Ger‐
many, and he is the first scholar to undertake a detailed study of King's links with
the German community in Berlin, Ontario. His important essay explores the im‐
pact of the unusual community in which King matured upon his later political
attitudes. Frisse details for the first time the close ties that King forged with Ber‐
lin's German population and reveals how much these ties influenced King's dis‐
tance from the British imperialist fervour of Victorian and Edwardian Canada.

rych mills's paper on King and Victoria Park complements Frisse's work on
King's youth in Berlin. Based upon careful research, mills describes how the new
park became the focal point of civic life in turn-of-the-century Berlin. As a Berlin
politician, King used the park for his major political rallies, where he confronted
his opponents and convinced the local audiences of his talents, which included
speaking German. The importance of ethnic support — if that term can be ap‐
plied to Germans in Berlin — was fundamental, and King surely took a lesson
from his early experience.

Geoffrey Hayes, of the University of Waterloo, recognizes that Waterloo
County and its German character influenced King but argues that King and oth‐
ers have created a myth about his life here. That life was neither so idyllic as King
imagined in his last years nor so free from defeats and disappointments as some
histories suggest. The King family had also been mired in major controversies that
brought some shame upon the family. Perhaps King's distance from his home‐
town in his prime ministerial years was not so much the product of the disap‐
pointment arising from his political defeat as a reflection of the economic and
political failures of his family in Waterloo County.

Bill Waiser looks at King and the Regina Riot of 1935. He argues that King was
unimaginative and unresponsive to the riot of the unemployed in Regina. Believ‐
ing that the Bennett government was collapsing, King took a conservative course,
one that did not support the demands of the workers. King, who instinctively
avoided conflict, did not support his Liberal counterparts in denouncing the
harsh response in Regina in 1935.

Robert Wardhaugh, the author of a recent study of King and the West, explores the reaction of J.W. Dafoe, the distinguished editor of the *Winnipeg Free Press*, to King and his policies. Wardhaugh recognizes that the problems of the Liberal Party in western Canada far antedate Lester Pearson and Pierre Trudeau. Dafoe was an early skeptic about the leadership of Mackenzie King; yet Wardhaugh demonstrates that Dafoe eventually came to assess King's leadership favourably, albeit grudgingly. King, like other leaders, dwelt upon the national unity questions that meant so much to vote-rich Ontario and Quebec, but he did convince Dafoe by the 1940s that others could not have done better.

Stephanie Bangarth takes the reader to British Columbia and King's interest in the so-called "Oriental question." She explains that King reflected his times in his attitude toward Asians and finds important clues in King's earlier attitudes that may explain why he reached the decision in early 1942 that Japanese Canadians should be removed from the West Coast and, in some cases, interned.

Galen Perras also concentrates on King's policies in the West, particularly his approach to the war in the Pacific. Perras demonstrates how cautious King was when confronted with demands that Canada become more deeply involved in the Pacific war. Although British Columbia strongly supported such involvement, King was extremely hesitant. In this richly detailed paper Perras demonstrates that Ottawa was far away from the Pacific in the war years.

Whitney Lackenbauer examines King's attitudes toward Arctic sovereignty questions. Drawing upon extensive archival research, Lackenbauer demonstrates that King did protect Canadian sovereignty in the north, that he was always cautious, that he was often pessimistic, and that he evaded confrontation. Still, King tried to ensure that "his colleagues did not become too comfortable with the bilateral embrace, even when military officials were stressing expediency."

Jim Struthers, the leading historian of Canadian social welfare programs in the twentieth century, finds consistency in King's caution and in the approach of later governments. He concludes that the needs of Canadian men, women, and children were never the major consideration in the minds of most politicians. The introduction of family allowances, an important social program in the 1940s, was an initiative to deal with inflation worries and the "threat" from the Left rather than a carefully considered approach to income redistribution and child poverty.

Kenneth Westhues, a sociologist, argues that King was Canada's first significant sociologist. King's attraction to sociology, a fresh subject in North American universities at the turn of the twentieth century, is, in Westhues's opinion, fundamental to understanding some of the practical choices he later made. Why, Westhues asks, did King pursue studies in such a fresh field, one so different from the classical approaches so characteristic of Canadian universities of the time?

These essays consider what citizenship has meant in Canada and what Mackenzie King's unique contribution to that debate has been. This book explores how King was very much the product of the community where he spent his early years and indicates how those experiences may have influenced his later career.

The photographs and cartoons and their placement have been chosen by the editors of the book.

The conference and this book reflect the work of many at Waterloo. Lena Yost, the major conference organizer, did an outstanding job, expertly coordinating myriad details. Irene Majer and Nancy Birss of the University of Waterloo's Department of History most ably assisted her. The organizing committee of the conference was extremely important in making the conference an event in which the community was deeply involved. We would like to thank Kim Seward-Hannam and Rob Rowe of Woodside National Historic Park, Myrta Rivera of the Kitchener-Waterloo Multicultural Council, Klaudios Mustakas of the Department of Citizenship and Immigration, two wonderful special librarian-archivists: Susan Bellingham of the Doris Lewis Rare Book Room at the University of Waterloo and Susan Hoffman of the Grace Schmidt Room at the Kitchener Public Library, Andrew Telegdi, M.P., and our colleagues in the Department of History at the University of Waterloo.

This project was supported by assistance from the university's Department of History, Woodside, and the Millennium Bureau of Canada. Speakers and participants from across Canada joined us to discuss the legacy of William Lyon Mackenzie King. It was an interesting and insightful debate, and we are deeply grateful to all of those who now share our fascination with the constant evolution of Canadian society. David Wright, then the chair of the Department of History, encouraged us, supported the conference financially, and attended its sessions. His premature death shortly after the conference saddened us all. We remember him fondly and miss his wonderful wit and great generosity of spirit.

The Editors, Waterloo, Ontario, April 2002

About the Contributors

John English is a Professor of History at the University of Waterloo. He and Ken McLaughlin are co-authors of *Kitchener: An Illustrated History*. He is co-editor of *Mackenzie King: Widening the Debate* and has also written a two-volume biography of Lester Pearson.

Kenneth McLaughlin is Professor of History at St. Jerome's University in the University of Waterloo, where he was formerly Vice-President and Academic Dean. He has published extensively in Canadian history and is especially interested in the relationship between community identity and national interests. He has also been an advisor to the government on museum policies for Canada and is currently director of the University of Waterloo's Public History Program; he is also the Associate Chair, Graduate in the Department of History and Director of the Tri-University (Waterloo, Laurier, Guelph) Graduate Program in history.

P. Whitney Lackenbauer was identified by Maclean's magazine in January 2000 as "one of 100 Canadians to watch for." He is a graduate of the University of Waterloo and a research associate with the Centre for Military and Strategic Studies at the University of Calgary, where he is also enrolled in the Ph.D. program. He has been awarded a Killam Memorial Scholarship and is the recipient of an SSHRC Queen's Fellowship.

Ian Wilson is National Archivist of Canada and a member of the Order of Canada. He previously served as Archivist of Ontario and Provincial Archivist for Saskatchewan.

Ulrich Frisse is completing a Doctorate on German Settlements in Canada, particularly Berlin–Kitchener in Ontario, and Lunenburg in Nova Scotia. He is a student at Marburg University in Germany, and was a visiting graduate student at Memorial University in St. John's, Newfoundland.

rych mills has attended the University of Waterloo and is a well known expert in the local history of Waterloo County. He is a director of the Waterloo Historical Society and Victoria Park Historical Committee and the author of several books and articles relating to the history of Berlin/Kitchener. His new book on Kitchener's history, *Kitchener 1880-1960,* was released in September 2002.

Geoffrey Hayes is Associate Professor of History at the University of Waterloo. He is the author of the award-winning *Waterloo County: An Illustrated History* and is currently working on a study of the formation of the Canadian officer corps in World War Two.

William (Bill) Waiser is Professor of History at the University of Saskatchewan. He has served on the council of the Canadian Historical Association and is a board member of Canada's National History Society. He is the author of *Loyal Till Death* and several other books.

Robert Wardhaugh has edited *Towards Defining the Prairies* and has recently published *Mackenzie King and the Prairie West.* He recently joined the University of Regina.

Stephanie Bangarth is currently a doctoral candidate in the Department of History at the University of Waterloo. Her dissertation, "The politics of human rights: Canadian and American advocacy groups and the 'defence' of the internment of North America's citizens of Japanese ancestry," employs a case-study approach to explore the roots of human rights advocacy in North America. She received a Fulbright Scholarship in 2000-2001 and a Princeton University Library Fellowship to conduct research for this comparative study.

Galen Perras has an M.A. in War Studies from RMC and a Ph.D. in Canadian and American history from the University of Waterloo. His first book, *Franklin Roosevelt and the Origins of the Canadian Security Alliance, 1933-1945: Necessary But Not Necessary Enough,* was published by Praeger in 1998. His second book, *Stepping Stones to Nowhere: The Aleutian Islands, Alaska, and American Military Strategy, 1867-1945,* will be published by UBC Press in 2003. Dr. Perras, who has taught at several Canadian universities, is currently employed at the National Archives of Canada.

James Struthers is Professor and Chair of Canadian Studies at Trent University in Peterborough. He is the author of *The Limits of Affluence: Welfare in Ontario 1920-1970* (University of Toronto Press, 1994). He is also author of another book on the history of the Canadian welfare state, *No Fault of Their Own: Unemployment and the Canadian Welfare State, 1914-1941* (University of Toronto Press, 1983). He teaches courses on Canadian community identities and Canadian social policy.

Kenneth Westhues is Professor of Sociology at the University of Waterloo. He teaches courses on the sociology of work as well as that of demographics and social change in Canada. He is the author of numerous books and articles in journals, including *The Working Centre: Experiment in Social Change* (Working Centre Publications, 1995), and *In Search of Community: Essays in Memory of Werner Stark,* edited jointly with Eillen Leonard, Vassar College, and Hermann Strasser, Universitt Duisberg (Fordham University Press, 1993).

Caricature of William Lyon Mackenzie King by Ivan Glassco from *Bigwigs: Canadians Wise and Otherwise* by R.T.L. (Charles Vining). The acerbic Charles Vining wrote of King in August 1934:

> He does not mind being Leader of the Opposition because it gives him more time to work on his memoirs.
>
> He would, however, like to have a few more years as Prime Minister in order to give the book a happier ending and intends to manage this as soon as he is sure the depression is over. ...
>
> Most of his best speeches to date have been those delivered with an emotional spontaneity born of necessity, and his poorest have usually been the most elaborately prepared. ...
>
> He has a hearty laugh, but hardly a proportionate sense of humour. ...
>
> He has a tendency to procrastinate until a crisis is upon him and he then improvises under fire with a skill which sometimes has transported his followers from desperation to delight. ...
>
> He has a genius for detecting the approach of trouble and an equal talent for avoiding it. ...
>
> To visitors at Laurier House he is a solicitous and generous host and takes a justifiable pride in his top floor library, where he would spend all his time if he did not have to bother about his career. ...

1

"One of the Closest and Truest of Friends I Have Ever Had":

Mackenzie King, Arthur Doughty, and the Public Archives of Canada

Ian E. Wilson

Every biographer of Mackenzie King examines King's friendship with Bert Harper, a fellow student and later civil servant with whom King shared rooms, an interest in the Arthurian legend and the poetry of Alfred Lord Tennyson, and a commitment to the Victorian ideal of the chivalrous gentleman. It was King who led the campaign to commemorate Harper's heroic and tragic death in 1901 with a statue of Sir Galahad, now located on Wellington Street in front of the Parliament Buildings in Ottawa. The Arthurian legends, notes King biographer Joy Esberey, "were more than just a story to Mackenzie King. They represented an ideal which he sought to recreate in twentieth-century Canada."[1] King longed to be a "knight" himself. Bert Harper was not the only friend who shared these ideals; there was another with whom King shared similar interests: Arthur George Doughty.

At first glance Mackenzie King and Arthur Doughty were very different, in age, background, and station in life. The details of King's life are well known to those who have studied almost any aspect of Canadian history touching on the first half of the twentieth century. Doughty was senior to King by fourteen years, an emigrant from England in the 1880s, a writer and romantic as comfortable in the storage areas of the archives as King was in the corridors of power on Parliament Hill.

In spite of their dissimilarities, both King and Doughty had considered a career in the church, and both were involved in social work as young men: King at Hull House in Chicago, Doughty at All Hallows Mission in London. Both men were cultured and refined in the Victorian sense; they were well read and broadly educated. Both King and Doughty held the rank of deputy minister in the Laurier government; indeed, both of them knew the prime minister personally. They met and socialized frequently, and for several years prior to the First World War, King was a regular visitor to the Public Archives. Following the war and King's return to Ottawa, first as leader of the Opposition and then prime minister, the two men renewed and deepened their friendship.

In a relationship that lasted some thirty years, their careers often crossed. Each had a sense of the past that came to bear on that relationship; it provided a common ground, a true meeting of minds. From Doughty, King learned the value of archives, the need to preserve documents and to make them available for research purposes. Over the course of his long life King created an invaluable archive of his own, one that is safely preserved in the house that Arthur Doughty built, now known as the National Archives of Canada.

King was well versed in history and valued historical knowledge as a key element in the creation of a national consciousness, if not a national consensus. In other ways, his use of history was very personal; he was conscious of his familial connections to William Lyon Mackenzie as well as his own personal place in history as participant and observer. For thirty years as dominion archivist, Doughty was consumed by archives and history; he dedicated his career to the archival record, ensuring that a national history could be written by collecting the documents necessary for the task.

King and Doughty had a personal and professional relationship, but more than this, the dominion archivist was the head of an institution that for many years was the only national cultural institution of note in Ottawa. When Mackenzie King thought about culture in the 1920s he inevitably thought about his friend and confidant Arthur Doughty and the Public Archives of Canada. Federal government involvement in Canada's cultural landscape of Canada during the interwar years left much to be desired, but the Public Archives, established in Ottawa in the 1870s, partially filled that void.[2]

Arthur Doughty, at work in his office with his secretary. (National Archives of Canada C-11602)

Although King was conscious of and interested in cultural activity in Canada, he was unlikely to offer public funds in support of the arts. But the Public Archives of Canada resonated well with his personal sense of history: he understood the work of the Public Archives, and he believed that it had a role to play in fostering national consciousness and a sense of history. During King's years in Ottawa the Public Archives thrived, growing from a few basement rooms in the Langevin Block in 1904 to a well-designed and modern building on Sussex Drive in 1907. By the mid-1920s it was an institution that combined the functions of an archives, a library, and a museum. At the time Canada had no national library or museum, while the Public Archives, taking a holistic approach to documenting and presenting the Canadian past, had acquired a vast array of documents, art work, and artifacts. The main-floor exhibition rooms displayed documents, books, art, maps, flags, Sir Isaac Brock's uniform, the Duberger model of Quebec, General James Wolfe's chair, the French Royal Arms taken from above the gate of Quebec in 1759, and countless other items acquired by the Public Archives since its establishment in the 1870s. The

Public Archives was popular with tourists and visitors to the capital, and by the 1920s was a magnet for a growing number of academics interested in the study of Canadian history. When the English novelist Mary Augusta Ward visited Ottawa in 1908 she commented that the "Archives represent the birth and future of Canadian history, and a Canadian patriotism … and already it is influencing ideas and politics, among a young people who did not know they *had* a history."[3] King often acknowledged the value of archives; in November 1923, speaking at the inaugural meeting of the Canadian History Society in London, England, he argued that archival collections "served to throw a flood light on the history of the country."[4]

Arthur George Doughty, Canada's second dominion archivist, was born on March 22, 1860, at Maidenhead, England. He was educated locally and in London, and in 1884 he spent two or three months at Oxford University. He considered the Anglican priesthood in the early 1880s and for a time worked at the All Hallows Mission at Southwark in London. But in June 1886 he emigrated to Canada and settled in Montreal.

Doughty was young, intelligent, charming, and bilingual. He soon found employment at the Legal and Commercial Exchange for the next eight or nine years, but his first love was literature, theatre, and the arts in general. In his spare time, he wrote drama reviews for the Montreal *Gazette* and pursued a personal interest in Alfred, Lord Tennyson. In 1889 Doughty self-published *The Idylls of a King by Alfred, Lord Tennyson* (in shorthand) and followed this in 1893 with a biography, *Tennyson: His Life and Work*. He wrote poetry, a libretto for a comic opera, songs, and reviews.

In 1895 Doughty worked briefly at the Post Office in Montreal, and in the following year he was employed by Quebec's inland revenue department. Between 1896 and 1899 he was private secretary to the province's minister of public works and the provincial treasurer. In 1899, at the insistence of Felix Gabriel Marchand, premier of Quebec, Doughty embarked on an ambitious history of the fall of Quebec in 1759. Two years later, with financial assistance from Charles Fitzpatrick, the federal minister of justice, Doughty collaborated with G.W. Parmelee and published, in six elaborate volumes, *The Siege of Quebec and the Battle of the Plains of Abraham*. Doughty's work was well received, earning him an honorary degree from Laval University in 1901 and appointment as joint librarian of Quebec's legislative library. With fellow librarian, N-E. Dionne, he subsequently produced in 1903 a two-volume history, *Quebec Under Two Flags: A Brief*

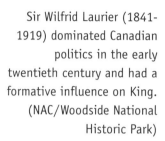

Sir Wilfrid Laurier (1841-1919) dominated Canadian politics in the early twentieth century and had a formative influence on King. (NAC/Woodside National Historic Park)

History of the City from its Foundation to the Present Time. Doughty also had political connections with the Liberal Party in Quebec, and in the fall of 1903, almost a full year after the death of Douglas Brymner, Canada's first dominion archivist, Doughty was offered the position; he held out for better terms and finally accepted a government offer in the spring of the following year. On May 16, 1904, Arthur Doughty was formally appointed dominion archivist and keeper of the records.

In the next thirty years Doughty put his personal imprint on the development of the Public Archives of Canada, in the process transforming it from a small, almost hidden repository in the Langevin Block to an institution of national cultural significance. He was personally responsible for expanding the role of the Public Archives, increasing staff and budgets, and adding to the collections. Doughty succeeded in linking the discovery, preservation, and opening of original documentary evidence to the government's political desire for national cohesion and harmony. The emergence of the "scientific" approach to historical research and historiography, national in scope and founded on the dispassionate, non-partisan examination of all historical documents, would end the divisive regional approaches to the past and provide a common historical basis and understanding of the new Dominion of Canada – or so a whole generation of scholars, Doughty included, confidently expected. The Public Archives, with its active programs of acquisition, exhibition, publication, and assistance to the research community, embodied the cultural policy of the Laurier era and provided the cultural equivalent, at times explicit, of the economic policies known as the National Policy. Similarly, during the First World War Doughty's keen interest in acquiring war trophies and preserving war records and art was closely tied with Canada's sense of national identity as fostered by Prime Minister Robert Borden and won on the battlefields of France.

The emergence of "scientific" history in the nineteenth century, most often associated with the work of the German historian Leopold von Ranke, the influence of the positivists, and the concept of "ultimate" history proposed by Lord Acton, were all closely allied to the potent forces of nationalism and liberalism; the establishment of state-run public archival repositories all across Europe followed in their train. Impressed by the dramatic opening of Italian archives following the war of 1859, Acton felt that it was the overthrow of governments that led to the opening of archives. Major political upheavals were required, and he characterized historical study "not only as a voyage of discovery" but also as a "struggle" with "men in authority" who had a "strong desire to hide the truth." The link between the study of history and nationalism was generally accepted by nineteenth-century liberals. Providing access to archival records for the study of the collective past of the nation was one indication of a government's interest in fostering the evolution of a national consciousness. John Stuart Mill emphasized this connection by stressing that the strongest factor generating a sense of nationality was the "identity of political antecedents; the possession of a national history, and consequent recollections; collective pride and humiliation, pleasure and regret, connected with the same incidents in the past."[5]

In the Canadian context Mill's views were shared by politicians and public figures intent on moulding a nation out of disparate sectional interests and rivalries. Two years before Confederation, D'Arcy McGee had voiced the opinion of many of his contemporaries when he said: "Patriotism will increase in Canada as its history is read."[6] Sixty years later Mackenzie King reaffirmed this faith in the value of history when he told schoolchildren: "You have inherited a great past, endeavour to be worthy of it and remember above all things that history is not only the guiding light, the pillar, history is not only the foundation stone of patriotism – history carries with it the title deeds of nationalism itself."[7]

History, national in scope and patriotic in character, was expected to provide both the spirit and the justification for the new Dominion formed at Confederation, nourished by Sir John A. Macdonald's National Policy and seemingly achieved by the prosperity of the Laurier years. The need for a common history, a national history, was the cultural extension of that grand design. "The surest basis of national feeling," stated the Toronto *Globe* in October 1907, "is found in interest and pride in the past, and the sooner Canadians study and understand the complex movements involved in their origin, the better for their ambition to be a nation."[8]

While the objective was clear – Canadians should have a greater understanding of their past – achieving the goal was proving to be a more difficult task. In his first annual report as dominion archivist in 1904, Doughty condemned historical writing in Canada as unsatisfactory and without substance: "Written from so many standpoints, and necessarily based upon insufficient evidence, no uniformity exists or is possible. And yet it is upon this imperfect, and oft times narrow view of the past, that our textbooks are formed and our youth are examined for academic honours."[9]

Doughty's innate artistic sense and dramatic feelings were repelled by the style of presentation that he dubbed a "dull, lifeless story," but more importantly he felt that the growth of national feeling in Canada was inextricably linked with historical knowledge. Critical as he was, Doughty hoped that those involved in researching and writing Canadian history would feel "the need of a national history, based upon the most ample documentary evidence."[10] He found his own inspiration in the work of Lord Acton and in the "construction of history on scientific principles." Doughty believed that unfettered access to the complete archival record would serve to overcome bias and disagreement in historical interpretation. For him, as for many of his time caught up in "scientific" methodology, the "ultimate history" of Canada would result from co-operative work among specialists, accumulating their research and their writings until all available archival material had been explored, assimilated, and brought together for a final, unbiased and unifying national history.

With cogent and relentless arguments, Doughty tied archives and history to the development of Canadian nationhood; in the same breath, he related the Public Archives and archival activity to one of Laurier's principal objectives. In 1904 Laurier confided to a correspondent: "My object is to consolidate Confederation and to bring our people long estranged from each other, gradually to become a nation. This is the supreme issue. Everything else is subordinate to that idea."[11] There was no doubt in Doughty's mind that the business of archives was clearly linked with the predominant political sentiment in the Laurier years: the need to foster a truly Canadian nationality.

If Doughty placed his confidence in the scientific approach to historical research, a similar approach was employed by Mackenzie King in addressing divergent and conflicting views often found at the heart of industrial disputes. King was a firm believer in the power of investigation and the gathering of impartial evidence to root out the causes of labour disputes in order to demonstrate the wider common interests that existed between workers and management. "All industrial strife is a form of anarchy," King explained in his 1918 book, *Industry and Humanity*, adding: "Investigation gives to the worker, where his claims are just, a better chance of redress than striking affords. ... Injustice will not necessarily be remedied by force. Investigation, if it reveals injustice, is irresistible. It can marshal to its support an informed public opinion and the agencies that create it, which in the use of force are antagonized rather than made sympathetic."[12] Doughty too expected that history, firmly rooted in the rapidly expanding archival collections, would similarly eliminate bias and sectionalism.

Not all historians shared this faith and optimism in the scientific approach to historical research. William D. LeSueur, a one-time colleague of Doughty's at the Public Archives, observed in his presidential address to the Royal Society of Canada in 1913: "Let two men work independently on the same period of history; give them access to the same documents and other sources of information, let them agree as to general methods, and let them be as free from prejudice as is possible for poor humanity, yet they will not tell you exactly the same tale. On some points they will agree, but not in all."[13] LeSueur asked: "Can history be written to any good purpose, or at all, without a point of view?"[14]

LeSueur had, of course, already encountered King's approach to history, an approach to the past that focused on and revolved around the career of his maternal grandfather, William Lyon Mackenzie. King viewed his own political career as a fulfilment and, in large measure, a justification of his grandfather's commitment to social reform and his role in the 1837 rebellion in Upper Canada. This is a recurring theme throughout King's public and personal life – in his diary, in his correspondence, and in his speeches. In February 1898 he confided to his diary that Mackenzie's "mantle has fallen upon me and it shall be taken up and worn. ... His voice, his words, shall be heard in Canada again and the cause he so nobly fought shall be carried on."[15] King prized his appointment to the British Privy

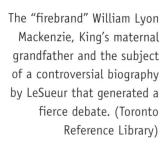

The "firebrand" William Lyon Mackenzie, King's maternal grandfather and the subject of a controversial biography by LeSueur that generated a fierce debate. (Toronto Reference Library)

Council in June 1922 because it was "the vindication of a great purpose & aim in the life of Grandfather and of his name in history."[16]

Much of King's sense of purpose and achievement throughout his long political career was bound up with fulfilling his inherited destiny. To impugn or even to question his grandfather was to cast doubt on the very basis of King's career in public life. He defended his family heritage fiercely, and for several years he waged a battle with LeSueur over the latter's interpretation of Mackenzie's role and the events in Upper Canada in the 1830s. Brian McKillop has detailed the legal battles fought by King, his uncle, Charles Lindsey (1820–1908), and his cousin, George G.S. Lindsey (1860–1920), with LeSueur over the publication of a manuscript of William Lyon Mackenzie written for George Morang's *Makers of Canada* series.[17] The case dragged through the courts from 1910 to 1913. As early as 1908 King had been in the Public Archives checking facts for himself. Although LeSueur sought and eventually won the return of his manuscript from Morang – as well as of his research notes from the Lindsey family, who had custody of the Mackenzie family papers – the King family alleged that LeSueur had gained access to the collection under false pretences: that he would depict Mackenzie as a "Maker of Canada" or, in the legal terminology, a "builder up rather than a puller down."

George Lindsey was aware that even before LeSueur used the papers he was very likely on a collision course with King. In a May 1908 letter to John Willison, LeSueur complained that "my competency to write the life of his grandfather had been violently impugned by his cousin WLMK."[18] Nonetheless LeSueur thought himself in good company when he was informed that Adam Shortt, in his draft of a biography of Lord Sydenham for the Morang series, observed that Mackenzie "by his extravagant and reckless agitation ... did more than all of the enemies of reform to retard those liberal measures which the conduct of the Family Compact had rendered indispensable."[19]

King was not pleased; he asked for and commented on Shortt's manuscript. Writing to his cousin, George Lindsey, King noted that Shortt "took out altogether, or changed the references to which exception was taken, and sent the corrected proofs on to Morang. He said he thought he would be quite satisfied with the matter in the form in which it now stood."[20] LeSueur soon discovered that Shortt had altered the Sydenham manuscript in accordance with King's wishes. Morang informed LeSueur that "whatever his [Shortt's] private and confidential opinion may once have been ... he has shown a prudence and discretion in that respect that I feel bound to say is well timed and judicious."[21] King's opinion of the role of the historian is clear enough: the process revealed "a very poor lot of men, with small minds & abilities. Shortt is a bit double faced in the estimate of Mackenzie he gives. Stephen Leacock the one square dealer in the lot. The whole transaction is a reflection on all save Leacock & a disgrace to Canadian letters."[22] King was successful in having the manuscript suppressed – hardly an accolade for one who preached objectivity and impartiality in labour–management relations.

One person conspicuously absent from all this legal wrangling was Arthur Doughty, friend and colleague to both parties. The Public Archives was called upon to produce documents supportive of one side or the other, but Doughty himself was never personally involved in the controversy, although King had his suspicions. In January 1912 King set aside a day to read documents in the Public Archives, but he observed Doughty "withdrawing some typewritten copy from a bundle of Mackenzie's papers & sneaking them away, presumably unnoticed by me. ... I conclude he is a bit of sneak & & is party to a conspiracy with LeSueur & others to injure Mackenzie's name & fame."[23] In spite of these concerns, the King–Doughty relationship did not suffer any permanent damage; if anything, the two men drew closer, especially after the First World War, when King returned to Canada and Ottawa to lead the Liberal Party.

By the time Doughty assumed his duties as dominion archivist in 1904 he had published several monographs, including books on aspects of Canadian history, in addition to his earlier work on Tennyson. In 1907 he played a key role in the launch of the Champlain Society, and he continued his own writing, especially on the history of New France and Quebec. Doughty pursued his vision of Canadian history in several ways, through research and publications, his involvement with the Quebec Tercentenary celebrations in 1908 and the multi-volume series *Canada and Its Provinces*, his encouragement of the use of archives and archival collections, and his zeal for acquisitions of new material.

For a fortnight in July 1908 Quebec was the focus of the entire British Empire.[24] The British, French, and American naval fleets were in port, the Prince of Wales presided over society functions, and a replica of Champlain's ship, the *Don de Dieu*, arrived from France; for two weeks fleet reviews, receptions, illuminations, historical re-enactments, and speeches were the order of the day (and night). The Plains of Abraham battlefield had been purchased through an eloquent appeal to the schoolchildren of the British Empire, and on their behalf the Prince of Wales entrusted the title deed to the Plains to the newly constituted National Battlefields Commission. Day after day the Plains witnessed a series of elaborate and almost magical historical pageants. For the astute authors of *The King's Book of Quebec* it was more than a commemoration Quebec's three hundred years of existence; it was an opportunity to celebrate Canada:

> It would be difficult to exaggerate its importance in Canadian history. It was the first occasion on which all the Provinces and, more significant still, both the great races of Canada spontaneously united to commemorate, at a single centre, an event in the national history of the Dominion. It is not too much to say, then, that the commemoration is itself a crucial event in the development of Canada as a self-conscious nation, united as one land, and united in a common past.[25]

Through it all, from initial inception to realization, and then in the production of the subsequent commemorative volumes, Doughty worked tirelessly with the governor general, Lord Grey, Prime Minister Wilfrid Laurier, a large coterie of businessmen, and the producer of the historical pageants. The Public Archives collections provided detail for the pageants, the costumes, and the speeches. More importantly, Doughty's interpretation of the events of 1759–60 lay at the very heart of bringing French and English together in mutual celebration on that famous battlefield. "It was on the battlefields of Quebec," observed Lord Grey, "that French and British parentage gave birth to the Canadian nation." He continued in eloquent fashion: "If the battle of the Plains decided the fate of North America, it is equally certain that the battle of Ste. Foy won for the French Canadians for all time the full and absolute right to the secured enjoyment of their language, their religion and their laws."[26]

For his part Doughty was attempting no less ambitious a project than establishing the historical basis for the Dominion of Canada. This was myth-history, seeking in the most public and engaging way possible to change the popular perception and understanding of what Doughty, and many others, considered the seminal historical event in Canadian history. The Quebec Battlefield Association's widely published and distributed appeal for support, addressed to the children of the British Empire, was written in an equally grand manner: "The Plains of Abraham stand alone among the world's immortal battlefields, as the place where an empire was lost and won in the first clash of arms, the balance of victory was redressed in the second, and the honour of each army was heightened in both."[27]

John Stuart Mill had identified "a national history" as a prerequisite for a strong nationality. Despairing of existing history texts, Doughty was trying in the most public and theatrical manner possible to present a unified understanding of the events of 1759–60 to replace the divisive connotations then held in the public memory. King, too, was associated with the celebrations. In March 1908 he was dispatched to London to speak with Winston Churchill, David Lloyd George, and others to stress the need for co-operation in the "Battlefields" movement. When he returned to Canada, King made a whirlwind tour of Canadian Clubs, speaking out on the historical significance of the Quebec Tercentenary and the need for a national history. "We should realize," King told his audiences, "that as a country we have a *history*, and a history in which we all share with infinite pride."[28]

Doughty was determined to bring the story of Canada to a broader audience through the publication of a comprehensive history of Canada based on archival collections and modern "scientific" research. The twenty-three volumes of *Canada and Its Provinces* stand as a monument to that generation of Canadian historians and to Doughty's driving spirit. Through the collaboration of more than one hundred authors from coast to coast, this ambitious multi-volume series was to provide a cultural dimension to the economic forces that had been tying Canada together, especially during the Laurier boom years.

Doughty and his co-editor, Adam Shortt, viewed this series explicitly as the intellectual counterpart of the railways and canals linking the country: "To the end that a broad national spirit should prevail in all parts of the Dominion, it is desirable that a sound knowledge of Canada as a whole, of its history, traditions and standards of life, should be diffused among its citizens, and especially among the immigrants who are peopling the new lands."[29] The series was, as W.A. Mackintosh observed some years later, "one of those important works which are not likely to be models for the future but which really create much of the future."[30]

Creating a vibrant Canadian nationality was one of the main objectives of the active archival program that Doughty had put in place after 1904, and it was supported by all of the prime ministers under whom he served: Laurier, Borden, King, and Bennett. To bolster his claim that the Public Archives should be the centre of Canadian historical studies, Doughty pursued an aggressive campaign to acquire new material as part of his growing collection of treasures. He was confident and innovative in his approach to potential donors, and during his career he directed an unprecedented acquisitions program.

During the First World War Doughty inaugurated a "War Records Survey" to acquire in an orderly fashion the official records of Canada's participation in the Great War, a war that Doughty regarded as "the greatest event in our history."[31] But he was interested in more than the "paper" record of the war. The scope of Doughty's activities had widened considerably in 1918, when he was appointed director of war trophies, responsible for gathering captured enemy weapons from the Western Front and exhibiting them to raise funds for war bonds. After the war the Public Archives handled the distribution of the guns and tanks to armouries, universities, and cities and town across the nation.[32]

Doughty's greatest triumphs as a collector occurred in the parlours and drawing rooms of Britain and France, where he took full advantage of the gratitude those nations felt for Canada's wartime contributions. The Durham, Murray, Monckton, and Townshend papers, the impressive Northcliffe Collection, the Elgin–Grey correspondence, and a host of other family records and artifacts found their way into Doughty's keeping. His reputation preceded him; when he was presented to Queen Mary she remarked that she "had been warned not to leave any loose things about."[33]

Doughty also made every effort to make archival collections available to as many users as possible. On the publication front, the annual reports of the Public Archives included extensive selections of historical documents, journals, guides, catalogues, and collections of constitutional documents. Soon familiar to generations of history students, these documents were published regularly throughout Doughty's tenure. To facilitate research and public use of the collections Doughty opened the reading room for twenty-four hours a day, and as early as 1907 he initiated a summer employment program, thus introducing university students to archives and to the study of Canadian history. Under Doughty's guidance, the Public Archives assisted teachers at all levels with the loan of historical lantern slides, tours, and publications; documents and art were exhibited regularly, and one floor of the Public Archives building was devoted to artifacts, thus making it a museum of Canadian history.

The growing collection and the collegial atmosphere of the Public Archives and archival services had a significant impact on a whole generation of scholars. In July 1926, in the midst of one of his annual research trips to Ottawa, A.L. Burt was struck by the changes at the Public Archives in a few short years. "Today the Archives presents a contrast with what it was five years ago," he wrote his wife. "For some while then I was the only visitor digging in the mine of the manuscript room. Now there are about a dozen."[34] These researchers, coming from universities across Canada and the United States, spent their summers exploring the wide range of records acquired and made available by Doughty and his staff. When Burt listed the names of researchers in the archives reading room – Frank Underhill, Lester Pearson, Duncan McArthur, Arthur S. Morton, W.A. Mackintosh, D.C. Harvey, General E.A. Cruikshank, and James Brebner – he identified most of the leading scholars of that generation. With greater prescience than he knew, Burt concluded: "It is very interesting to see the actual renaissance of Canadian history in the course of preparation."[35]

In 1925, while immersed in the details of adding a wing to the Public Archives building, Doughty received an offer from the Hudson's Bay Company to return to England and become the company's archivist in London. Although he was sixty-five years old, Doughty was enticed by the offer and submitted his resignation to the government on August 20. When news leaked that Doughty might be leaving the Public Archives, various academics, newspaper editors, and others urged the government to offer whatever was needed to retain the services of Dr. Doughty in Canada. In May 1926 Mackenzie King took a direct hand in retaining Doughty's services when he established a Public Records Commission to advise the government on the "control, custody, preservation, indexing, making accessible and publishing the public records of Canada in the most economical and expeditious manner for the benefit of the Dominion at large."[36] This was immediately followed by a second order-in-council appointing Doughty as chairman of the commission; three thousand dollars per annum was added to his base salary of nine thousand dollars as a junior deputy minister. No other members were appointed to the commission; its establishment did nothing but increase Doughty's salary. King's motives in ushering through the increase were clear enough. "I hope this means," he wrote to Doughty, "that for the remainder of your days your services will continue to be given to Canada and to its past and future greatness."[37]

The net effect was that the dominion archivist became the third-highest-paid civil servant in the federal government, after the auditor general and the deputy minister of finance. More importantly, Doughty banished thoughts of the Hudson's Bay Company to remain at the helm of the Public Archives until his retirement.

Doughty grew old in the public service, retiring on his seventy-fifth birthday in March 1935 to become dominion archivist emeritus. Since his seventieth birthday there had been rampant speculation and open campaigning for his position. There is a large file in the R.B. Bennett papers on this issue; it includes letters from nearly every Roman Catholic bishop in Canada, supporting either a francophone Catholic, Gustave Lanctôt, or an anglophone Irish Catholic, James F. Kenney – each of whom were long-time Public Archives employees. Dr. Kenney became acting dominion archivist, and with the very active political campaigning for the succession Bennett decided to defer any appointment until after the 1935 election. It was on his recommendation, though, that Doughty received his knighthood in the King's Birthday Honours List. On assuming office in October 1935 King also was besieged with suggestions for a successor to Doughty, but he too refused to name a new dominion archivist while Doughty lived. Throughout 1937 the main contenders, Lanctôt and Kenney, continued to campaign for the appointment. A number of pamphlets and documents concerning William Lyon Mackenzie and the centennial of the events of 1837, bound in red leather in the Public Archives' bindery, now sit on the shelves of King's Laurier House library – gifts, it seems, from competing candidates. Lanctôt was finally appointed in November 1937, nearly a full year after the death of Sir Arthur Doughty.

King lost a close friend and kindred spirit when Doughty died. He recognized, as many of his contemporaries did, that Arthur Doughty had been an extraordinary individual. For it was Doughty who articulated the enormous value of archives to the Canadian identity. In 1924 in a small booklet, *The Canadian Archives and Its Activities*, Doughty asserted: "Of all national assets, archives are the most precious. They are the gift of one generation to another and the extent of our care of them marks the extent of our civilization."[38] It was a bold and confident assertion, and it summarized in a few well-chosen words Doughty's philosophy for the Public Archives and the role that it might play in the evolution of a true Canadian identity. No less significant is the fact that on the evening Doughty died, December 1, 1936, Mackenzie King was familiar enough with Doughty's writings that he was able to locate the quotation and use it in his official press release.

Doughty and King were friends for more than thirty years. As well as meeting Doughty socially, King occasionally would visit the Public Archives to consult records pertaining to his grandfather, William Lyon Mackenzie. In his biography of King, *A Very Double Life*, Charles Stacey reveals that it was Doughty who first introduced King to "table-rapping" in 1933, in a memorable session in which King's father and mother communicated with their son.[39] On Doughty's death three years later, King wrote that he had been "one of the closest and truest friends I have ever had," adding a few days later that "I know of no man who seemed, to be more a true knight in pursuit of the ideal."[40] This was indeed high praise for a Victorian gentleman. In a private letter to Lady Doughty, King went even further:

I loved the doctor with all my heart. His spirit came closer to my own than that of any other man with whom I have been associated in my years in Ottawa. Fortunately, to that intimacy of soul, death itself is no barrier. If anything, it lets downs bars and barriers which, in our sojourn here, all too frequently make their presence felt.[41]

After Doughty's death, King immediately accorded him two distinct honours unique for a civil servant. First, he directed that the flag on the Public Archives building be flown at half-mast and that the institution be closed on the day of the funeral; second, he secured cabinet approval for an official statue to honour his departed friend and "the great work he had done for Canada."[42] Over the years there had been other, more tangible, indications that Doughty was held in high esteem by Mackenzie King, including his appointment as chair of the Public Records Commission. Doughty was a frequent guest of King's before and especially after the First World War and in 1926 he was invited to accompany the Canadian delegation to the Imperial Conference in London. The two men were, in many ways, kindred spirits.

After Doughty's death, however, there is little evidence that King took any further interest in the Public Archives until the end of the Second World War, when his thoughts turned to the writing of his memoirs and to the preservation of his personal papers and diaries. As early as July 1945 King had considered the possibility of hiring a research assistant to organize material for his memoirs. W.A. Mackintosh of Queen's University recommended Frederick W. Gibson, a young graduate student who had just completed the first year of his doctoral studies at Harvard University (King's alma mater); Gibson was hired for a six-month term in September 1946. Gibson in turn engaged a young assistant, Jacqueline Côté, and the long and intensive process or organizing the King papers began in earnest. Oddly enough, the dominion archivist had no involvement with the project. Over time, portions of the King papers were turned over to the custody of the Public Archives, although full ownership was not transferred to it until 1977.

In the final few months of his tenure as prime minister, King took action to appoint a new dominion archivist. Lanctôt had applied for an extension of his appointment beyond the age of sixty-five, and while this would have been normal for a senior official in good health, King refused the request. In one of his final acts as prime minister he appointed Dr. W. Kaye Lamb as dominion archivist in September 1948. In Kaye Lamb, King found the man he wanted; he was comfortable enough with Lamb to select him as one of the literary executors responsible for his papers and diaries and to transfer responsibility for Laurier House to the Public Archives.[43]

King's sense of mission and historical destiny are borne out by the care and attention he devoted to his diary and his well-known efforts to document his every action, deed, and thought. Yet, in spite of his sense of history and family heritage, King directed that certain portions of his diary and all of his notebooks on spiritualism be destroyed. Fortunately, wiser heads prevailed; the King papers now constitute one of the most significant collections for the study of Canadian politics and society in the first half of the twentieth century. Regardless of how one interprets his politics, his social policy, his execution of the Second World War, King has left all Canadians an inestimable gift, a documentary treasure to enable Canadians to understand their past. His friend Arthur Doughty would have approved. For he, too, ensured for all Canadians that their national archives would be preserved and made available for historical research.

2

The Missing Link: *Mackenzie King*
and Canada's *"German Capital"*

Ulrich Frisse[*]

Canada's longest-serving prime minister, William Lyon Mackenzie King – the "least typical of Canadians"[1] – was born in Berlin, Ontario, the least typical of Canada's communities. The relationship between King and Berlin's German-speaking community is not just a matter of local historical interest but an essential element for understanding the prime minister's political philosophy. "An adequate understanding of King as a person," Blair Neatby once said, "would take us back into the nineteenth century, to small-town life in Ontario."[2] King's early socialization among German Canadians left a deep impact on the future prime minister and affected his decisions in both domestic and foreign politics.

Many of King's personal and political beliefs as well as his perception of ethnicity in the Canadian context originated in nineteenth-century Berlin. The experience of having grown up in Canada's "German capital" was fundamental to the development of the prime minister's most distinguished political skill: his ability to understand the power of diversity for Canadian society, which enabled him to lead the country through the challenging years of the Second World War. King's notion of Canada as "a cultural partnership"[3] included not only French and English Canadians, but also the German Canadians of his hometown com-

* Research for this paper has been made possible through a Ph.D. research scholarship by the German Academic Exchange Service (DAAD).

munity of Berlin and Waterloo County. For the prime minister this community was evidence that conflict was not insurmountable in relations among Canada's various ethnic groups and between the German and the English nations in Europe. This firm belief in the possibility of a peaceful coexistence of the British and German peoples eventually led to one of King's most contested foreign-policy decisions: his decision to visit Adolf Hitler in 1937.[4]

Berlin, renamed Kitchener in 1916, was in many ways an atypical Canadian community. Mennonites from Pennsylvania had founded the community at the beginning of the nineteenth century, and the extended migration of Europeans to North America starting in the 1830s brought large numbers of German-speaking settlers from Europe to Waterloo County.[5] After becoming the seat of the newly established county in 1852, Berlin became a significant Ontario manufacturing centre[6] and – as a result of continuing immigration from Germany – became Canada's "German capital." Through German choirs, musical societies, and large-scale choir festivals that included participants from across Canada and the United States, the residents of Berlin and neighbouring Waterloo proudly exhibited the German ethnic character of their communities.[7] Berlin's cultural distinctiveness, which further manifested itself in various local German-language newspapers, German-language church services, a German school society, and various other associations such as the *Turnverein, Schützenverein,* and *Landwehrverein,* culminated in the erection of a monument to the late German emperor, Wilhelm I, in Berlin's Victoria Park in 1897.[8] Prior to the First World War, German was the language most commonly heard on the streets and in the homes, churches, shops, and factories of Berlin, Ontario. In the 1911 census people of German ethnic origin made up 70 percent of the city's population.[9]

The link between the King family and Berlin had been established by the prime minister's father, John King, who in 1857, at the age of fourteen, had come to the community with his widowed mother to stay with her brother, Dougall McDougall.[10] In 1869, after studying law at the University of Toronto and practising for a short time in Toronto, John King returned to Berlin with his wife, Isabel, and established a law practice. The politically ambitious young lawyer became engaged in local politics and was elected president of the North Waterloo Reform Association in 1878.[11] Nominated to run for Parliament in 1872 and for the Ontario legislative assembly in 1875, King turned down the nominations on both occasions,[12] thereby leaving it to his eldest son, William

Lyon Mackenzie King, to become the first member of the family to represent the riding.

John King actively contributed to the "German" cultural activities of Berlin in the 1870s. When the community celebrated the end of the Franco-Prussian War and the founding of Bismarck's German Empire on May 2, 1871, the future prime minister's father was one of three representatives of Berlin's "English" residents who presented an address to their celebrating German fellow citizens. In the typically glorifying language of the day King and his co-authors, William Jaffray and George Davidson, expressed their admiration for the German character of the community and for the virtues of "Germanness." They emphasized the good relations between Berlin's German- and English-speaking residents and pointed to the close family ties between the British and the German royal families. By stressing the similarities and the mutual accord between German and English Canadians with regard to their "aspirations after true liberty" and their "reverence for truth, morality and religion, the observance of law and order, and respect for constituted authority," King, Davidson, and Jaffray assured German Canadians that "Germany has truly challenged the world's admiration." Berlin's Germans were referred to as "friends" and "neighbours" and as "fellow-workers with ourselves in the erection, on this continent, of a great Canadian nationality."[13] On February 24, 1874, John King again participated in the cultural life of Berlin by delivering a speech at the official opening ceremony of the German *Gesangsverein Concordia*. Another public appearance followed at the *Sängerfest* in 1875.[14]

The early optimism of the Kings, as expressed in John King's political involvement and in his contributions to the cultural life of the community during the first half of the 1870s, soon came to an end. King came to realize that Berlin did not offer enough of a market for a lawyer of his ambitions. Berlin's lawyers competed in a community that in 1871 hosted not more than 2,743 inhabitants, only 662 of whom belonged to the English-language group.[15] The days in which an English-speaking lawyer was guaranteed success in the legal profession of the community were coming to an end. Not only did King have to compete with the already well-established law offices of Ward Hamilton Bowlby and Alexander Millar, but, from 1878 on, Berlin's first lawyer of German origin, Preston-born Conrad Bitzer, had set up practice.[16] Both Bowlby and Bitzer spoke German and had strong personal ties to Berlin's German community.[17]

When John King first decided to practise law in Berlin he hoped that his connections to his uncle, Dougall McDougall, would help get his business successfully established in Berlin. He was wrong. McDougall's editorship of the German-language newspaper *Deutscher Canadier*, his various public offices, especially as county registrar, and his involvement in Liberal Party politics as a leading member of the local branch of the Reform Association had given him prominence; but McDougall was also a very controversial public figure. When, in 1861, County Registrar William Davidson disappeared after allegations of fraud and misappropriation of thousands of dollars while serving as Berlin's postmaster and county clerk, the *Berliner Journal* linked McDougall to him and created the impression that those Scottish residents involved in the political affairs of the county were corrupt and only concerned with their own financial interests.[18] McDougall finally had to cease publication of the *Deutscher Canadier*. In 1891, after a provincial investigation, allegations of embezzlement and the misappropriation of funds led to McDougall's dismissal as county registrar after more than twenty-six years in office.[19]

The King family in the 1890s. Left to right: Bella King, Mrs. John King, W.L. Mackenzie King and John King. (Photo by James Esson / National Archives of Canada C-007348)

John King's own reputation in the community was negatively affected by his uncle's many conflicts and scandals. In 1878 King himself was fined ten dollars by the Magistrate's Court for punching the editor of the *Waterloo Chronicle*, Thomas Hilliard, after the latter had publicly called him a "*Trunkenbold*," the German-language equivalent of a drunkard.[20] In April 1880 the editor of the *Berlin Daily News*, P.E.W. Moyer, was sentenced to pay King one hundred dollars' compensation for slander and libel in a lawsuit that involved allegations raised by the *Daily News* that King's uncle McDougall was using the services of prostitutes.[21]

By the time John and Isabel King finally left Berlin for Toronto in 1893, John King's reputation had been further damaged by his uncle's embarrassing dismissal from the office of county registrar. King had also clearly limited his chances to obtain clients from among Berlin's business community when he challenged the local industrial establishment. He had first done so in 1887, when he sued the Breithaupt tannery in one of Ontario's earliest environmental pollution cases, after refuse from the tannery had polluted the creek that ran through the Woodside property on which the Kings had been living since 1886.[22] In 1890 he again confronted the Breithaupts by representing a former tannery employee in a compensation claim against the company for the loss of his hand in a work-related accident. Regarding King's involvement in the case, Louis Jacob Breithaupt expressed this opinion in his diary: "King seems exceedingly anxious again for a lawsuit, as times no doubt are also dull with him and his style of living is expensive. He is more conspicuous for the latter than for fair principals [*sic*] to my way of thinking."[23] In a community that defined itself primarily in terms of the economic success of its businesses, criticism of the industrial establishment was problematic for the success of a law firm that largely depended on clients from Berlin's local business elite.

Young Mackenzie King was probably unaware of the extent of his parents' growing disillusionment with their social position and their strained economic status in Berlin. For the future prime minister and his siblings, growing up in Berlin during the 1870s and 1880s seemed to provide a harmonious family life and close contacts with children of recent German immigrants and with first-generation Canadians of German origin. Like most other children from English-speaking families in Berlin, the King children studied German at school. From time to time, John and Isabel King also employed German tutors and governesses to teach the German language to their children.[24] Much later, on returning to his native community in 1925, Prime Minister King recalled that he was unaware of ethnic tensions in the Berlin of his boyhood years.[25]

King's close relationship with German-Canadian school friends during his formative years in Berlin resulted in a deep interest in all things German, which expressed itself in various ways. In March 1900 the twenty-six-year-old Harvard doctoral student, while in Europe on a travelling scholarship, visited the German imperial capital of Berlin. His stay there, with the family of Professor Anton Weber, established a lasting friendship.[26] Against the background of King's close ties to Canada's Germans, it is not surprising to learn that two years before his visit to the German capital the twenty-three-year-old Harvard graduate had fallen in love with Mathilde Grossert, a nurse who had recently emigrated from Germany.[27] Most importantly for King the politician, however, was the fact that growing up among German Canadians helped create a firm and idealistic belief in the possibility of a peaceful coexistence of German- and English-speaking people. This belief not only became the basis of the prime minister's understanding of ethnic diversity in the Canadian context, but also of his rather simplistic understanding of the relationship between Great Britain and Germany during the 1930s.

The King family's move from Berlin to Toronto in 1893, Mackenzie King's student years at the universities of Toronto, Harvard, and Chicago, and his move to Ottawa in 1900 only temporarily severed his ties to his hometown community. After gaining his first political experiences in Canadian federal affairs as deputy minister of labour, the thirty-four-year-old returned to his native community in 1908 to run for Parliament in his hometown riding of North Waterloo. His decision to face the vote here was free of any kind of nostalgia for his hometown. King's diary of that year presents a young, ambitious federal politician in search of a safe riding in order to become minister of a separate department of labour within the Laurier government. Returning to the place of his childhood in the first of his many political campaigns, however, re-established his links with Canada's "German capital" and reinforced his admiration for Germany and the German people.

Mackenzie King brought into his first political campaign the experience of eight years in office as deputy minister of labour. In March 1902 he had successfully settled a strike in Lippert's furniture factory in Berlin,[28] which added weight to the Liberals' claim that a vote for King was a vote for the representation of workers' interests in Ottawa. When Prime Minister Wilfrid Laurier spoke on

King's behalf at the Liberals' central campaign meeting in Berlin's Victoria Park on September 24, 1908, he explicitly confirmed the Liberal candidate's prospect of joining the cabinet table if he carried the riding. In a campaign that was clearly focused on the urban workforce King described the labour question, at a rally in Berlin's auditorium on October 10, 1908, as "the one of all questions which is of the utmost importance to the working classes. The happiness of the nation depends to a very large extent upon the contentment and prosperity of its working classes."[29] The voters and the Liberal local newspapers were impressed. The *Berliner Journal* asked its readers to vote for King, "who is a friend of the worker and the workers interests."[30]

It was not, however, only the impression that the Liberal candidate had the workers' interests at heart that contributed to King's popularity in the riding during the 1908 campaign. He also impressed his German-speaking electorate by appealing to their distinct identity. At the meeting in Victoria Park on September

Mackenzie King, Sir Wilfrid Laurier and an unidentified lady in 1915. (National Archives of Canada C-046319)

24, the future prime minister expressed his admiration for Germany, the German people, and Canada's population of German extraction. In the presence of Prime Minister Laurier, Minister of Railways and Canals George P. Graham, Postmaster General Rodolphe Lemieux, and an audience of several thousand people King reassured his electorate in German that since he had left Berlin,

> my heart and my soul were always longing for the old beloved Waterloo, where I was born, and for my native country here and for the friends and playmates of my youth. My school years awakened inside me a lasting and deep love for the German people, whose extraordinary characteristics have always made them an example for all nations. When Harvard University sent me to study in a foreign country, I chose Germany and the old, beloved city of Berlin. During my stay there I visited many historically interesting places, such as the River Rhine with its old castles, also Potsdam and the grave of Frederick II, Nuremberg and its castle and the Heimat of Hans Sachs, also Weimar and the places of birth of Schiller and Goethe, Breslau, Heidelberg, Hamburg and many other places, whose names we have adopted here in our County. At the University of Berlin I studied the history of the Fatherland and I had the great honour to meet Emperor Wilhelm, whose grandfather I have been keeping in dear memory since the time of my youth. ... Finally I have to thank you for your patience, with which you listened to my faulty attempt of a German speech.[31]

Although the Liberal candidate's political objective to win the election in North Waterloo cannot be severed from the content of this speech, his expression of appreciation and admiration for Germany and the German people was more than mere lip service to his voters. It reflected the way King thought about the country to which the majority of his voters were so closely linked. The effect of the speech was tremendous. The German-language *Berliner Journal* published it in full, and the *Berlin Daily Telegraph* remarked that Mackenzie King spoke "fluently and with great ease in German."[32]

By addressing his electorate in their native language King not only proved that he acknowledged and appreciated their distinct identity, but he also put his Conservative opponent, his former teacher, and, at the time of the election, the president of the Conservative Association of North Waterloo, Richard Reid, under pressure to follow his example by addressing the voters in their native language as well. Reid, however, did not deliver a single German speech throughout the entire campaign, although his German seems to have been quite good. The *Berlin Daily Telegraph* added to the pressure on Reid by presenting him as an opponent of German-language education in the public schools of Waterloo County, referring to the stand he had taken earlier on the matter as a member of the local school board.[33] On October 7, 1908, the *Daily Telegraph* asked under the headline "Richard Reid As A German":

> Mr. Richard Reid is being held up by his organ as a great friend of the Germans and as one who understands and speaks the German language. Was not Mr. Reid at one time in favor of having the teaching of German in our public schools abolished? He might enlighten Berlin citizens on this point by a speech in the German language at the Conservative meeting in Berlin tonight.[34]

While the *Berlin Daily Telegraph* did not hesitate to use the language issue to diminish the Conservative candidate's chances of carrying the riding, Berlin's main German-language newspaper, the *Berliner Journal*, remained completely silent on this matter. Reid, despite the frequent attacks by the *Daily Telegraph*, did not deliver a German speech, although his campaign supporter, Dr. Lackner, a local member of the legislative assembly, speaking in German, assured the voters at a Conservative meeting in Berlin "that Mr. Reid was the friend of the Germans and could speak the language."[35]

King's various appeals to his German-speaking electorate, the prospect of having the riding represented at the cabinet table, and the traditionally strong Liberal vote in rural parts of the riding contributed to his success in a campaign the *Daily Telegraph* described as "one of the hardest and most exciting struggles ever experienced in this riding."[36] Despite his inability to break the traditional Conservative majority in Berlin and neighbouring Waterloo, the successful Liberal candidate was able to reduce Berlin's Conservative majority to 153 votes. He carried the riding with an overall majority of 263 votes.[37]

King's appointment to cabinet as the minister of labour necessitated a by-election in North Waterloo, which he carried by acclamation in June 1909.[38] On July 10, Berlin honoured its native son with a picnic in Victoria Park.[39] The speech

King delivered then is of central importance for an understanding of the future prime minister's perception of the relations between Britain and Germany later, during the 1930s. Addressing the growing tensions between the two major European powers, King for the first time discussed the ethnic composition of his riding in the context of world politics. He offered the example of the harmonious relationship between Waterloo County's German- and English-speaking populations as a model for the two contesting nations in overcoming their differences:

> I would like to say one word which will come as a word from the County of Waterloo to other parts of the world. I would say to the people of England, to the people of Germany and to the people of the continent … stop your talk of war and the possibilities of war and look over to the County of Waterloo, in the Dominion of Canada, look at the gathering we had on the 10th of July and see us there, English and German alike, united in doing honour to what is best in the traditions of the two great peoples … the voice of the County of Waterloo is going to be heard in the affairs of the Old World as well as in the affairs of this country. And I feel we can make it felt with pride, we can point over yonder to the Statue of Emperor Wilhelm, of Germany, we can tell our English friends and those who are of English descent how we are pledged to protect that statute from defilement here in the park of a British people, and that as English subjects we are going to defend that statue and all it stands for. And our German friends who are here can turn to their German friends of the old land, and say we are erecting in the same park a statue of Queen Victoria, and as Germans, British subjects and citizens in Canada we purpose [*sic*], with the last drop of blood in our veins to respect and defend all that is typified in that monument.[40]

It was a rather simplistic understanding of the realities and complexities of world affairs that expressed itself in King's recommendation to the two European nations only five years prior to the outbreak of the First World War. Twenty-seven years later, in 1937, the same simplistic approach to European politics, together with the prime minister's firm belief that conciliation and goodwill were enough to overcome conflicts between nations, resulted in his attempt to make the voice of Waterloo County heard in world politics, when meeting high-ranking officials of Nazi Germany and the *Führer* himself.

At the time he spoke in Victoria Park in 1909, however, King was still far from entering the stage of world politics. The next major challenge for the minister of labour was the federal election of 1911, in which he ran in North Waterloo again. This time the Liberals and King were on the defensive. While in 1908 the prospect of becoming a member of Laurier's cabinet had contributed to King's success in his hometown riding, this time his rank as a cabinet minister made him partially responsible, in the eyes of the electorate, for the Liberals' unpopular stand on reciprocity. He had been spared major personal attacks in the 1908 election, but this time King's involvement in the controversial settlement of the Grand Trunk strike made him an easy target for personal attacks by his political opponents. The result of the strike settlement was frequently used by the Conservatives to discredit Mackenzie King for not having the true interests of the workers at heart.[41]

Although King repeatedly stressed that the Liberal government would not eliminate protective tariffs for domestic industrial products, fears among local manufacturers and labourers about the consequences of reciprocity and reduced tariffs on a limited number of manufactured articles, as suggested by the government, were strong in Berlin. For the majority of Berlin's local industrialists and workers, protective tariffs rather than reciprocity guaranteed further prosperity and the economic success of "Busy Berlin's" export-oriented industries. King's Conservative challenger, W.G. Weichel, the former mayor of Waterloo, in a public address published by the *Berliner Journal* appealed in particular to fears within

William George Weichel, MP for Waterloo North, who defeated King in the 1911 election. (William James Topley Collection / National Archives of Canada PA-043128)

Berlin's workforce by stating that voting for reciprocity would be a vote "for the easy introduction of stars and stripes in Canada and for an empty dinner-kettle for the worker."[42] King, who had been previously warned by Berlin resident G. Debus that "if your Government goes for Reciprocity I don't think that there is any show for your future here,"[43] noted in his diary that if the government interfered too much with Ontario's manufacturers on the tariff and reciprocity issue he would not be returned to Parliament by his constituents.[44]

The extent to which the naval question – the controversy over Canada's contribution to England's armament at sea – affected the outcome of the 1911 election in North Waterloo cannot be determined with any certainty. The question did, however, add a distinct feature to the campaign by raising the loyalty issue for the first time in North Waterloo. That issue would lead to the demise of Berlin's proud German identity during the tumultuous years of the First World War.

It is striking that while Weichel and his campaign activists in various election meetings addressed the voters in German, King this time did not even try to make use of the German-language skills that had so clearly contributed to his popularity and success in 1908. On the one hand it was impossible for him to compete with Weichel for the position of the "German candidate" in this campaign because Weichel, whose parents had emigrated from Germany, was of direct German extraction and perfectly fluent in German. On the other hand King's unwillingness to use his German-language skills at the time was a clear concession to his long-range political ambitions, which he felt were threatened by his close personal associations with a riding whose loyalty was increasingly being put into question with regard to German Canadians' stand on the naval question.

The *Berliner Journal* had earlier reflected the feelings of many Berliners in its rejection of Great Britain's plea for a Canadian contribution to the mother country's dreadnought program, which was clearly directed against the potential German threat.[45] So had Pastor Oberländer of Berlin's St. Peter's Lutheran Church when, in a sermon on loyalty to God and the Fatherland in November 1909, he had also rejected the alternative option of Canada establishing its own fleet to be employed in support of Great Britain in case of war against Germany.[46] At a time when Canada's English-language press began adopting the British papers' propaganda-like agitation against German imperialism, many Berliners were unwilling to support Canadian contributions to a British fleet that was so obviously directed against the Fatherland and the German emperor. It is important to keep in mind that up to the eve of the First World War, Emperor Wilhelm II was celebrated in Canada's "German capital" as the guarantor of peace in Europe and as a man who had prevented war in Europe since his ascension to the throne in 1888. It was obvious to King that in such a situation the reinforcement of his close personal ties with his German constituents had the potential to publicly stigmatize him as a sympathizer with German interests.

Such fears were not unfounded; in contrast to the situation in 1908, King this time ran as a high-ranking public figure whose moves were closely observed by the national press. The *Belleville Intelligencer's* immediate response to the minister of labour's public stand on the naval issue at a campaign meeting in Waterloo was to link it to his political involvement in the affairs of German Canadians. The newspaper asked its readers: "Wouldn't it be a stroke of political genius if Hon. Mackenzie King got an autographed letter from Kaiser Wilhelm advising all German residents of Waterloo to vote for him?"[47]

Along with Prime Minister Laurier and five of his cabinet colleagues, King lost his seat in the 1911 "reciprocity election" that swept the Liberals out of power and marked the end of the Laurier era.[48] Despite his defeat King did well in North Waterloo. As in 1908 it was a very close race, and in the end only a couple of hundred votes decided the final outcome. While the vote in the rural parts of the riding remained stable in support of the Liberal cause, it was the loss by 563 votes in Berlin that caused King's defeat.[49]

After defeating the incumbent minister of labour, North Waterloo's new member of Parliament, W.G. Weichel, openly accused King in Parliament of having tried to gain political profit from appealing to the resentments of Waterloo County's German Canadians with regard to the naval issue. Quoting from the Toronto *Globe*, Weichel confronted his fellow parliamentarians on November 27, 1911, with the following statement, which King had made at the convention in Waterloo on August 22:

> Are the people of this country going to place at the head of affairs a man who will be precipitated into such a position as this, who will take from the treasury of this country and who would have taken money enough to build two Dreadnoughts and send that money to England so that they could spend it as they pleased? And against what country? He was ready to send money to build warships to fight Germany."[50]

Weichel reassured his fellow MPs that

> every man, woman, and child in that constituency resented the implication
> contained in the statement of Mr. Mackenzie King. … I would like to ask
> Wm. Lyon Mackenzie King whether he thinks we are subjects of King
> George or subjects of the Emperor of Germany. I can assure the members
> of this House that there are no more loyal subjects in this Dominion than
> the German people of North Waterloo.[51]

The fact that he had failed in North Waterloo in 1911 did not prevent King
from later developing a nostalgic view of his hometown, which for him – despite
its name change to Kitchener in 1916 – always remained Berlin. He named parts
of the grounds of his summer residence Kingswood after Woodside in Berlin,[52]
and he used his personal contacts with his friend and former campaign manager
Harvey Sims and with Kitchener's mayor, Mortimer Bezeau, to add two old Berlin
lamp poles to the eclectic collection of artifacts he assembled at his summer home,
Kingsmere.[53] In retrospect, the Berlin years represented for the prime minister the
time when his whole family had lived together for the last time. In a letter to Louis
O. Breithaupt in 1944, King referred to the Woodside years as "the years that left the
most abiding of all impressions and most in the way of family association."[54]

During the First World War, King was primarily preoccupied with his work for
the Rockefeller Foundation and the loss of his sister Bella and of both his parents.
In spite of this, the dramatic developments that his hometown community under-
went then did not go unnoticed by him. The loyalty of Berlin's and Waterloo
County's German-Canadian community to the British Empire's cause was put
into question over the community's contributions to the war effort, particularly
with regard to the county's ability to provide recruits for Canada's overseas contingent. In September 1916 – as a demonstration of loyalty – Berlin's name was
changed to Kitchener.[55] With the name change came the end of the community's
proud German heritage which was replaced by the glorification of Waterloo
County's Mennonite pioneer past.[56] King stayed informed about Berlin's loyalty
crisis through his friend Harvey Sims.[57] In light of Waterloo County's dramatic
loyalty crisis during the First World War, King's strong pledge against conscription in the 1917 election and later during the Second World War is even more
understandable.

A youthful King on the political hustings. (NAC/Woodside National Historic Park)

Even though, with the end of the First World War, Canada's "German capital" became a matter of the past, in King's political philosophy Berlin survived as a model for the possibility of a peaceful coexistence of the German and the English nations. As prime minister, King expressed his critical stand on the city's name change in a letter to C. Mortimer Bezeau, the mayor of Kitchener, in 1931: "Personally, I never cease to regret that its name does not continue to be that which rightfully belongs to it, which is the only name that could have been known to its founders and many of those who have since passed away."[58]

One of the driving forces behind King's highly contested decision to pay German Chancellor Adolf Hitler a visit in 1937 was the prime minister's perception that his upbringing in Canada's "German capital" had particularly qualified him to mediate between the German and the English people. Reflecting on the reasons he had given to British Foreign Secretary Anthony Eden for his intention to travel to the German capital and to meet Hitler, King wrote in his diary on October 1, 1936:

I then said to him that I had been born in Berlin in Canada, in a county which had several communities of German names, and had represented that county in Parliament. Had also lived one winter in Berlin and I felt I knew the best sides of the German people. That I understood the difference between the Prussians and the Bavarians. I said if I were talking to Hitler I could assure him what was costing him friends was the fear which he was creating against other countries. That there was not so far as Canada, for example, and other parts of the Empire were concerned, any thought of continued enmity toward Germany but a desire to have friendly relations all around.[59]

King's 1937 trip to the German capital almost had the character of the closure of a life circle for the Canadian prime minister: "Certainly it would seem to be the day for which I was born – Berlin 1874, and came to Berlin, Germany … 37 years ago. May God's blessing rest upon this day and the nations of the world – And His peace be theirs." While travelling to Berlin by train from Paris during the night of June 26, recollections of his hometown occupied the prime minister's mind and got mixed with memories of his earlier visit to the German capital as a Harvard doctoral student in 1900:

Seeing where I lived 37 years ago, the association with Berlin, etc., all is most remarkable. My thoughts went back to earliest days in Berlin. Ont. to many Germans there whose names I have not thought of since to any extent, all seemed to come back – part of the cloud of witnesses who are helping today.[60]

In 1909 the thirty-five-year-old minister of labour had promised his electorate in Berlin's Victoria Park that the voice of Berlin and Waterloo County would be heard in world politics. Now the time had come to fulfill his promise. Writing down his impressions of the meeting with Hitler, King reflected:

As we were about to be seated, I placed a de luxe copy of Rogers' biography on the table, and opened it at the picture of the cottage where I was born, and of Woodside, of Berlin. I told Herr Hitler that I had brought this book with me to show him where I was born, and the associations which I had with Berlin, Germany, through Berlin, Canada. That I would like him to know that I had spent the early part of my life in Berlin, and had later represented the county of Waterloo in Parliament with its different towns which I named over. I said I thought I understood the German people very well. I mentioned that I had also been registered at the municipality of Berlin 37 years ago, and had lived with Anton Weber at the other side of the Tiergarten. While I was speaking, Hitler looked at the book in a very friendly way, and smiling at me as he turned over its pages and looked at its inscription. … I told him I had been anxious to visit Germany because of these old associations, and also because I was most anxious to see the friendliest of relations existing between the peoples of the different countries.[61]

Unfortunately the voice of Waterloo County fell on deaf ears. Adolf Hitler continued to take the steps that within two short years led to the most devastating war humanity has experienced.

3

"On the Hill Over Yonder ... "

rych mills

William Lyon Mackenzie King often returned to his hometown, and the sense of community that he carried with him was evident whenever he spoke of Berlin. In his speeches and political addresses, King sought to reconnect with this community by incorporating local sites, events, and themes into his remarks. His parents' first home and King's birthplace was on Benton Street, near Church Street, in a small frame cottage later numbered 43. Here "Willie" was born on December 17, 1874.[1] Willie King's return appearances in Berlin–Kitchener are tied to much of his political career. He had grown up in a community that was rapidly progressing from a small but industrious town to a city that was known widely as "Busy Berlin."[2]

Victoria Park, the focal point of many of King's speeches, did not exist when the Kings lived in Berlin. In 1894, however, the Berlin Park Board purchased twenty-eight acres of farmland and swamp from Samuel Schneider, grandson of the Mennonite pioneer Joseph Schneider, whose 1816 home is now an active historical site in the centre of Kitchener.[3] At the same time the board bought an adjoining five-acre plot that had been developed in the late 1880s as a private athletic field. It came complete with a grandstand, a race track, and well-kept grounds.[4] Knowing that young Willie King was both an enthusiastic participant in and a spectator of sports, one can easily imagine that as a youth he sometimes trod on this pre-Victoria Park sports field: chasing a cricket ball, kicking a football, or watching a lacrosse match.

The birthplace of King on Benton Street in Berlin/Kitchener. It no longer exists. (NAC/Woodside National Historic Park)

By 1905 an enchanted idyll, Victoria Park, had been created in downtown Berlin. Structures such as a boathouse, the 1897 Peace Memorial topped with a bust of Germany's Kaiser Wilhelm I, a pavilion, a bandstand, several bridges, and a drinking fountain added to the park's attractions. Such a transformation never failed to amaze those who had moved away and then returned for a visit.

The first appearance by the future prime minister in Victoria Park had as much to do with John King as with Willie. John was president of the Toronto Association of the Old Boys of Berlin. When a three-day celebration was organized in August 1906, he and Willie came back home. In light of the Kings' departure and the unresolved debts, it was perhaps not surprising that this was John's first visit in more than a decade.[5] Having departed Berlin a high school graduate, Willie returned with several university degrees, a well-respected civil service position as deputy minister of labor, a CMG [6] behind his name, and political nirvana ahead.

Willie did not speak that day but John did, and it is likely that his words echoed Willie's feelings. For his father "it seemed ... as if the wand of a magician had passed over the town and transformed it."[7] Father and son enjoyed an evening of music and fireworks, part of a throng of seven thousand packed into Victoria

Park's athletic field. Before the night's entertainment, Willie was honoured with an impromptu banquet and a "Welcome Back Willie" banner strung across King Street. Those paying tribute to their "becoming-famous" friend made up a who's who of future hometown political support: H.L. Staebler, A.L. Breithaupt, D.S. Bowlby, Oscar Rumpel, David Forsyth, and H.J. "Peter" Sims, among others.[8] Friendships renewed and cemented in 1906 would come in handy two years hence.[9]

After the final rocket faded in the night sky, John and Willie followed the crowd downtown, where bands played until the wee hours. It is tempting to visualize John King, forgetting his financial worries for the moment, enjoying himself thoroughly with the son he admired so much. One also imagines the more pragmatic younger King enjoying the revelry but also realizing that his hometown had not forgotten him and had indeed been watching his rising career with interest. Was a spark ignited on this occasion?

As deputy minister of labor King reported directly to Rodolphe Lemieux, one of the government's most popular ministers and the one who some predicted might replace Sir Wilfrid Laurier when the prime minister eventually stepped down. In cabinet, Lemieux held the combined position of postmaster general and minister of labor. King's goal was a separate ministry for labour, with himself as the minister. Lemieux was encouraging, but it was Laurier who would make the decision, and he was in no hurry. King was learning important political lessons early – especially the need for allies and the importance of timing.[10]

On July 4, 1907, in response to an invitation from the town's board of trade to speak at its twenty-second annual banquet, Lemieux came to Berlin with his young deputy minister. The inclusion of King was probably due equally to Lemieux and the board's president, Willie's long-time friend, Peter Sims.[11]

At an afternoon public reception in Victoria Park's pavilion, each guest was presented with an illuminated address. The wording of King's address noted that "we have watched with interest and expectation as we beheld you a rising star in the sociological firmament." King replied briefly, stating that this day was the most memorable of his life. His success, he said, was due to "the training he had received from his father and mother and his early associations while a resident of this progressive town." [12]

During the evening Board of Trade banquet at the elegant Walper Hotel, Lemieux and King gave lengthy speeches. Lemieux had certainly paid attention during his Victoria Park tour. If he were a Frenchman, Lemieux noted, he might

Rodolphe Lemieux, MP for Gaspé, in 1917. (William James Topley Collection / National Archives of Canada PA-028135)

have taken exception to the bust of the German, Wilhelm I. Instead, as a Canadian, he believed that "the quarrels that brought about the Franco-Prussian war may concern France and Germany but they should not mar the good feeling existing between Canadians of French and German origin."[13] It was this theme, introduced here by Lemieux, to which Mackenzie King would return time and time again in later hometown speeches, simply substituting the word *British* for *French*.

King's wide-ranging address that evening touched on several other subjects. First, he recalled life as a graduate student in 1900, living in Germany with the artist Anton Weber. At that time King had visited the grave of Wilhelm I. He also recalled that as a child in hometown Berlin, he had mourned Wilhelm's 1888 passing. This memory included streets draped in black, flags at half-mast, muffled drums, tolling bells, marching from Central School to St. Peter's Lutheran Church for the service – and the profound mystery of the event to a thirteen-year-old Canadian boy of Scottish heritage. Like Lemieux, King also pointed to the presence of the Kaiser's bust in Victoria Park.

A second topic evolved from an early experience that had taught King a lesson about community. As a youth, he and his father had often taken evening strolls together. Along the way they would pause to watch as a simple artisan built his

"Reminiscence of Berlin," July 4, 1907. Photo by Willie Schmalz. (National Archives of Canada C-28570)

own home, brick by brick, and though this took two years it showed Willie the value of honest toil.

As a third point King remarked that if any lesson needed to be learned about mingling of races and devotion to the British Crown: "No better example could be afforded ... than the town of Berlin with its German and English customs, its German and English languages, its German and English points of view, with its British patriotism for all."

The fourth point of his 1907 speech to some two hundred Board of Trade members concerned a visit he had hoped to make to the Williams, Green and Rome shirt and collar company on Queen Street South to learn more of its employee-welfare plan. Today, King recounted, he was firmly told he could not visit the plant! The factory would be closed this week. Was it a strike? A lockout?

No, but, forsooth, that the employees might go on a camping expedition, and enjoy, as employers also like to enjoy, a two-weeks' vacation under canvas in the open air. Gentleman, if there was much of this sort of thing the word strike and lockout would soon disappear from our vocabulary.[14]

King's feelings may now appear naive at best, cynical at worst. But this was a thirty-three year-old idealistic progressive trying to express his beliefs. And the year was 1907. On a non-political level, King's tour through Victoria Park perhaps gave him some ideas for decorating, in a Romantic landscape style, his expanding estate at Kingsmere.

The 1907 visit with Lemieux exposed King to an experienced politician's methods and reinforced his knowledge that he might find support in Berlin for a hometown boy. His next visit to town would put him in company with Canada's master politician and show just how well he had absorbed the lessons of Ottawa.

The 1908 Canadian general election had been preceded by several years of frustration for King: frustration while he was being groomed by the prime minister, Sir Wilfrid Laurier, for the political life everyone knew was coming.[15] During this period he was also learning another political lesson: that any one man, however brilliant, was only a small facet of what a political leader must juggle in maintaining a government.

King's triptych of political fantasies still stood above all else: a seat in Parliament, a separate cabinet role for labour in a renewed Laurier government, and a minister of labor named Mackenzie King. As early as 1905 King had been proposing this course of action to Sir Wilfrid.[16] Over the next three years the discussion would come up again and again between King and Laurier; between King and his early political mentors, such as Governor General Earl Grey, Sir William Mulock, and Rodolphe Lemieux; and between King and his diary.[17] In the fall of 1908 King's frustration ended and his public political career began at Berlin's Victoria Park.

It seemed inevitable that King would challenge the Tories in North Waterloo. One is tempted to believe that the impressive Berlin and Victoria Park receptions of 1906 and 1907 played a role in his choice of riding.

There is a wonderful picture of the crucial moment drawn in the King diaries. It is Ottawa, September 9, 1908. The aging leader, Laurier, and the thirty-four-year-old political "wunderkind," King, have been deep in discussion. The snapshot of that pivotal point in Canadian political history is in King's own words, written shortly after the decision was made.

> I then said Well Sir Wilfrid if you will agree to make the Department a separate Dept., & announce it during the campaign, I will run in North Waterloo against Joe Seagram or any one else. Sir Wilfrid said "Very good." I replied All right I will run in North Waterloo. Sir Wilfrid got up off his chair & struck his knee with his hand and say [sic] "I am delighted." ... He looked long and steadfastly, and his face was lighted with his smile. I looked steadfastly at him, through it all he looked so worn and feeble. There was great spirit & fire there, but there seemed to be no constitution on which it could thrive. ... He shook hands with me a second time, & I told him I would bring back that riding, that I would try to win, that I would win.[18]

Now to let the public know.

King was nominated on September 21 by the North Waterloo Reform Association at its convention in Waterloo's Town Hall.[19] His movers were Leander Bowman, of Bloomingdale, and John Hostetler, of Wellesley.[20] The rural areas in the riding would be strong for the Liberals but a little early cement wouldn't hurt: in fact, it proved crucial.

Following incumbent Joseph Seagram's retirement, the Conservatives nominated King Edward Public School principal Richard Reid, but only after several higher-profile Conservatives declined.[21] Ironically, Reid was one of King's former teachers at Central School in Berlin. The two men had great respect for one another, and at times during the campaign took lunch together. They never met in public debate.[22]

A visit by Laurier on September 24, 1908, not only gave the local Liberal campaign a tremendous kickoff but also launched King's public political career. This was Sir Wilfrid's first trip to Berlin since the 1896 election, when he had travelled with Sir Oliver Mowat to address a crowd at the old Gaukel Street skating rink.

(In recalling this event the Liberal paper, the *Daily Telegraph,* made one of the great typographical blunders of the campaign: "He was then [1896] leader of Her Majesty's loyal Opposition with no administrative record. To-morrow he will appear before the electors with a record of twelve years of *failure* and distinguished service to his country as its prime minister."[23] One can imagine the poor

Mackenzie King in the buggy and other members of the family at Woodside, Berlin, during the 1890s. Bella and Jennie stand, with Mrs. King sitting at the table and Max on the porch. (National Archives of Canada C-007310)

Jennie King on horseback at Woodside. (National Archives of Canada C-63268)

The party press supports its favourite. (NAC / Woodside National Historic Park)

Telegraph editor, D. Alex Bean, becoming apoplectic as he read this in his own newspaper during supper. Perhaps the next day's headline, stretching across the entire front page of the *Daily Telegraph,* had its basis in the gaffe: "Berlin Welcomes Sir Wilfrid After Twelve Years *Prosperity.*"[24])

Along with Laurier came Rodolphe Lemieux and Sir George Graham, the minister of railways and canals. This was the Liberals' "A" Team, and it was in Berlin for William Lyon Mackenzie King!

The day, September 24, began with a reception at St. Jerome's College, then luncheon at L.J. Breithaupt's home, Sonneck, on Queen Street North. In the afternoon came a parade through Busy Berlin's streets. More than fifty carriages made up one of the town's largest-ever processions. Sir Wilfrid, Mackenzie King, Waterloo South candidate Dr. Sylvester Moyer, and Dr. J.F. Honsberger, president of the North Waterloo Reform Association, sat in the lead carriage. The first twelve carriages were detailed in the newspapers: they contained a roster of Waterloo

County Liberals and civic politicians. Waterloo mayor John B. Fischer was in the second carriage. In number nine was Berlin's mayor, Allen Huber. Organizers probably wished they could have put Huber in number fifty-one out of fifty. He had become a year-long embarrassment, and he sat fuming and scheming in carriage nine.[25]

At Victoria Park, the athletic field was ready: a special platform had been set up and decorated with bunting, flags, and a striped awning. Several bands from the county were ready to entertain, and a huge crowd awaited the official party. As the carriages entered the park, those seated in the grandstand and the throngs standing about the sports field let out a tremendous cheer. Noah Zeller's Band of the 29th Regiment entertained with popular and patriotic airs before the speeches. And speeches there were, made without a microphone, to upwards of twelve thousand people.[26]

One can easily imagine John King's feelings as he sat on the platform watching this gathering and knowing it was intended to sanctify his son. This is the same John King who just twenty-five years before had harboured ambitions of his own in this very riding.[27]

The entire King family, apart from Willie's brother, was on hand. Over the course of the afternoon they listened to Dr. Moyer, a former teacher of Willie's, now the candidate in South Waterloo; Prime Minister Laurier; and cabinet members Graham and Lemieux. Each paid tribute to the brilliant young man from Berlin. When civic officials and local Liberals spoke, they too lauded King for the work he had done since leaving Berlin. Following Moyer's opening address, Mackenzie King spoke. He didn't talk very long. Although it was his day, he was, after all, the warm-up act. It was the last time he would warm up for another politician.

As the band played "The Maple Leaf Forever" King basked in the ovation. His speech included more than fifty occurrences of the first-person singular pronoun, a fact the Tory papers would bring up later in the campaign.[28] Not only this day, but this entire campaign, was destined to focus more on King than on the issues. The beginning of his address is worth quoting at length:

I cannot thank you enough for the great honor … in nominating me as your candidate in the grand old riding and county of North Waterloo. Perhaps it may be a little difficult for me to tell you to-day just how fully and deeply and truly I appreciate that honour. Most of you know…that most

of my life has been spent in the town of Berlin and you all know that the
early training, the high standard of character, and the high and holy associations I then formed have gone with me out into the world ... it is therefore with a feeling of deep gratitude that I announce to you my intention
of making my home with you for the rest of my life. This is a proud day for
me; but what does it all mean? Here I was born a little boy on the hill over
yonder, here I was raised, here I went to school and collegiate institute, and
now I have come back and bring with me as my friend that illustrious and
distinguished statesman, the Prime Minister of the Dominion of Canada.

The cheers rang out, and King paused before continuing:

I have with me to-day my father and mother and my sisters, whom you all
know, and you do not wonder that I am deeply stirred to find that the
dreams of my boyhood days have come true. I find it hard to tell you how
much and how strongly this day and this hour appeal to me.

He also spoke of his work as deputy minister of labor, trying to reconcile the
relationship between industry and labour.

I have devoted my life to it for the reason that I believe that industrial peace
is the beginning of international peace. ... I hope that the young men of
Canada will follow my example. There are too many of our young men
interested in making money, and to any such if they are here I say that they
do not know the greatness and grandeur of life consists in getting out and
trying to make life better and happier for the rest of men.[29]

King soon concluded the English-language portion of his address, but the boy
from Berlin had not quite finished. He read a speech in German recounting time
spent in Berlin, Germany. Although it was not translated in the English-language
papers, this speech was similar to his previous year's talk to the board of trade.
This time King hoped to reach out and touch the hearts of the German Canadians in the crowd as he explained that his childhood years gave him "a deep and
lasting love for the German people whose extraordinary characteristics have always made them an example for all nations."[30] The first public speech of King's

political career concluded, and to great cheers he sat down, ready to bask in the acclaim that was to follow.

Next, Rodolphe Lemieux praised King's ideals and work, and he linked King's future to the great Reform-Liberals of the past: William Lyon Mackenzie, Alexander Mackenzie, George Brown, Oliver Mowat. He predicted that King would soon bring even greater honour to his native county.

A great ovation rang throughout Victoria Park, increasing as Sir Wilfrid rose to speak. It was the last stop on a gruelling southern Ontario campaign swing, and the prime minister had not been well. After the band played "O Canada" and two civic addresses were read, Laurier began: "There is inspiration in the air ... Mr. Mackenzie King ... is one of the men of the future ... a champion of Reform worthy of his predecessors in the cause."

He then went on to give what was probably his standard campaign speech, touching on the Liberals' twelve-year reign. Laurier left until the end of his speech what most had hoped to hear, indeed, had expected to hear. In this speech in Berlin's Victoria Park on September 24, 1908, the political career of William Lyon Mackenzie King took flight.

> The cause of labor has taken on a new aspect. The laboring man to-day is no longer the semi-slave he was formerly. He is a fellow-citizen now in every particular. He has rights which must be protected and which are protected by the present government ... we have abolished the sweating system ... we have brought in the law of conciliation. ... There is a Department of Labor ... my friend, Mr. King has taken an active part. I think that at the first opportunity I shall submit to my colleagues that the time has come when we should have the Department of Labor under a separate minister. [31]

As the cheers went up, the prime minister sat down. The crowd cheered as much for what Laurier didn't say as for what he did. To Berliners, it was a given that if the Department of Labor was to come under a separate cabinet minister, there was only one man to head it: William Lyon Mackenzie King.

George Graham punctuated the rally with a brief statement emphasizing that "we want Mr. King in the House of Commons." [32] As the meeting came to an end amid a series of cheers for the guests on the platform, Rodolphe Lemieux stepped forward and proposed a cheer for the ladies of the audience. Not allowed to vote in those days, women were often noticeable by their absence in political gatherings; but the *Toronto Star* made particular note of the large number of Waterloo County women that attended the rally.[33]

Berlin's Conservative newspaper, the *News Record*, suggested that only four thousand unenthusiastic people were at the park for the rally and that Mackenzie King's speech had been disappointing.

> To very many this was the first time they had seen Mr. King who is brought in from Ottawa by the government in its determined attempt to wrest the riding from those who are upholding the principles of Conservatism. Mr. King did not deal with the political issues that are before the people ... the only reference he made to the unpunished misdeeds of those sheltered by the Liberal administration was that these matters should not be discussed in Parliament as other countries reading about grafters and bounders tends to hurt the credit of the Dominion.[34]

The *News Record* was also delighted to publish a piece from the Clinton newspaper revealing that Sir Wilfrid travelled one day behind and one day ahead of a team of "professional decorators, the Turner Co of Peterboro," who arranged for all the bunting, flags, banners, brass bands, and fancy awnings.[35] Sending the volley back, the Grit *Daily Telegraph* scolded the Tory *News Record* for its crowd count of four thousand and quoted several Toronto papers that had guessed at a crowd of around ten thousand.[36]

Allen Huber, as noted earlier, was originally relegated to carriage nine, accompanied by three ordinary aldermen. After the Victoria Park rally broke up, the official party had to dash to the train station to catch the Toronto express. There was a scramble to get into the carriages, and the first now contained, as it did on the way to the park, Laurier, Moyer, and King. But, surprise, now it also held Huber, who had buttonholed the prime minister and asked if he did not think the town mayor should be in the first carriage? [37]

One day later, at King's first meeting of the campaign in rural North Waterloo, Huber showed up in Winterbourne, declared himself an independent candidate, demanded speaking time, got fifteen minutes, and claimed that King would be beaten because

> He goes around the country in a gas buggy owned by a representative of
> the Standard Oil Co, along with a member of the Leather Trust ... every
> woman should have the vote – and a voter also ... [I] too had a grandfa-
> ther, in fact [I] had two grandfathers ... [King is] not like his grandfather.
> The latter had warred against those whom he believed to be thieves, the
> grandson is with a political party of thieves. [38]

Huber went on to be nominated and proved to be a gadfly in the campaign, especially to King, but his vote total had no influence.

King won the election, but the margin of 271 votes came entirely from rural
voters: the three towns of Berlin, Waterloo, and Elmira all preferred Richard
Reid.[39] Almost immediately, King was asked to undertake a special mission to
China for the renewed government. He returned to Ottawa only in May 1909, just
in time to hear Laurier table a bill making labor a separate cabinet department
and naming King the new minister. Under the rules of Parliament at that time a
newly named cabinet minister had to resign and attempt to win his seat again in a
by-election. This King did. He moved to Berlin, rented a house at 96 Queen
North, and awaited the Tories' next move.[40] Would they nominate someone? They
did not. Allen Huber, no longer the town's mayor but still the riding's loose cannon, was urged by some to run. He decided not to.[41] King was acclaimed, and to
celebrate, local Liberals threw a "Monster Picnic" for him in Victoria Park on Saturday, July 10, 1909. Music, sports, fireworks, speeches! It would be a day to anoint
the "Berlin Boy" for his two election victories.

One little hitch: both the Berlin and the Waterloo bands had been hired to
play. The Berlin band was unionized; Waterloo's was not. Union rules forbade union bands from playing at events with non-organized bands. So Berlin's Band of
the 29th Regiment withdrew; a bit embarrassing for the minister of labor. Not
surprisingly, the *Daily Telegraph* made no mention.[42]

The program consisted of races and dashes for under-tens, for farmers, for
men over two hundred pounds; aquatic activities such as canoe and tub races,
swimming races in the park lake, and of course baseball, tug-of-war, and football.
And, yes, there would be a Mackenzie King speech. It was his first chance to address his constituents since the October election nine months earlier.

Berlin's mayor, Charles Hahn, welcomed King back and said how proud he
was that the first minister of labor came from Berlin. Hahn himself was seemingly

a contradiction: a dyed-in-the-wool Conservative but also vice-president of the Trades and Labour Congress of Canada, which had urged a labour portfolio. Industrial workers were in favour of the Conservative policy of protection for Canada's manufactures during this era, thus explaining this anomaly. "No member of any Government … has ever taken the interest in the cause of labor that Mr King has," said Hahn to the crowd of 3,500 in the park. They cheered long and loud as the Waterloo band played "O Canada."

Finally King was able to speak. "I am sure that if any man ever born under a lucky star had reason to rejoice at his lot, that man is the one who is addressing you at this moment," he began. But his main theme was peace: peace in labour, peace in the county, peace in the country, and peace around the world. He welcomed the many Conservatives he saw in the crowd and said he harboured no grudge against them.

> I don't believe in keeping up party strife … we are working and co-operating together for the good of the County of Waterloo for the good of this province and for the whole Dominion. Give me my chance to show you whether I am going to be an independent-minded Liberal or a party slave.

Moving to the international scene, King used the friendly feelings between the peoples of German and British background in his hometown as a metaphor for what could happen on the world stage, especially in Europe, where war clouds were already gathering.

> I would say, stop your talk of war and the possibility of war and look over to the County of Waterloo, in the Dominion of Canada, look at the gathering we had on the 10th of July and see us here, English and German alike, united in doing honour to what is best in the traditions of the two great peoples … we can point over yonder to the statue of Emperor Wilhelm of Germany … [we] of English descent … are pledged to protect that statue from defilement here in the park of a British people…our German friends … can turn to their German friends of the old land and say we are erecting in this same park a statue of Queen Victoria … and as Germans, British subjects and citizens of Canada we purpose, with the last drop of blood in our veins, to respect and defend all that is typified in that monument. … I

> hope that to-day from this park that a voice which is a voice of every man and every woman here will go out across the waters ... and bid [others] to cease looking with angry eyes across the [English] Channel and cast their looks to this County.[43]

King's delivery was arousing and vibrant, reflecting a young man's passionate beliefs. He created a theme of racial harmony in Berlin, relating it to the national and world stages. This theme served two purposes: to keep King's link with the area meaningful and to give his constituents a feeling of actually influencing the Canadian and international scene.

Victoria Park's two monuments (the Peace Memorial, with its bust of Kaiser Wilhelm I, and the soon-to-be-erected statue of Queen Victoria) symbolized the local experience for King. They were a concrete link for both him and his constituents to hopes for world peace. How tragic those links would become within five years.[44] But this was the summer of 1909, not 1914: idealism was in the air.

Less than two months later King was back in Victoria Park: the minister of labor attended Labour Day celebrations on September 4. Mayor Hahn again in-

King with his parents in Berlin. (NAC / Woodside National Historic Park)

troduced King, who said he was glad the mayor had outlined what he was to do, because a list of the afternoon's events showed that the minister of labor was to appear between an acrobat and the baby show. King quipped that perhaps he "might be able to qualify for a little of each." [45]

That was the sum of his levity. Naturally, the speech was devoted to the role of labour and the labouring man and woman. King gave a shocking description of working conditions he had seen around the world: in India, in China, in Japan, in England. Nowhere on earth, he claimed, had the worker such a life as in the Dominion, particularly in Berlin and the other towns of Waterloo County. It was "necessary that the labour unions should seek not only to preserve the rights they had attained in this country, but endeavour to extend them to people of other countries." [46] Asking, then answering his own question about the real strength of a nation, King pointed out that more than 70 percent of the franchise holders in Berlin owned their own homes and that each of them had their own vegetable garden. That was the strength of the Canadian worker. King invited everyone to continue to co-operate with him in his role as labor minister, "not only to maintain Labor but to rouse Labor to a full consciousness of its duties." [47]

King's speech was relatively short and quite radical for a minister of the Crown, but he was addressing a Labour Day gathering. With less than a year under his belt as a member of Parliament and only a few months in cabinet, he was learning his political lessons well. Today it is called demographics; back then it was audience. King knew to whom he was talking.

His idealism and background originally made him a small-l liberal – once he was in professional politics he became a large-L Liberal. He may have thought in his Victoria Park speeches of 1909 that he could bridge both camps, but reality and party discipline in Ottawa ensured that he could not be all things to all people, not even back home in North Waterloo.

Almost two years passed before King next appeared in an official capacity in Victoria Park. In Berlin, the Imperial Order of the Daughters of the Empire (IODE) had spent years raising money to commission a statue honouring Queen Victoria. The granite base had been erected in the park in late 1909, but the statue itself was a long time coming from Italy. Finally, on October 20, 1910, it arrived. That evening's *Daily Telegraph* let readers know that "there were no duty charges, thanks to the efforts of the Minister of Labor making the necessary arrangements" on the importation of the six-thousand-dollar sculpture.

Governor General Earl Grey officiated at the May 29, 1911, unveiling of the Queen Victoria monument. Following a civic reception at Berlin Town Hall, the carriages headed for Victoria Park. King was in the second carriage, with Earl Grey's daughter, Lady Sybil, and Mrs. Mahlon Davis, regent of the local IODE. Among those invited to ride in the early carriages was Richard Reid, King's 1908 opponent.[48]

Atop the granite base and die stood the bronze statue. All winter it had been shrouded in canvas, hidden from view. For the ceremony, a huge Union Jack replaced the canvas. As the *Daily Telegraph* reported the next day:

> Earl Grey was then requested to perform the ceremony ... [and] gracefully complied ... as the flag fell to the ground, the crowd cheered enthusiastically and the band played the National Anthem. The crowd gazed in wonderment and admiration as they saw the familiar figure of the late Queen Victoria standing before them.

A chorus of five hundred school children sang for the crowd of ten thousand. Both Dr. H.G. Lackner, MPP, and the governor general noted the appropriate presence in Victoria Park of statues honouring both Queen Victoria and Kaiser Wilhelm I. Each speaker alluded to the previous week's unveiling in London, England, of the Buckingham Palace memorial to Victoria. There, her grandson, Kaiser Wilhelm II of Germany, was an honoured guest of another grandson, King George V of Britain.

Mackenzie King's brief speech again focused on the theme that the world could learn so much from the friendly relations between two diverse peoples in Waterloo County. His talk noted the memorable and historical significance of the occasion: memorable for Berlin and Waterloo County; historical as regards the Dominion; and significant in the context of the British Empire. Locally, King offered, the day allowed

> citizens the opportunity ... of expressing their loyal attachment to the British Crown ... and we believe that Your Excellency will find here a community after your own heart ... whose industry and prosperity abound ... of model industrial establishments ... a city of schools and churches, without slums and without poverty, a city of parks and gardens ... of happy and

contented and cultured homes; a community sense and a community pride, a law-abiding, a peace-loving and God-fearing race.

In addition the IODE had added "a very special adornment to this park ... and to the town of Berlin ... the conception and the artistic quality of Its execution ... [make it] ... in every sense a national possession."

For King the international importance of the day "in the community which is proud to bear the name of the capital of Germany ... [occurs because] ... people of German and British origin and their descendants have the honor of uniting in the ceremony of unveiling a statue of the same beloved sovereign." Now he introduced a point that he had not mentioned when his political friends of French descent, such as Laurier and Lemieux, were on stage with him. He noted that the situation in this community showed a "common devotion on the parts of the German and British peoples of the old world and the new ... here in this County of Waterloo, a name which itself bespeaks of the deeds jointly wrought by German and British alliance." That allusion would not have won any points with a French-Canadian audience or political boss: again, King knew his audience. He concluded by linking the ceremony in London, England, and the one in Berlin, Ontario, as similar events symbolizing "the loftier ideal of mutual service, the larger conception of world duty." [49]

Within two months of this special day in Victoria Park, the 1911 "reciprocity election" was called. King's 1909 pleas to rise above party politics bore little fruit in what was a particularly bitter campaign. The popular mayor of Waterloo, W.G. "Billy" Weichel, returned the riding to the Conservatives, and on September 21, 1911, Mackenzie King's political career in Berlin – in Waterloo County – was over.[50] But he did return to Victoria Park in 1912 to help Berlin celebrate its cityhood.

On July 17, 1912, "Busy Berlin" became a city. The festivities encompassed many sites and took many forms. Speechmaking certainly was not ignored. On the afternoon program at Victoria Park, Mayor W.H. Schmalz expressed pleasure at welcoming the ex–minister of labor back to Berlin. Sharing the platform with Weichel and several other Conservative politicians, King chose to speak briefly. He offered congratulations to the citizens on the great progress the community had made and noted how proud he would always be to look upon Berlin as his home, no matter where he was located.[51]

The Prime Minister comes home. King at the residence of W.D. Euler, MP, in Kitchener on September 13, 1922. (Kitchener Public Library)

With that visit, William Lyon Mackenzie King said goodbye to the public of Berlin. Not for ten years did he return to Victoria Park: Kitchener's Victoria Park and Prime Minister King, if you please! The 1922 celebration would be stirring and the press coverage stellar. By this time the two rival papers, the *Daily Telegraph* and the *News Record*, had amalgamated. More importantly, the combined paper was co-owned by King's North Waterloo lieutenant and member of Parliament, W.D. Euler. There would be no sniping at King from the Kitchener press for the remaining three decades of his life and career.

It is September 13, 1922. In a series of triumphant revisitations to his hometown, this visit reigned supreme. In 1906 King had come back as an "Old Boy" with his father. In 1907 he had arrived as a civil servant with an important cabinet member. In 1908 he had appeared as a candidate with the Prime Minister. In 1911 he had come as a cabinet minister with the governor general.

But to return as prime minister! And the community recognized this. The *Daily Record* declared:

> Kitchener is en fete today ... a community wide non partisan appreciation and acknowledgement of the achievements of a native boy coupled with a compliment to Canada's premier. [52]

In a strange way, King's earlier pleas for a party-free political scene in North Waterloo had come to pass. Starting with Euler's election in 1917, the Liberals controlled federal politics in the riding until 1958. In that period there was no significant Conservative opposition: Euler was in cabinet or the Senate; King was in the prime minister's office; and the local press was half-owned by Euler; the other half by W.J. Motz, a friend and confidante of the prime minister.

Under threatening skies on that September afternoon in 1922, Victoria Park was thronged with schoolchildren, several local bands, and thousands of area residents. The crowd joined the bands, and their voices roared "O Canada" as never before. Graciously, Kitchener mayor Charles Greb handed the speaker's platform to Waterloo's mayor, W.G. Weichel, for the introductions – the same "Billy" Weichel who had defeated King in 1911. He lost to Euler in 1917, returned to municipal politics, and again won the mayor's chair. Weichel welcomed King and recalled "the memorable meeting in this park in 1908, when another Prime Minister stood on the platform beside you and made the announcement that if successful you would receive cabinet rank and become minister of labor."[53]

Weichel's misremembered welcome didn't detract from his sincerity.[54] King responded with a remarkable speech. He thanked everybody for their hospitality and then turned to Weichel and paid tribute: "We have been opponents on the political field but the elections have been fought out on the square and while we have been old time political rivals Billy Weichel will always remain a life-long friend of mine."[55]

King knew he owed much to Weichel. Suppose that Weichel had not won in 1911: King would have been in Parliament, a leading Opposition figure in the First World War years, and would likely have become embroiled in his hometown's ferment. The political casualty list in the politics of that era mimicked the overseas casualty list. Few survived the turbulence of Parliament unscathed. Instead, for much of this period King toiled in relative obscurity in the United States, always keeping a close watch on events in Canada.

Sir Wilfrid Laurier died in 1919. King had a fairly clean slate when the infighting and side-taking began at the Liberal convention, and he was able to call in some political debts to win the leadership. Had he been in politics during those years, enemies would have been made and his elevation to leadership would not have been so simple. The Weichel setback made King's path to victory, if not possible, at least easier. There was a dynamic between the two men on this day that most of the public, perhaps even Weichel, did not understand when King paid Weichel tribute in Victoria Park.

Much of King's speech was a long and rambling recollection of his memories of Berlin; from stealing neighbour's apples and church-going at St. Andrew's to riding the family horse and being with favourite teachers. King traced his political career, pointing out that in this riding, his score was about even: one loss, one win, one acclamation. With this in mind, he claimed that "I have yet to discover the individual whom I could term either a personal or a political enemy."

Wrapping up, King looked into the more recent past. Even in 1922 it was evident that the First World War years were a twentieth-century turning point.

> We shall have missed the first of all lessons of the period thru which we have passed if it has not taught us a larger toleration and a greater deference and respect for opinions which may differ from our own. ... You have shared in that anguish of mind and heart ... is it to mean the arousing of new bitternesses, the deepening of old prejudices or is to mark the birth of a larger tolerance. ... Or is it to mean the re-birth of goodwill, as the spirit of a new brotherhood uniting in common, higher purpose, men, communities and nations alike?

In a message of special import to Kitchener, which in the past few years had experienced more hatred than most communities, King said: "if in anything there remains aught of difference between you, let me remind you that time brings many changes, that nothing born of prejudices or passion is likely long to endure."[56]

What a change from his pre-war theme of perfect harmony in Waterloo County! King's tacit acknowledgment that his hopes for a German–English utopia had been shattered can be read into this scolding of his hometowners. In the ensuing applause it was several minutes before King could take his leave. This was his final Victoria Park crowd and appearance. (During his 1947 farewell tour of the area, he chose to speak and make a national broadcast from Waterloo Park.)[57]

* * *

Does all this mean a new facet of William Lyon Mackenzie King has been discovered? Will past studies be superseded? Of course not.

King ... the man, the politician, the hometown boy, the handsome young idealist, the aging frump, the statesman: whatever Mackenzie King you want, he was much more than the sum of his Victoria Park parts. He was a sum greater than all parts of him yet discovered.

A man easy to fault, to dislike, to criticize, to mock, to satirize; but also a man who managed his patchwork country for so long and welded some of his labour, industrial, and social welfare idealism into its fabric.

A man whose many facets and intellect invite study, a certain respect, even admiration; a man who in his younger days possessed ideals, convictions, and great hopes for a better world.

A man born in Berlin, Ontario, just three blocks from Victoria Park, "on the hill over yonder ... "

* * *

There's a postscript to Mackenzie King in Victoria Park.

It is Sunday afternoon, July 23, 1950. The long-awaited new bandstand is to be officially opened on Roos Island.[58]

The Kitchener Musical Society Band, descended from the Band of the 29th Regiment, which had serenaded King and his father, King and Lemieux, King and Laurier, King and Earl Grey, King the prime minister ... the Kitchener Musical Society Band, under director George Ziegler, plays "Nearer My God to Thee" as its tribute selection on the brand-new bandstand.

A crowd of two thousand fills the island in Victoria Park. Some weep. Most reminisce.

Seventeen hours earlier, William Lyon Mackenzie King had died in his sleep.

Mackenzie King and Waterloo County

Geoffrey Hayes

In the first volume of his great biography of Sir John A. Macdonald, subtitled "The Young Politician," Donald Creighton depicted the impact on the young Scottish immigrant of growing up in Kingston, Ontario. Who can forget Creighton's description of the sombre, grey Victorian Kingston that greeted Macdonald and his family as they arrived from Scotland? The business failures of Sir John A.'s father and the bonding with his Macpherson cousins were important formative influences on the young Macdonald.

In contrast to Macdonald, William Lyon Mackenzie King was born in Berlin, Ontario, and grew up in social and political circumstances that differed dramatically from those of the Macdonalds in Kingston. What were the relationships between the political values King experienced in this unusual Canadian community, and how did they influence his later political decisions? Were his political values drawn from his experiences in accommodating the German majority of Berlin? Was there something about the place that helps explain his political success? King said as much.

In September 1947 King arrived in Kitchener for a two-day visit. As he related in his famous diary, his arrival caused him a great deal of fear and trepidation. "I do not think there is any occasion in my life when I was less prepared for what was before me than when I arrived at the station platform in Kitchener." The day, however, was a resounding success, and it left the aging prime minister sincerely moved. He confessed later that the area's "strong influence of home, school and church, and simple community life among all classes" had well prepared him for public life: "I was astonished to find myself feeling much more belonging to Kitchener and Waterloo County than either to Ottawa, in which I have lived for the past 47 years, or Toronto."[1]

This homecoming became a pilgrimage in King's mind. The most important feature of the trip was his visit to Woodside, his boyhood home. He had come believing that Woodside was best torn down and that a simple cairn should be built to commemorate the site as a public park. But as he walked through the house and the surrounding properties, he came to believe that the site should be preserved. A small group of local businesspeople and politicians shared this view and fought to preserve Woodside.

King's sentiments were sincere, but his view of Waterloo County was largely based on a myth, a simplified, idealized view that overlooked many of the complexities of his boyhood and early political life in the area. In this King joined a progression of local historians, librarians, novelists, and public officials who helped create the notion of a stylized rural-pioneer existence in Waterloo County.[2] Like so many others, King helped sustain the myth of Waterloo County; in turn, the myth sustained him.

Waterloo County was not always a good place for Mackenzie King. As prime minister, King never represented the area; nor did he visit it very often. That might be because his permanent departures from the area, in 1891 and 1911, were extremely difficult periods in his own and in his family's life. Woodside National Historic Site is "situated" in the year 1891. King first left Berlin and Waterloo County that year and headed for University College in Toronto to study political economy. Then as now, the family home was removed from the centre of the town, suggesting that the King family experienced a certain distance during its time here. Although William's father, John King, was a prominent lawyer, he struggled financially.[3] He was the county solicitor for some time, an appointment developed through the intricate web of political connections cast by his uncle, Dougall McDougall.

McDougall was a second father to John King, so much so that John's second son was named for "Uncle Dougall." By most accounts McDougall was a lively fixture on the county scene as a newspaper publisher, editor, printer, and political operative. Despite his Scottish roots, he owned and later edited the German-language *Deutsche Canadier* newspaper from 1857 until it ceased publication in

King attended the universities of Toronto, Chicago and Harvard, studying political economy and sociology. (NAC/Woodside National Historic Park)

1865. When that enterprise failed, he turned to English-language newspapers, publishing the *Berlin Telegraph*. Newspapermen were highly visible members of the community then; that McDougall chaired the local high school board in the 1870s also says something of his social position.

McDougall also worked tirelessly for the Reform-Liberal cause. In the days of old Liberal Ontario, such loyalty was rewarded. In 1864 McDougall became the registrar of Waterloo County, taking up his office in the new brick registry office just beside the courthouse on Weber Street.[4] When he was not working to ensure that the Liberals stayed in power, his task was to accept and record the deeds and land transactions of the county. In 1889, when Ontario premier Oliver Mowat came to Berlin, Dougall McDougall was there – in a county council photograph he can be seen sitting in the front row, his loyal nephew, John, proudly at his side.

The next year everything fell apart for McDougall and, by association, for the King family at Woodside. In 1890 he was the victim of an extortionist. His assistant, William Stanton, early in 1889 informed Premier Mowat, who was then also attorney general, that McDougall's 1888 accounts were short by more than $1,400. Stanton later withdrew his complaint, but in April 1890 he wrote a desperate letter to McDougall asking for a personal loan of four hundred dollars ("for unless I have it inside of a couple of days, I shall lose all I have in the world"). McDougall refused to make the loan. In May 1890 Stanton charged the county registrar with making false returns. An investigation by the provincial registry office followed.

Two county court judges and the mayor of Berlin swore to McDougall's good character, but no one was willing to testify as to his bookkeeping. The provincial inspector of registry offices concluded that McDougall "was not a man of business accustomed to or skilled in dealing with figures, and that he was generally careless in money matters." McDougall kept no fee book through his time as registrar. "At the end of the year, it is said, [the receipts at the Registry Office] were put away in a drawer and were never looked at."[5]

The investigation revealed that the registrar's cash books to 1882 had been destroyed and that more recent accounts "were permitted to disappear." McDougall's record was undeniable: every year from 1873 to 1888 he had sworn that his financial returns were correct, and every year they were not. As a result, the registrar owed more than five thousand dollars to the County of Waterloo. McDougall paid up, apparently to the satisfaction of county council, which resolved in December 1890 that it did not wish to see him removed from office.[6]

Still the issue would not go away, and the premier himself had to act. In August 1891 Mowat thought it prudent that McDougall resign as Waterloo County's registrar. In making its decision the premier's executive council noted:

Mr. McDougall is now advanced in years. He has been registrar for more than a quarter of a century; and seems to have lived simply, to have had no extravagant tastes or habits, to have been charitable and generous with his money, and through improvidence and want of business ways to have saved nothing; and we have already referred to his high character in the community. … We have also been reminded on his behalf, nor have we forgotten or been indifferent to the further facts, that he has been all his life an out-spoken member or friend of the political party which is represented by your Honor's present advisers, and has for many years been on terms of personal friendship with some of ourselves.[7]

Neither his age, his character, nor his Liberal connections could save Dougall McDougall.

For the King family the revelations must have been devastating. The Kings stayed on at Woodside until July 1893, but the embarrassment (and possibly the expense) of Uncle Dougall's misappropriations must have made it clear that the Kings had no real future, political or otherwise, in Berlin.

What impact did the scandal have on young Willie, who had gone off to University College in 1891? When his uncle died in August 1894, King noted the sad event in his new diary. But he did not go to the funeral; he was vacationing in Muskoka at the time.

> Poor old man I trust that he is happier now than he could have been while on earth. His death was to some degree expected[,] the last two years have been full of worry and anxiety to him and it is better that he should not be longer kept on "the rack of this tough world." He has helped many and will doubtless be rewarded for this.[8]

King's musings are of interest for several reasons. They hint at his uncle's difficulties, but more importantly they reveal a common pattern of reflective thought. The next day, August 29, 1894, King recorded, after reading his uncle's obituary: "this naturally threw me into a very thoughtful mood so I drew up a chair along side the fire and let my mind take me where it would. I could trace the life of a man in a log burning and finally turning to ashes. … I tried to place myself in father's position and share his sorrow, I thought of the changes that must necessarily follow."[9]

King's associations with Berlin remained in correspondence and friendships, but his path as an academic and civil servant took him to Ottawa by way of Toronto, Chicago, and Harvard. When he decided to run for political office, North Waterloo was not his first choice; no family connections remained in the riding. Even with Sir Wilfrid Laurier's urgings, it took King several months to decide to run in his hometown. He knew it would be a tough race, for North Waterloo had long been in Conservative hands – not just in any hands, but those of the prominent distiller Joseph E. Seagram. Although Seagram chose not to run in 1908, his influence was widespread. King trailed in the two towns of Berlin and Waterloo and in Elmira village; only wide margins in the three rural townships gave him the victory in North Waterloo.[10] The next year he held the riding in a by-election that saw him become Laurier's minister of labour. He was then not quite thirty-five years old.

Like all politicians through this period, King contributed to his constituency in several ways. The promise of rural mail delivery helped him win the townships, and he returned the favour. A post office in Elmira, and the still-impressive postal building in Waterloo, remain as visible reminders of his time as the member of Parliament for North Waterloo.

But his parliamentary duties were short-lived. The people of North Waterloo elected him for only one term. In 1911, King and the Laurier Liberals went down to defeat in the reciprocity election that saw Robert Borden and the Conservatives come to power. This time the Tories' anti-reciprocity campaign in Berlin, Waterloo, and Elmira could not be offset by the farmers' support for the Liberals and free trade. For such a young, ambitious, and able cabinet minister, the loss must have been difficult. Yet, as he did so often throughout his life, King placed his defeat on a lofty plane, in highly moral, sanctimonious terms. On September 25, 1911, he replied to the condolences of a long-time Berlin correspondent, C. Mortimer Bezeau:

I agree wholly with you that the result has been brought about through much misrepresentation and prejudice fostered by selfish interests. I doubt, however, whether it is wholly fair to assume that the result is due to any conscious or unconscious ingratitude on the part of the laboring classes. I have often felt in my rounds of dreary canvas in the factories how hopeless to attempt to enlighten on a great question the minds of men whose time is so wholly given over to work which, where it is continuous, must have a deadening effect upon the faculties. ... The task of gaining moral and intellectual liberty for the mass of the people has been the task of the ages, and will continue to be such through time. One must, therefore, be prepared for all the ignorance it may be responsible for and strive the harder to bring enlightenment. Passion and viciousness are harder forces to contend against. As I have studied the psychology of the peoples in my limited public experience, I have become more and more impressed with the truth that in the last analysis, by whatever names we call our different parties and issues the struggle at bottom is between right and wrong, between justice and injustice, between righteousness and unrighteousness.[11]

King would make a habit of consoling himself by elevating defeats, electoral and otherwise, into lofty moral battles.

For King the results of 1911 were a watershed. After his defeat he committed himself "to becoming better informed on Canadian affairs & history." Though he felt a certain pull, he realized his temperament was not well suited "to the Christian Ministry." He thought that "a professorship at McGill might prove attractive, or the presidency of some college." But business was not for him: "the making of money has no attractions for me." For a passing moment, King contemplated marriage, "if I can only find the one that will be the helpmate needed thro [*sic*] life I will certainly marry." But as he concluded in this revealing entry, dated September 24, 1911, the real choice was political: "If I can get a seat in parliament, I feel that to be the wise thing to do."[12]

Through the next decade, King's road back to politics was not easy. He worked for the Liberal Party and briefly dabbled in pacifism before becoming an industrial relations specialist with the Rockefeller Foundation. He had a busy, safe, but troubling war. Between 1915 and 1917 he lost his older sister and both parents. His brother contracted tuberculosis in 1916, and with William's help moved west. In that year King consulted a psychoanalyst.[13] In 1917 he ran for the Liberals, and lost. His political fortunes reversed in 1919, when he became the leader of the Liberal Party following Laurier's death. In 1921 he became prime minister, albeit the first to lead a minority government. The Mackenzie King era had begun.

One of the many challenges King faced as prime minister was the nation's "memory" of the First World War. It is here that his path converged with Waterloo County once again. As Jonathan Vance has pointed out, the memory of the war in Canada prompted an extraordinary emotional outpouring that embraced the memory of the fallen soldier and cast suspicion on those who did not enlist. Eager to "remove the perceived stain of failing to enlist," King recited in the House of Commons a record of his family's losses through the war; he also went to considerable lengths to demonstrate that he helped nurture the memory of Canada's war dead.[14]

In a place that had once proudly proclaimed itself the German capital of Canada, a pall of suspicion hung over Berlin and much of Waterloo County. During the war, as cries of disloyalty became more shrill, the area's long-cherished German cultural institutions – its clubs, its school classes, its newspapers – came

King speaking during the federal election campaign, Cobourg, Ontario, ca. July 1926.
(F.J. Skitch photo / National Archives of Canada PA-138867)

under attack and were closed. On September 1, 1916, the city of Berlin became
Kitchener, Ontario.

In the years following the war a more innocuous, German-Canadian myth
emerged in Waterloo County, one not based on "Busy Berlin" but on the trek of
the Conestoga wagon that had brought the area's early Mennonite settlers from
Pennsylvania. Led by W.H. Breithaupt, the first president of the Waterloo Historical Society and later a president of the Ontario Historical Society, Waterloo County's Pennsylvania-German origins were elevated through publications, com-
memorations, and memorials. The most famous of these was Mabel Dunham's
book *The Trail of the Conestoga*, first published by Macmillan in 1924. Dunham, a
Kitchener librarian, wove a wonderfully gripping story around the lives of some
of the area's first settlers. The book provided an imaginary tapestry for a fascinating historic site, the Pioneer Memorial Tower, that was conceived by Breithaupt,
financed by private subscription, and opened in an elaborate ceremony in August
1926. As the long line of speakers reiterated that day, the pioneers' bravery, loyalty,
and industry, as well as the pacifism of the county's first German-speaking settlers, were much-overlooked aspects of Canada's beginnings.[15]

King was more than glad to give national status to the founding myth of Waterloo County. In 1924 the prime minister penned (or at least put his signature to) the foreword of Dunham's first edition:

It is such literature that makes us realize the background of our country's story. We know and appreciate too little the initiative, patience and self-sacrifice which characterized the struggles of our forefathers in laying not only the material but also the political foundations of our country. If we go back to early days, we shall find that the problems which perplex us are no greater than those they successfully solved. In their example we should find alike strength and inspiration.[16]

That same year, and despite the objections of some local Mennonites who rejected the ostentation of such a memorial, the Historic Sites and Monuments Board recognized the Pioneer Memorial Tower as a national historic site. The founding myth of Waterloo County, one that firmly placed its Pennsylvania-German-Canadian founders at the very heart of Canada, was firmly in place – thanks in no small measure to Prime Minister King.

King signed thousands of portraits with his distinctive handwriting. (NAC / Woodside National Historic Park)

Waterloo County would continue to serve as a kind of mythical place for King. As he grew older and his immediate family died or moved away, his memories of the area only brought to mind a simpler, gentler, happier time. In 1931 King was out of office, hanging on as leader of the Opposition. He confided to C. Mortimer Bezeau, then Kitchener's mayor, that he preferred the name Berlin: it was "the only name that could have been known to its founders and to many of those who have since passed away."[17] The next year, he asked the mayor to locate and salvage some old gas street lamps of the kind King remembered as a child. The wording of his request reveals a interesting turn of phrase:

> One of my earliest recollections of old Berlin was the lamp lighter who went his round ere the close of day, hooked his ladder to an iron rod that ran through the lamp post about a foot or more from the lamp itself, and then proceeded to light the oil lamp which found its place in a four-sided glass enclosure covered by a tin top.[18]

With the help of Kitchener hardware merchant William Knell, Mayor Mortimer Bezeau sent the lamps to Kingsmere, King's estate outside of Ottawa.

With its out-of-place gothic church arches, Kingsmere is often a target of ridicule, a place where King nurtured his yearning for a simpler, quieter age. He was not alone in this. His old friend John D. Rockefeller was building Colonial Williamsburg at the same time, and Henry Ford was re-creating the "typical" American pre-industrial town in Michigan. These people were not making history; they were trying to find some psychic foundations as members of a generation that had experienced the leap from horses to automobiles, from farming to industry, from country store gossip to radio.

That King's memories would encompass old Berlin are not surprising. Nor is it unusual that he would befriend Homer Watson, this area's most famous landscape artist. In a time when the Group of Seven seemed to be redefining the Canadian artistic landscape, Watson's highly romantic vistas – often of Waterloo County scenes – were far more suited to King's eye and imagination.[19]

Some of this background – his triumphs, his failures, his imaginative sense of Waterloo County – may help explain why King was so nervous when his train approached the Kitchener station in September 1947. Would the real County of Waterloo tend to strengthen or weaken his memories? Despite his accomplish-

Mr. and Mrs. John King outside Mackenzie King's cottage at Kingsmere, Quebec, September 1904. (National Archives of Canada PA-124447)

ments, would this place of his youth – the site of his first and most painful political defeat – reject him again?

Old memories flooded back as King was driven to the city hall. "I was immensely pleased with the changed appearance of King Street through the removal of car tracks and what appeared to be the widening thereby of the street. As we passed building after building, I found I could recall almost instantly the old places and possibly by whom they were occupied and the purposes they served. Going by my father's offices, other memories were revived."[20]

"At the City Hall, the scene was a different one and very pleasing," King continued. "The new city hall itself is an exceptionally fine building, put up in [former Kitchener mayor and then MP] Louis Breithaupt's day." Here King surveyed the pictures of former mayors, "practically all of whom I had known but most of whom had passed away."[21] He was flustered, for he needed time alone to prepare his thoughts. He disliked his impromptu speech, later regretting that he did not mention his father and uncle. He laid a wreath at the cenotaph and then enjoyed a pleasant lunch at Kitchener's late-Victorian Walper Hotel.[22] Another speech and a busy walkabout followed at a crowded reception in Waterloo Park.

This visit moved him deeply, for it affirmed the myth of Waterloo County in his mind; it also reminded King of his advancing years. Shaking hands with people he did not know made him remember friends and political colleagues from old Berlin: "I was of course not expecting to see them but it all made me realize how much older I am than what I really believe myself to be and how nearer I must be drawing to the end of my earthly days." Nevertheless, "I realized the day had brought something very real to my life; that its experiences had left memories much greater than those I had anticipated it would be possible to enjoy."[23]

The next day proved even more memorable. King toured his old riding, greeting long-time supporters in Bridgeport, Linwood, and then Elmira, "where the whole community had been gathered together for an open air meeting." He also returned to his boyhood home, Woodside. Long neglected, the property was then being reclaimed by a trust led by then local MP Louis Breithaupt and Kenneth Sims, with whom King had enjoyed a long correspondence. King's imagination took hold as he approached the grounds. "On the way, I was amazed to find we were driving along a road above the tracks, near the High School, which ran all the way to Woodside. I recall some time ago having a vision of walking in the other direction across a ground that was yet unopened in part, along the very route on which we were driving. It seemed extraordinary that this street should be called 'Breithaupt St.' and that I should be driving with Louis Breithaupt along it."[24]

A great deal had changed, but King immediately recalled the landscape of old Berlin. "I recognized at once the familiar contour of the hills and fields – [the] one which belonged to uncle Dougall; one time an orchard, now a site of many residences and then Woodside itself, the approach to which unhappily has been badly marred by a railroad crossing over a bridge constructed just a little on this side of what was a gateway leading up the Avenue." A young resident of the home greeted the prime minister. "A little girl of the people who are living there at the moment looked out of a window and then came around and put a flower in my buttonhole. She was wearing a Scotch skirt and white waist."[25]

As he did in so much of his political life, King understood the visit as part of a vision fulfilled, even if he had to create a boyhood memory to do so:

I told Louis [Breithaupt] that I recalled vividly and had the thought while lying there under the pine trees [many years before] in the orchard, wondering if some day I might be able to come back after years of public service and secure as my own home the place of my childhood days 'Woodside.' I can remember that impression coming over me vividly. The thought of a life of public service to follow with the reward at the close of it – of having as my own, the home of my boyhood. I do not recall having had thoughts of the kind elsewhere or if I had, I no longer recollect them but this impression was very vivid at the time and comes back very strongly at this moment. (I come to see a little later one how significame [sic] this was. I did not realize it fully at the time.)

He walked through the thick grass to where his family had buried Fanny, their dog. King recalled Old Bill, the family horse, summer days spent playing cricket on the lawn, and his brother Max sliding down a wintry slope. As he wandered through the home he realized "what a tremendous influence that environment must have had on my thought and imagination."[26]

This visit became Mackenzie King's pilgrimage. He had returned fearful of his reception in a place that had once rejected him. Woodside saddened him, for he had no sense of his family's spiritual presence that day. King admitted that he was "too filled with regrets to be … conscious of the influences from Beyond." Still, he left inspired that Woodside might be "rebuilt and used for some useful historical purpose."[27] William Lyon Mackenzie King retired as prime minister in August 1948 and died in July 1950, at the age of seventy-five.

In his psychological essay on Mackenzie King, Paul Roazen concluded: "Nations, like families, live by myths, which are often incomprehensible to outsiders."[28] The same could be said of a nation's leaders. For William Lyon Mackenzie King, Waterloo County became a mythical region that reminded him of family and youthful happiness. In one of his last visits to the area, the focus of that myth became Woodside. Consistent with his wish, it is now a national historic site, carefully rebuilt to resemble the seemingly innocent days when the King family were last together. Gone from memory were the bad events, the setbacks, the bitter defeats. King would have been pleased.

5

King and Chaos: *The Liberals and the 1935 Regina Riot*

Bill Waiser[*]

On October 14, 1935, Mackenzie King ended five years in the political wilderness and led his party into office with the largest and most lopsided Canadian general election victory to date. In contesting the campaign, the Liberal Party leader reasoned that the electorate wanted to punish Prime Minister R.B. Bennett and his five years of Tory rule and that the Liberals would prevail if they held their traditional support. The federal Liberal Party consequently campaigned on the slogan "It's King or Chaos" – in other words, the best policy was to have no policy. But, ironically, there was no shortage of chaos in 1935.

First, in response to the Great Depression, several new political parties had come into being. A record number of candidates sought the 245 seats in the 1935 Parliament. Next was the depression itself, which had shaken the Canadian economy to its foundations while calling into question traditional values about social welfare and the role of the state. Finally, there had been actual chaos on the streets of Regina on Dominion Day, when a bungled police attempt to break up the On-to-Ottawa Trek had provoked a riot, resulting in at least one death, tens of injuries, more than a hundred arrests, and thousands of dollars' damage to the city. How King dealt with the On-to-Ottawa Trek and Regina Riot says much about how the wily Liberal leader placed returning to power above everything else.

---

* The author gratefully acknowledges the research assistance of Jacki Andre.

That the On-to-Ottawa Trek even reached Regina was a testament to the Canadian government's failure to deal with the country's single and homeless unemployed during the Great Depression. In early April 1935 hundreds of dissatisfied, disillusioned men walked out of federally run relief camps in British Columbia and descended on Vancouver in a bold attempt to reverse their dead-end lives and bring about some kind of "work for wages" program. But no one wanted to provide any support for, let alone negotiate with, the men — least of all the federal government, which believed that the Communist Party of Canada had orchestrated the protest. At first the "strikers," as they were dubbed, eked out a hand-to-mouth existence as best they could, thanks to the sympathy and kindness of Vancouver's citizens. But as the stalemate dragged on week after numbing week and more and more men slipped away from an increasingly hopeless situation, the trekkers decided to travel to Ottawa and lay their grievances directly before the government.

About one thousand On-to-Ottawa trekkers left Vancouver by freight train in early June 1935. No attempt was made to stop them. Police and government authorities confidently assumed that the proposed trek was nothing more than a desperate bid to prevent the collapse of the Vancouver strike and that the trekkers' resolve would melt like the snow in the interior mountains. Even Prime Minister Bennett, convinced that the communists had misplayed their hand, announced that his Conservative government would simply watch from the sidelines. There

Caricature of R.B. Bennett, the Conservative prime minister of Canada from 1930 to 1935, by Ivan Glassco from *Bigwigs: Canadians Wise and Otherwise* by R.T.L. (Charles Vining). Vining wrote of Bennett in 1933: "He is seldom afflicted by doubts as to the correctness of his conclusions and misguided obstruction to his plans is likely to induce a metamorphosis which renders him as domineering and highly unpleasant as he has been affable and charming two minutes before. ... He has the quality of courage which burns brightest with necessity and is probably the most combative leader among our modern statesmen."

was no apparent need to do anything; the near-breakdown of the trek at Kamloops seemed to suggest that it was nothing more than a crazy scheme. But the same kind of organizing zeal that had kept the strike going in Vancouver soon took over, and various committees ensured that the trek ran as smoothly as possible. The trekkers also came to realize that they would never reach their goal, never get to Ottawa, unless they worked together as a disciplined unit. They were no longer an aimless group of individuals, hitching a ride on a train, headed for nowhere, but men with a cause – and a mission.

Just as the freight trains the men were riding gained momentum as they rumbled down the Alberta foothills, so did the trek as it headed across the drought-stricken prairie. In fact, it assumed a symbolic significance when it reached the prime minister's home riding of Calgary West. The sheer audacity of the trekkers stirred the imaginations of citizens who had suffered through five terrible years of drought and depressed prices. Here were hundreds of young men – some of them could have been their sons – headed to Ottawa to tell the country's political leaders that they were not doing enough to ease the hardship and deprivation. The Bennett government, however, saw things differently. Whereas many ordinary people understood the trekkers' sense of frustration and loss of patience, the federal government saw only an army of single and homeless unemployed people who had nothing to lose and might do anything. Although people were struck by the trekkers' youth and referred to them as "our boys," the government regarded them as easy targets of communist propaganda. And whereas people appreciated the trekkers' good behaviour and no-nonsense organization, the government feared that the trek's outward appearance – a peaceful, orderly protest – masked its sinister motives.

As the trek continued east from Calgary, the Bennett government made plans to bring it to an end. A sense of urgency now informed Ottawa's response. Not only had the ranks of the trekkers swollen to 1,500 because of a number of new recruits from Alberta, but hundreds more were expected to join in Winnipeg. The federal government consequently turned to the Canadian Pacific and Canadian National Railways, which had willingly been transporting the men, and secured their co-operation. On June 12, the day the trekkers entered Saskatchewan, Ottawa's plan was in place: the railways would complain that the men were trespassing on their trains, and in response to their plea for federal help, the Royal Canadian Mounted Police (RCMP) would be instructed to stop the unlawful movement at

Regina. The next day, in a prepared statement read before the House of Commons, the minister of justice branded the trek a communist plot whose very purpose was "to disturb the peace, order, and good Government of Canada by unlawful means."[1] Ottawa believed that it had no alternative but to intervene and derail the trek before it was too late.

Meanwhile the Conservative government had another problem on its hands: Jimmy Gardiner, the Liberal premier of Saskatchewan, branded Bennett's decision "the most diabolical conspiracy ever perpetrated on the people of any province or any city."[2] Gardiner was infuriated by the federal order to dump the men on the doorsteps of the provincial capital like unwanted waifs, and he insisted that the railways were obligated to take the men out of Saskatchewan since they had brought them in. He also deeply resented federal interference in provincial affairs – he was not consulted – and predicted that the massing of the RCMP could lead to only one outcome: a riot. But Gardiner's ranting and hand-wringing were dismissed as partisan theatrics, and all the Saskatchewan government could do was prepare for the arrival of the trek, now numbering an estimated two thousand men, in the early hours of Friday, June 14.

The federal Opposition leader, Mackenzie King, also watched the unfolding Regina drama with interest – but characteristically, from the sidelines. King had represented a Saskatchewan riding since February 1926, when Gardiner had arranged for a Liberal backbencher to give up his Prince Albert seat so that King, who had been personally defeated in the 1925 general election, could run there. King greatly appreciated the gesture, partly because his mentor, Sir Wilfrid Laurier, had been elected in the same riding in 1896. He also considered a western seat as a counterbalance to his strong Quebec bloc, as well as another step in wooing the Progressive Party into the Liberal fold. But sentiment and regional representation aside, King's attachment to Saskatchewan had its limits; in keeping with the national organization of the party, he looked to Jimmy Gardiner to run the provincial machine. He also relied heavily on Tommy Davis, Prince Albert's representative in the Saskatchewan legislature, to attend to his interests in his riding. King even ignored the wonderful cabin that he had been given for his work in establishing Prince Albert National Park, one hundred kilometres north of the city, in 1927; it fell to others to maintain the cabin.[3]

Premier Gardiner first contacted King about the On-to-Ottawa Trek on the same day that he learned Ottawa planned to use the RCMP to stop the trekkers at

Regina. Over the next few days Gardiner sent King copies from the escalating "telegram war" that he was waging with Bennett. The Saskatchewan premier denounced his federal counterpart for taking over the administration of justice in the province. He also accused Bennett of deliberately misleading the country by portraying the men as trespassers, especially when the railways had willingly transported them to Saskatchewan – to the point of delaying train departures until the men had boarded safely. King was thankful for the correspondence – it might prove useful at a future date – but he failed to sympathize with Gardiner's predicament. Nor did he offer any advice to his Saskatchewan lieutenant. King was more interested in the wider political implications of the Regina showdown and simply observed that the trek had "been as badly bungled by the Government as was possible"[4] and that a satisfactory settlement would be elusive.

This sense that larger issues were at play in Regina was confirmed when Gardiner, after a more detached assessment of the situation, suggested that Bennett might use the apparent communist role in the trek to call for the formation of a national government to deal with subversion and unrest in the country. King agreed, with a warning that the Liberals "shall have to be on guard against all kinds of manoeuvres on the part of those who hope to see the Tory party, under one guise or another retained in office."[5] Beyond that, however, he was not prepared to take a position on the trek or on attempts to derail it. When the matter was raised in caucus on June 26, King reminded his fellow Liberals that there was no need for an official statement on the matter because they were not in office.[6]

The much-anticipated Regina showdown became a prolonged stalemate. On June 17 two federal cabinet ministers, Robert Manion and Robert Weir, met with the trek leaders in Regina and, after failing to reach any agreement, invited them to send a delegation to Ottawa to deal directly with the prime minister. The meeting soon degenerated into a shouting match between Bennett and the trek leader, Arthur "Slim" Evans. The trekkers refused to give up, though, and tried to send a group of men east by car and truck, only to have the convoy intercepted by the RCMP on the outskirts of the city. With no way out of Regina, with federal meals cut off, and with their own funds nearly exhausted, the trekkers decided by the end of June to return to the West Coast. But Ottawa insisted that they had to disband on federal terms – namely, go to a hurriedly erected holding facility at Lumsden, a town near Regina, where the men would be processed.

The trek leadership balked at this proposal – it saw Lumsden as a "concentration camp" – and turned to the Gardiner government for assistance on the afternoon of July 1. Later that evening, while the provincial cabinet met to discuss the trek request, the RCMP, with the support of the Regina city police, decided to execute warrants for the trek leaders at a public rally at Market Square. The mounted men could easily have made the arrests at any time during the day, but with clubs and tear gas at the ready they chose to pluck the men from a peaceful fund-raising meeting – with the expected results. The raid quickly degenerated into a pitched battle between the police and the trekkers and other citizens that spilled over into the streets of downtown Regina. Order was not restored until the early hours of the next day, and only after the police had fired directly into crowds of rioters.[7]

Premier Gardiner was enraged by the brutal breakup of the trek and the resulting destruction to the provincial capital. With Attorney General Tommy Davis he took immediate steps to defuse the situation and extract a measure of revenge. Gardiner and Davis first demanded that the federal minister of justice return control of the RCMP to Saskatchewan. They then met with hundreds of trekkers who were being held under armed guard in the stadium at the Regina exhibition grounds and arranged to send them by train, over the next few days, wherever they wanted to go. Finally, on July 10, they authorized the establishment of a three-person public inquiry into the riot and into the questionable role of the federal government and the police. This last action alarmed the Bennett Conservatives, especially since the commission included the former Liberal provincial premier, William Martin, and they protested that Saskatchewan had neither the right nor the approval to proceed in such a manner.

King was much more circumspect and cautious, particularly since Bennett had decided to remain at the Tory helm and fight the next election, which was expected in the early fall. The leader of the Opposition was genuinely worried that the Conservatives might accuse the Liberals of being soft on communism if they were too outspoken in their criticism of the handling of the trek. This perception was something that King wanted to avoid at all costs, especially in Quebec. Indeed, if the attitude of his own caucus was any indication, many Canadians applauded the government's no-nonsense treatment of the trekkers.[8] King consequently decided to let J.S. Woodsworth, the leader of the fledgling Co-operative Commonwealth Federation (CCF), raise the matter in the House of Commons on July 2, the day after the riot. He also chose to limit his comments during the emergency debate to reading the Gardiner telegrams into Hansard in an effort to counter the government version of the events in Regina.

Later that night, in a moment of reflection, King confided to his diary that the riot was symbolic of Bennett's years in office: "this tragedy … discloses the complete failure of his government to provide work and solve the unemployment problem, which was the ground on which they obtained office."[9] He repeated these remarks the next day at caucus, admonishing his members that unemployment, not communism, was the real issue at Regina and that Bennett was trying to use the threat of subversion to divert attention away from his sorry record.[10] Two days later King regretted that he had not spoken in defence of the homeless men during the Commons debate on the riot. "I should have made one of the great speeches of my life," he noted in his diary on July 5. "Had I been faithful to that end, I would have had a veritable crown of life."[11] His change of heart safely coincided with the end of the parliamentary session, and just a few weeks later King told Tommy Davis that the riot had "increased rather than lessened the problems with which a new Liberal government will be faced, should we be returned."[12]

On August 17, 1935, Prime Minister Bennett finally set the general election date, for October 14. It was widely conceded that the Conservatives would go down to defeat. The question was, by how great a margin. Many Liberals looked to King to propose new programs or talk about new ideas during the campaign, but the federal Liberal leader remained noncommittal. King did not want to give his opponents anything to attack or criticize, and he believed that the best strategy was to hammer away at Bennett's mismanagement of the unemployment crisis, while at the same time portraying the Liberals as the only viable and trustworthy alternative government. He consequently steered clear of the trek and riot and the larger law-and-order issue, except to promise that a Liberal government would repeal the notorious section 98 of the Criminal Code. Otherwise, he deliberately left it to the CCF and the Communist Party of Canada to attack Bennett and his infamous iron heel of ruthlessness – which they gladly did, by means of protest rallies, petitions, and newspaper commentary, including a series of devastating political cartoons in *The Worker*.

When King returned to power, the new Liberal administration took immediate steps to remove some of the irritants from the Bennett years – irritants that had figured in the trek and riot. In 1936 the new government repealed section 98

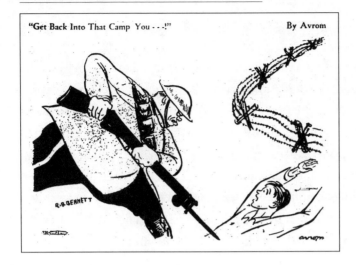

"Get Back Into That Camp You - - -!"   By Avrom

The Communist Party of Canada savaged Prime Minister Bennett in a series of editorials in *The Worker*. These cartoons are from the July 2 and 4, 1935, issues.

First Notch--Estevan 1931; Second Notch--Regina 1935   ---by Avrom

and closed all federal relief camps, in the belief that their purpose was well past. These actions were popular and non-controversial at the time; other parties had called for the repeal of section 98, while even Bennett had toyed with closing the camps in 1934. The bigger question is how the King government dealt with the riot and the government and police roles.

The Regina Riot Inquiry Commission, delayed until after the federal election, finally got underway on November 12, 1935. Over the next three months 359 witnesses provided fifty-three volumes of testimony and one inescapable conclusion: the police had provoked the violence by trying to arrest the trek leaders at a public rally. But in their two-volume report, the commissioners assigned the blame for the riot to the trekkers; the police were completely exonerated.

The findings were not surprising. The trek smacked of communism; after all, trek leader Slim Evans willingly testified that he was a communist organizer. The trekkers' behaviour on the night of the riot also went against the Canadian public's deep-seated allegiance to the prerogatives of peace, order, and good government. Besides, Jimmy Gardiner, the one man who might have exerted some influence on the commission, had left Saskatchewan to join the King government as the new federal minister of agriculture. It was now much easier for the fiercely partisan Gardiner to let the trek and riot simply be remembered as the legacy of Tory governments in general and the Bennett administration in particular.[13]

Despite any misgivings he might have had about the handling of the trek, King not only stood by the RCMP but accepted their interpretation that communism constituted the greatest threat to Canadian life at the time. In fact, when RCMP Commissioner James MacBrien died suddenly in 1938, he was replaced by S.T. Wood, the man who had made the decision to arrest the trek leaders at the Regina Market Square meeting on Dominion Day.

But even though the Liberals and Conservatives viewed communism in much the same light, King believed that the fundamental difference between the two parties was apparent in the way they responded to dissent. He said as much in a personal letter to Tommy Davis a few weeks after the riot: "nothing could better illustrate the difference between the Liberal and Conservative attitude in dealing with human beings than the different methods of Bennett and yourself [a Liberal government]."[14] Later, however, King seemed to forget this difference, when his government adopted the Defence of Canada Regulations on the eve of the Second World War.

6

Considering Both Sides of the Ledger:
J.W. Dafoe and Mackenzie King

Robert Wardhaugh

William Lyon Mackenzie King, Canada's longest-serving prime minister, has not been well remembered. If the average Canadian knows anything about King, it is that he was a queer little fellow who consorted with prostitutes, conducted séances with his dead heroes, was far too close to his mother, and was far too reliant on his dog for attention. All of this is true. But it does tend to obscure what is undoubtedly a remarkable political record, and it certainly does nothing to help understand his amazing success and longevity.

Some historians have attempted to restore the miserable reputation of Mackenzie King that was constructed by the Canadian historical establishment of the 1960s and 1970s. Jack Granatstein and Michael Bliss have gone so far as to argue that King was the "greatest and most interesting of Canada's prime ministers" and perhaps even the "greatest" of Canadians.[1] This approach, however, also fails to present a realistic portrait of King. The prime minister's style and leadership were anything but awe-inspiring; some of his decisions, or lack thereof, were undoubtedly repugnant. But he did lead Canada for a very long time, through many challenging and arduous perils. For this he at least deserves a fair hearing, an attempt to "balance the ledger."

One way to balance the ledger is to approach King's success through the opinionated but insightful perspective of John Wesley Dafoe. The views held by a subject's contemporaries suffer from inevitable bias, but they can at the same time offer interesting first-hand revelations that are not available to the historian. Dafoe was one of the most influential Canadians of the first half of the twentieth century. His political insight from the editorial desk of the *Winnipeg Free Press* was unmatched. His views of King's long career, through its many meandering trails, provide a keen understanding as to its success. In addition, Dafoe's opinions of King offer an insight into the relationships among the federal government, the Liberal Party, and the Prairie West.

John Dafoe's initial views of Mackenzie King were shaped by his relationship with the Liberal Party and its previous leader, Sir Wilfrid Laurier. From his early days as a fledging journalist for the *Montreal Star* covering the parliamentary debates of 1884, Dafoe was more impressed by the Blakes and Cartwrights than the Macdonalds and Tuppers. He came to believe in the Liberal creed of lower tariffs and freight rates and Canadian autonomy in imperial relations. His Liberal partisanship was put to use in 1901, when he accepted the editorship of Clifford Sifton's *Manitoba Free Press*. Dafoe set out to strengthen Prairie Liberalism by explaining party policy to western readers, but his interpretation also included a warning to Ottawa about the needs of the new region. Dafoe learned quickly to "walk carefully in the heavily mined no man's land between the Liberal Government's national policies and the increasingly blunt agrarian attack upon them."[2]

Dafoe served on the paper from 1886 until 1892 and espoused the Liberal position on such issues as the Canadian Pacific Railway's "monopoly" clause and the Manitoba Schools Question. When he returned to Winnipeg nine years later the Liberal torch was again taken up with equal tenacity. Laurier's course on the Schools Question in regard to the Autonomy Acts of 1905, however, led to Sifton's self-imposed exile from the Liberal Party; and even after the prime minister's subsequent surrender on the issue, Dafoe's relationship with the party did not change.[3] It did, however, lead to his identifying more closely with western interests. Dafoe still found himself strongly in agreement with the Laurier line on imperial relations and the development of Canadian autonomy. The debate over the Naval Bill in 1910 only reinforced his support.

In the years preceding the First World War, Dafoe found it increasingly difficult to wade through debates on such key western concerns as tariffs, freight rates, railways, and natural resources in an attempt to "represent Western Canada without damaging the Laurier Government." The Liberal defeat of 1911, along with the end of the western dream of reciprocity, convinced him that the party was

Caricature by Ivan Glassco of John Wesley Dafoe (1866-1944) from *Bigwigs: Canadians Wise and Otherwise* by R.T.L. (Charles Vining). Dafoe developed a grudging respect for King during the interwar years. Vining said of him: "Mr. John W. Dafoe is editor of the Winnipeg *Free Press,* a high-minded journal which never swerves from the path of strict independence except to defend Liberal principles. He has been described as the last of the great Canadian editors but nobody on the *Free Press* knows who the others have been."

"dying a natural death."[4] The Liberals no longer seemed to represent the reforming spirit of the nation, and defeat would, Dafoe hoped, allow a progressive reformation. Increasingly his attitude toward the Liberal Party would coincide with that of western Canada in general. With the beginning of war in 1914, the editor shelved his opposition to the imperial policies of the Tories and threw himself completely behind a united war effort. Laurier's refusal to join Robert Borden's Union Government in 1917 led to the editor's final break with the old Liberal chief. For the first time Dafoe was "a man without a party."[5]

The concept of Union Government received the complete support of J.W. Dafoe and overshadowed his Liberal partisanship. Neither he nor the *Free Press* had advocated conscription prior to 1917, but after Borden returned from a trip to Europe advancing the joint causes of conscription and coalition, both men became ardent advocates. The editor joined the majority of English-Canadian Liberals in supporting the quest for a united war effort, but his biases against French-Catholic Quebec and its isolationist stance also fuelled his opposition to Laurier and his party.

Dafoe provided the Union Government with steady support both during the war and immediately after it. If the coalition could retain its Liberal elements and produce policies acceptable to the West, the support would continue. When this proved not to be the case and Borden's government displayed its Tory leanings, the backing of Dafoe and the *Free Press* faded. With the break of his friend, T.A. Crerar, from government ranks in 1920, it ended completely. Borden's subsequent retirement and Meighen's acceptance of the leadership turned this support into opposition, and Dafoe became a strong advocate of Crerar's Progressive Party.[6] Dafoe joined the majority of westerners in not returning to the Liberal fold.

Both Dafoe and Crerar favoured the selection of W.S. Fielding at the 1919 Liberal leadership convention as the only possible chance, however slight, of strengthening party fortunes on the Prairies. In the West Fielding was perceived as a Maritime protectionist, but he had supported the Union Government, whereas King had remained loyal to Laurier and worked for the Rockefeller family in the United States during the sacrifices of war.[7] "King would do well to go back to working for John D. Rockefeller," the *Free Press* thundered. "There is no future for him in Canada."[8] Dafoe agreed with Crerar in not considering "Mackenzie-King [*sic*] as a possibility." Regardless of the convention choice, however, Dafoe was certain that the Farmer's Movement would gain Prairie support and the two-party system would be disrupted. A fusion between Progressives and Liberals would become a necessity.[9]

After King's selection as leader, Dafoe critically observed his attempts to convince the West that he could represent Prairie interests. The editor believed that King genuinely belonged to the "liberal" and "progressive" end of the party[10] but also that he had become the puppet of the Quebec Liberals who had ensured his selection as leader. Dafoe did not believe that King would be strong enough to exert his own influence at party councils.[11] During King's first western speaking tour the editor noted that there were "no traces of any wild enthusiasm." If the trip was intended to put the party "back upon the political map," it was "a failure." If King was hoping for some form of "unofficial" alliance between the Liberals and the Farmers, Dafoe wrote, "he will by now have abandoned them if he has the faculty so necessary to a successful political career of seeing things as they are and refusing to follow phantoms."[12] The Liberal Party, Dafoe noted with the approach of the 1921 election, had "no strength whatever in the West. Laurier destroyed it in 1917 and Mr. King has not been able to revive it." The western Liberals had moved "almost solidly" into the Progressive ranks, and Dafoe "watched like a hawk" for signs of disintegration in the party. He was convinced that King was the party's "poorest asset."[13]

The Prairie drift toward the Progressives proved to be a stampede in the election of 1921. Dafoe was opposed to the Progressive leadership joining the new Liberal cabinet in Ottawa without an official coalition, and he viewed King's overtures to Crerar and Ontario's E.C. Drury as blatant attempts to absorb and destroy the movement within a Quebec-dominated party. The Progressives had to maintain their identity because King did not yet understand or appreciate the reasons behind the agrarian revolt. Personally, Dafoe believed the new prime minister would have been prepared to accept a coalition and co-operate fully with the Progressives, but "the thing that upset the applecart was his surrender to pressure from the Montreal junta."[14] By preserving their identity the Progressives would not only save their movement but also leave King's party to the "Liberal antiques" congregating at Ottawa.[15] A split would be inevitable, and "liberal" elements of the party would then be free to fuse with the Progressives.

King had little chance of impressing the *Free Press* editor until he rid the Liberal Party of the Montreal "junta" led by Sir Lomer Gouin. The problem was compounded, according to Dafoe, because this group constituted the most "Conservative" influence in the entire nation:

> I don't see how you can combine in one party members of Parliament truly representative of Western desires and interests and the members who represent say the district of Montreal. There is hardly a point of contact between them. As things are at present it is the Montreal element that will control the Liberal party, and if the West sends Liberal members to Ottawa they will find themselves subject to this control with only the right to make protests in the party caucus, which will be listened to tolerantly and ignored.[16]

Dafoe recognized King's expedient nature as well as his desire and intention to remain true to the Gouin Liberals from Quebec. Although the prime minister often espoused Prairie sympathies and claimed support for western issues,[17] Dafoe doubted that he had the "resolution to act in accordance with what appear to be his wishes." Gouin's exit from the cabinet would be a necessity, not only in providing King with a stronger grasp on the leadership, but also in advancing his cause on the Prairies. Dafoe did not believe that King had the courage to "bell the cat."[18] Governments often become more conservative in office, he observed, "but I never knew one which became more radical." Since the prime minister would

Sir Robert Borden during the Victory Bond Campaign, Ottawa, 1917. (A.G Pittaway photo / National Archives of Canada C-004755)

not "pay the price," Dafoe maintained his hopes for a reformed Liberal Party with a controlling western wing.[19] Charles Dunning, the Liberal premier of Saskatchewan who had maintained friendly relations with both Liberal and Progressive groups, would be the likely candidate to lead such a fusion.[20]

By 1923 it remained obvious that Dafoe had no faith in King's ability to lead the Liberal Party. The need to maintain the support of the Gouin group prevented King from acting to improve his position in the West or with the *Free Press*. An issue outside domestic politics would be required, and that issue arose during the Imperial Conference of 1923.

The Chanak Crisis of 1922 and King's firm stand in defending Canadian autonomy had demonstrated that Anglo–Dominion relations could provide common ground between Quebec and the West. The 1923 Imperial Conference would allow Mackenzie King to continue his quest toward autonomy while providing common ground to bring the Progressive and Quebec groups together. The gathering in London witnessed the struggle between the forces arrayed for and against imperial centralization, and the Canadian prime minister took command of those advocating dominion autonomy. Dafoe had been invited to attend the conference and report the proceedings for the Canadian Press. He found that King shared his position on the Dominion's role in Empire and was markedly impressed by the determined stand of the prime minister. "As for King," he indicated on his return,

> my regard for him has perceptibly increased by what I saw of him in London. He is an abler man than I thought; he has more courage than I gave him credit for; and he could be a very much better speaker than he is if he would cut out the platitudes and "get down to brass tacks." He really made some excellent speeches in London.

As a result of the conference, "Dafoe's regard for King rose for the first time to a high level."[21] The reaction demonstrated a notable improvement, but the praise could hardly have been more qualified. Dafoe agreed that King possessed "some excellent qualities for public life" but was "by no means sold on the proposition that he has the equipment for leadership for times such as these." In fact, he was "rather convinced to the contrary." If a fusion between the Liberals and Progressives occurred, however, it was "quite in the cards" that King might continue to lead the party. In the "right setting" and "with the right men behind him," King would be "a not unacceptable party leader."[22]

Although the conference allowed Dafoe to view King temporarily from outside the biases of regional politics, it did nothing to bring the two men together on domestic issues. Dafoe hoped the situation would improve when at year's end both Fielding and Gouin retired from politics. The opportunities for gaining Liberal support in the West were markedly increased, and King's leadership was strengthened. But as 1924 progressed, Dafoe's hope that King would use his newfound strength to distance himself from his Quebec support and reform the party diminished. The editor became even more pessimistic that a fusion would ever take place. Instead the prime minister seemed "pleased with himself" and confident that his strategy of absorbing the Progressives was working, without actually

offering an official alliance or any substantial concessions. Dafoe found this conclusion absurd. While King was "manoeuvring to prevent adverse combinations
in parliament against him; and hoping that something will turn up to better his
conditions," the government was "slipping" and Arthur Meighen's Conservatives
were reaping the rewards. Dafoe maintained no confidence in King's strength as
Liberal leader. "So you see I don't think much of King's chances as a party leader
in Canada," he told journalist J.A. Stevenson.[23] At the very least, he did "not see a
chance in the world in Western Canada for the Ottawa Government at the next
election."[24]

The Progressives maintained Dafoe's loyalty into the election of 1925. The
problem, he contended, was that King still had no understanding of the western
political situation or of how to handle the agrarian revolt. "My experience of politicians," he wrote Sifton, "is that they are peculiarly subject to pipe-dreams," and
this characteristic seemed particularly evident in King. The Progressives were declining, but they would not disappear as the prime minister believed before the
next election: "If Mr. King is allowing himself to be lulled by these stories of Progressive disintegration and the certainty of Liberal triumph he is preparing a disaster for himself." The editor continued to advance his notion of transforming the
Progressives into an ally – and eventually an element – of the Liberal Party. Such a
fusion could only occur if the Liberals paid more attention to the needs of western Canada, and at present this meant the Progressives: "If some magician could
only make the necessary shift for them they would be quite content to serve as a
sort of Western wing; but the stream divides them and no one is able to throw a
bridge over it." King was speaking on the Prairies about "sinking differences" and
"getting together" but the words remained "pious observations."[25] Candidates in
the West who offered themselves as direct supporters of the King government had
little chance of success.[26]

After the poor Liberal showing in the 1925 election, rumours abounded that
tied Dafoe and his "Winnipeg Sanhedrin"[27] to a plot to replace King with Saskatchewan premier Charles Dunning. Dafoe certainly viewed Dunning as "one of
the few public men who take a realistic view of the situation" and recognized his
ability to placate both western Liberals and Progressives. In other words, Dunning's views were "almost identical" to those of Dafoe.[28] There was also no doubt
that King's stock had reached a new low on the Prairies. Dafoe believed that he
had a following among "what are popularly called the Laurier-Liberals," but

Arthur Meighen (1874-1960), Conservative leader 1920-1926, and bitter adversary of Mackenzie King. (National Archives of Canada C-005799)

otherwise the consensus was that he was "not the right man for the present emergency." King would likely meet Parliament with no definite program and would expect to be saved by Progressive support. Dafoe was annoyed with King's refusal to contemplate a coalition and his belief that "if a couple of Progressives would come into the government everything would be lovely." The precarious position with the Progressives holding the balance of power in Parliament would at least force "more readiness" on behalf of the prime minister to heed the West. "Quebec has come off the high horse," Dafoe claimed, "under the whip of necessity."[29]

But Dafoe had no intention of conspiring to overthrow King: there was no real alternative to the Liberal leader, and this glaring fact became a major motivation in forcing Dafoe to reconsider his view of the prime minister. Dunning's name inevitably came up, even among the French-Canadian discontented, but a move to replace "Laurier's successor" with a western Liberal would have to come from Quebec. From the outset Dafoe disagreed with any attempt to change leaders and argued that "to swap horses at this moment would probably be fatal."[30]

The Customs Scandal, the King–Byng Affair, and the Constitutional Question quickened Dafoe's return to the Liberal ranks and set the stage for his further re-evaluation of King. The Progressives had shown their sterility and, more importantly, had demonstrated that their existence threatened to divide the Liberal vote and allow a Tory government. The time had come for some form of fusion, even if it meant the Progressives directly supporting the Liberals. The very real threat of Conservative victory played a dominant role in forcing Dafoe's hand:

> My idea of the political objective to be aimed at is to keep the Conserva-
> tives out for the next few years at any rate. If by any chance Mr. Meighen
> were to get into office with a substantial majority behind him he would
> probably smash this country trying to make it conform with his theories.[31]

The editor admitted that it was only the "probabilities" of the Conservatives coming into power that was bestirring him "to activity" on behalf of the government.[32] It was clear that any hope of the King Liberals forming a government
hinged on the West, and this would have to provide enough pressure in forcing
the party to pay attention to Prairie concerns. The 1926 election campaign would
see Dafoe, and the Manitoba Liberals led by Crerar, throw themselves wholeheart-
edly into the Liberal cause and behind Mackenzie King. A.B. Hudson, one of the
members of the "Winnipeg Sanhedrin," went so far as to herald the work of the
Free Press as the most important single factor in achieving complete success for
the Liberals in the province.[33] Dafoe and the West found they had little choice but
to return to the Liberal Party.[34]

If the *Free Press* editor had any thoughts of replacing King, they were dispelled
by the Liberal victory of 1926. Against all odds the prime minister had managed
to survive the turbulent years since 1921 and had succeeded in keeping his party
and leadership intact. For this feat Dafoe offered a grudging respect:

> The angels are certainly on the side of Willie King. He has a finer opportu-
> nity now than he had in 1921, and I hope he will be equal to it. I am begin-
> ning to think that probably he will measure up to his opportunities this
> time. It was certainly a Mr. King that I knew nothing about who has been
> performing in the last two months.[35]

The election and an ensuing decline in the editor's regard for Charles Dunning
also helped diminish any notion of a leadership change.[36] His view of the prime
minister had improved, but he still remained cautious:[37]

My regard for King has gone up a good deal since July 1st. The way he handled himself in the House and the admirable campaign which he has carried on suggest to me that there is more to him than I have been inclined to think there was. He certainly now has a magnificent opportunity and if he fumbles it his blood be on his head.[38]

King continued to travel the road to Dominion autonomy at the Imperial Conference of 1926. Dafoe's decision not to attend the conference was an indication of his support for the prime minister. As Ramsay Cook points out in *The Politics of John W. Dafoe and the Free Press*, Dafoe probably would have attended, but his vigorous backing of King during the recent election had endangered his "independence" as a newspaperman and he did not wish to become further identified with the Liberal government. King's overall performance, however, did not please Dafoe as it had in 1923. The Canadian prime minister now found himself in the moderate position, between Australia and New Zealand and the push for complete independence led by the Irish Free State and South Africa.

After 1926 Dafoe returned to his pre-war position of convincing the West to support the Liberal Party, and his relationship with King was further enhanced by provincial politics in Manitoba. The key to winning the province lay in healing the breach in the Liberal Party between the Laurier "Diehard" and Unionist "Free Press" factions, and although the prime minister worked to maintain the support of both sides he ended up courting the more influential Free Press group. As one of the leaders of this group Dafoe worked closely with King in cementing a fusion not only among Liberals but also between Liberals and Progressives at the provincial level.

In 1930 the Liberal government in Ottawa was defeated by R.B. Bennett's Conservatives. King's overconfidence and poor choice of an election date once again brought Dafoe's doubts and criticisms to the surface: "I felt a good deal of exasperation over King's performance in leaving the plough in the furrow, when there was great need for it to be ploughed through to the end." He had hoped the government would carry out its complete term and use the time to develop a new constructive program to handle the depression. King's "political sagacity" had been "a minus quantity" throughout the campaign, and although Dafoe looked to King "to show up well in Opposition" he doubted that the Liberal leader appreciated "the magnitude" of his task: "I do not think his chances again of being Prime Minister are very good."[39]

Prime Minister R.B. Bennett speaking in Toronto during the Depression. (National Archives of Canada PA-052387)

It was quickly made clear that while the *Free Press* was going to be "very much an opposition paper" there was "no intention of becoming a sort of organ and factum of the Opposition party and of Mr. King." As far as Dafoe was concerned, the Liberal leader had "wrecked the ship by the dumbest political strategy of this generation." If the federal Liberals expected the paper to "fly kites and do chores of various kinds for them" they were mistaken. The editor would lead the paper into his own "brand of war against Bennett without much regard as to whether or not it fits in with the plans of the Liberal board of strategy."[40] For Dafoe there was still room for western Liberals to take an alternative path from the federal party of Mackenzie King. He now seemed uncertain as to whether the Liberal leader would "muff" or "prove equal" to the situation.[41] "King has not been one of my heroes," Dafoe noted with a qualification, "(though my opinion of him has risen greatly in the past two years)."[42] He was prepared to continue backing King, but the support remained tenuous.

The Liberal return to opposition led to the usual calls within certain sections of the party for a leadership change. The rapid decline of Bennett stock made it apparent that whoever led the party would very likely end up in office after the next election.[43] Dafoe had been angered by King's "bungling" of the 1930 election but was now even less prone to discuss a change in leadership. "He is the best leader for the next battle," the editor told his Ottawa reporter, Grant Dexter. As long as the disclosures relating to the Beauharnois political donation scandal did not cause irreparable harm, Dafoe supported keeping King at the helm.[44] The quest for Canadian autonomy continued, and the editor hoped that the publication of his diary detailing the 1923 Imperial Conference would somehow "exonerate" the Liberal leader: "I have never been a worshipper of Mr. King, but upon the whole I think he has done valuable service to Canada ... he certainly has a truer idea of the policies necessary for Canadian prosperity than his adversary."[45]

Dafoe's position on King had gradually changed from outright opposition to grudging acceptance. When compared with the choices available, the editor told Frank Underhill, King "was the most truly Liberal in his views." There was "hope" for King, and although he was not "an ideal leader" Dafoe now admitted that he had never met one. King had a "better intellectual grasp of the fundamentals of liberalism than most of his colleagues,"[46] but it did not follow "that there is much enthusiasm for him." In fact, he had little personal following. Dafoe would admit King's "good many achievements to his credit" but also that they did not "stand out in the public mind."[47] The Liberal leader was effective but by no means charismatic. Such a combination, however, seemed to be well suited to Canadian politics.

Throughout the 1930s the Prairie West became increasingly alienated from Ottawa and the Liberal Party, but unlike the situation in the period prior to the First World War, Dafoe did not share the sense of alienation. As Ramsay Cook points out:

> Just as Dafoe admired T.A. Crerar as the leader of the Progressives because he stood in the tradition of nineteenth-century Canadian Liberalism, so he measured the politicians of the great depression against the standard of Mackenzie, Blake and Laurier. He found all of them wanting, except Mackenzie King.[48]

The Prairies were now moving in a political direction that the *Free Press* editor was not prepared to follow. He noted the increased power of the "Left" and that King made little appeal to this group. The Liberal Party had to win back discontented moderates by returning to its traditional "liberal" roots and ending its courting of the "big interests."[49] King would have to do what he did best – find the middle ground – and Dafoe would be right there, pointing the way.

King's handling of the Co-operative Commonwealth Federation (CCF) received praise from Dafoe. He agreed with the "stiff rejection" of the CCF by the federal Liberals and the attempt to show that "socialism is on a wholly different basis from the progressive movement which was essentially Liberal in its origins."[50] A Liberal meeting was held to discuss reaction to the CCF, and Dafoe advocated a leftward shift by the party to maintain western support. He also advanced strengthening the federal government to handle increasing provincial responsibilities in the face of the depression. In 1921 Dafoe had stood squarely opposed to the federal Liberal government of Mackenzie King, but now he was clearly on side. "The editor believed," Cook exaggerates, "that Mackenzie King was the Liberal Moses who could lead the Canadian people out of the economic wilderness and back to the Promised Land."[51]

As late as 1934 Dafoe still occasionally complained of King being the puppet of Quebec, but these grumblings were now uncommon.[52] In a letter to Harry Sifton he found himself in the strange position of defending King. "Theoretically," he wrote,

> the Liberals would be happier if they had a new leader who would be young, attractive, competent, etc. They would then be able to go before the public and play the usual confidence game, representing him as a man who would make the country rich, if not in a night, at least in a year or so. With King in charge a campaign of this sort is not possible, since both his virtues and his limitations are well known to the country.

Although King was uncharismatic he had mastered the art of brokerage politics, and these skills were far more valuable in governing such a diverse nation as Canada. Perhaps even more importantly, King represented the seemingly safe "Liberal" middle ground in a political spectrum increasingly shaped by a Right–Left dichotomy. Once again Dafoe reinforced his position that a leadership change was not "within range of practical politics." No practicable alternative had yet appeared, except perhaps Ernest Lapointe, but the problems this choice would pose to the unity of the party and nation were insurmountable: "Chief among

them would be his refusal to entertain the proposition if it were put up to him."
The frustration with King's leadership arose "more from restlessness and a desire
for some kind of a new deal" and ignored the "row" that would be created by a
leadership struggle. "I am very strongly of the opinion," Dafoe told Sifton, "that
the commonsense view of the situation is to accept the situation and make the
best of it. I am inclined to think that upon the whole the Liberal party is fortunate
in having a leader with as many qualifications for the job as Mr. King has."[53]

The 1935 federal election campaign and ensuing Liberal victory brought the relationship between King and Dafoe to a new level. King was so impressed and
thankful for the support given by the *Free Press* that he even offered Dafoe a cabinet
position. Dafoe assumed it was a "courtesy offer" and believed that King expected
him to decline; he had no intention of leaving his editor's desk regardless.[54]

Canada's external policy had consistently proven a valuable ally in strengthening Dafoe's relationship with King since 1921, but this ended in the late 1930s. The
two men had found themselves in agreement on Canada's role in the Empire but
disagreed over the nation's role in maintaining collective security. These contrasting positions, taken during the First World War, had demonstrated the potential
for conflict. By 1937 events in Europe were making this potential a reality.

In the face of threats to world peace by Italy, Japan, and Germany, King attempted to avoid involvement in foreign conflicts and fully supported the policies
of appeasement advanced by British prime minister Neville Chamberlain. Dafoe,
on the other hand, correctly analyzed the futility of appeasement and advocated
firm opposition. "Mr. King has very definitely decided upon a policy of one hundred per cent isolation," he angrily wrote after observing the prime minister's desperate attempts to avoid a position at the League of Nations that would censure
Italy's attack on Abyssinia:[55] "The League of the future which Mr. King envisages
will be a kind of recurrent conference with permanent organs functioning in the
interim, at which there will be debate and more debate about world affairs." There
would be little chance of Canada avoiding struggles in the future, he argued, regardless of desires for peace, however genuine.[56]

The 1937 Imperial Conference demonstrated that while Dafoe now disagreed
with King's foreign policy, the two men's relationship had advanced to the point
that there was little likelihood of a break. In advancing Canadian autonomy,
Dafoe noted that the prime minister

has certainly gone a long way and is likely to go still farther. ... I do not
think his contemporaries appreciate the part Mr. King has played in Canadian affairs during the last seventeen years. It has in fact been very notable
and it would not surprise me if his participation in Commonwealth affairs
now and hereafter should also be of outstanding importance.

The editor admitted to "occasionally" becoming "a little annoyed" because King
was "a little defective in making up his mind to take action," but he also thought
that King was "usually right when he does act."[57] On the other hand, Dafoe remained highly critical of King's obsession with appeasement even to the brink of
war, and he held nothing back in blasting these policies in the pages of the *Free
Press*.

With the outbreak of the Second World War Dafoe's criticisms came to an
abrupt end. There was no anger or resentment, no "I told you so" – just a grim
acceptance and determination to face the task at hand. In his characteristic style,
Dafoe led the *Free Press* fully into the quest for a united war effort, and this time
he was prepared to work personally for the federal government. His position on
the Rowell–Sirois Commission, designed to study the state of Dominion–provincial relations, was part of this endeavour.[58]

These years would demonstrate the complete reversal that had occurred in
Dafoe's view of King since 1919. The necessity of a united war effort had shaped
Dafoe's attitude toward Borden during World War One and made him an advocate of the Tory prime minister, but the editor's support of King during the Second World War cannot be explained solely along the same lines. Opposition
aimed at the Liberal government during the war, and King in particular, angered
Dafoe. In fact, he told journalist J.A. Stevenson,

the systematic disparagement and belittlement of everything he has done
has vexed me to the point that I have become somewhat of a partisan on
his behalf – something I never was previously. I am going wherever possible, to give him the benefit of the doubt when his policies are assailed by
his inveterate foes.[59]

According to the editor, the prime minister's opponents had to realize that the
government was going to be in office for the duration and should offer more gen-

erous support to Canada's agency for carrying out the war. Much of the opposition, he noted, was due to "a carry over from a former anti-King complex" that he himself had shared. It was now "ridiculous," he told Crerar, "to suggest any possible alternative to Mr. King."[60]

But the editor's defence of the prime minister also demonstrated a genuine respect that had developed over the preceding two decades. "There can be no question of the indispensability of Mr. King in the difficult days through which we have passed," he told Grant Dexter in 1941, "and history will of course make this clear."[61] King was not an infallible leader, but he was the least fallible of the alternatives. Dafoe then went on to produce what is probably the most insightful account of King's lengthy career and contribution:

> Every person, before God and man, has a right to ask that both pages in the ledger in which his deeds are recorded shall be considered in any accounting. On that basis, King stands up pretty well in my estimation. He came down to 1935 with a pretty fair balance in his credit. His external policies during those years were sound and right. ... His domestic policies during those years on many points did not command my enthusiastic support; but I do not know any man in public life during those years who would have done better from my point of view. ... From October, 1935 to September, 1939, the ledger account is heavily against King. I myself had to listen to his talk about Hitler and his apparent good intentions. ... If he had held my views ... he probably would not have been in office since he would have been at outs with Canadian opinion, feeling and prejudices. ... As for King's record since September 1, 1939, he has piled up a surplus which gives him a substantial balance in my judgement. ... No doubt he has made many mistakes; his methods of doing business may exasperate; he may at times have confused national and party interests. In short he is a miserable sinner. But aren't we all?

Peter Larkin, a prominent businessman and Liberal who would serve as King's High Commissioner in London during the 1920s, had told a skeptical Dafoe in 1919 that the future would demonstrate King worthy to be placed in the same ranks as Macdonald and Laurier. Dafoe now accepted the truth of this prophecy.[62] "My relations with King have never got to the point of warm friendship," he admitted in January 1943, "but they have been close enough to give me an impression, which grows with every contact, that there is more to this man than I have thought." This was a powerful confession for the forthright editor and reflected much about Mackenzie King. "I not infrequently think of you," he wrote the prime minister at year's end,

> with a sympathetic appreciation of your difficulty which, in comparison with mine, must be as fifty to one. … Of the four Prime Ministers of Canada in the first eight decades of the Dominion's existence who will be given the rank of greatness, you have had to carry the heaviest burden; and history will do full justice to the manner in which you have discharged this duty.[63]

In his last days Dafoe wrote King again with hopes that he would be "at the helm when the ship of state makes port after the voyage through perilous seas" and that he would be "accepted by all the people of Canada, after the passions of the day subside, as one who rendered the country invaluable service. At any rate that will be the record of history."[64] There was little doubt in Dafoe's mind that unlike Borden in 1920, King would emerge from the war and remain in power. His "political sagacity," so often the subject of Dafoe's scrutiny, would now lead him to a solid and effective programme of reconstruction:

> I see no adequate substitute for King in the leadership of the Liberal party or for that matter, in the premiership of the country. He is the best we have got by a considerable margin. Moreover, his personal stock is higher than it has been, even though the party stock is down. The country realizes that he is a very much abler man than he was given credit for being, even when his party was sweeping the country. … The Conservatives have abandoned their absurd attitude, in which they persisted for years, that King was a political accident whom they could push out of office with any kind of leader.[65]

Dafoe's views on many issues, as his biographer Murray Donnelly indicates, became "moderated by time and experience." His prejudices against French Catholics and immigrant groups had subsided, and in his last years he even "looked back on the conscription crisis of 1917 with some sympathy for the Quebec point of view."[66] According to Ramsay Cook, "at the centre of this change in Dafoe was Mackenzie King."[67] The editor always had a keen insight into the workings of Canadian politics, but in his early years his views were much more determined by religious, cultural, and regional biases. By the Second World War he was convinced that the King Liberals were the best option for preserving national unity. As Cook notes, the prime minister "had proven invincible against the years of Dafoe's criticism, as against the criticism of so many others."[68]

Dafoe's changing views provide an important perspective on the success of "the enigma" that is Mackenzie King.[69] The prime minister did not inspire enthusiasm and his brokerage politics were difficult to praise, but they were effective. Dafoe came to recognize this essential fact. When looking back on King's career, T.A. Crerar argued that Macdonald, Laurier, and Borden were statesmen and that Canada was very largely the "product of their statesmanship" but that King had no "similar monument."[70] On this count Dafoe, who was usually in accord with Crerar, would have disagreed.

7

Mackenzie King and Japanese Canadians

Stephanie Bangarth

The Second World War affected all Canadians, but particularly those from countries at war with Canada, such as Germany and Italy, and more significantly people of Japanese descent living on Canada's West Coast. Like those of German and Italian descent, many people of Japanese descent in Canada were long-time Canadian citizens. Their very presence, however, raised a cry of alarm among a population already prone to racial intolerance. The Canadian government, with the full co-operation of British Columbia's provincial government, responded to the popular outcry by evicting Canadians of Japanese descent to the interior of British Columbia and other points farther east.[1]

Under the direction of Prime Minister William Lyon Mackenzie King, the government announced its plans on January 14, 1942, to remove Japanese nationals from the West Coast. The policy bore the unmistakeable imprint of West Coast opinion. On February 24, 1942, under heavy pressure from B.C. politicians and citizens after the outbreak of the Pacific war in 1941, the federal government approved an enabling measure (order-in-council P.C. 1486) that permitted the total evacuation of all persons of Japanese ancestry from the protected zones in British Columbia. A racist animus had pervaded the motivations of the people and politicians of British Columbia, but what were the motivations of those in Ottawa? More specifically, what prompted King to endorse so extreme a policy?

In examining the attitudes of any group or individual (in this case, King) the researcher faces a dilemma. It is difficult to construct adequately a particular mindset and the factors that influenced those opinions. Often the problem is to avoid making sweeping inferences based on scanty resources. When the subject material is particularly rich, as in the case of Prime Minister King, the challenge is to determine the salient aspects of the subject's character, attitudes, and mores. The source material left by King, both for posterity and that uncovered by scholars, is vast, varied, and interesting. This paper has relied on various King diaries, spanning from 1893 to 1950; prime ministerial notes and memoranda; King's personal, published works; written commission reports (specifically dealing with the investigation into the 1907 Vancouver Riots, the Opium Commission, and various others dealing with "Oriental"[2] immigration); the War Cabinet Committee minutes, and Hansard.

In their assessments of King's political formation historians have largely neglected King's earlier careers as a public servant and politician. The "Oriental question,"[3] however, was a major issue from King's beginnings as a politician to the end of his career. An examination of the policies directed toward Japanese Canadians in 1942 conducted in light of how King's views on the "Oriental question" developed *throughout* his career suggests that the internment of the Japanese Canadians was not merely a phenomenon of the wartime circumstances of 1942. This interpretation is examined here in two parts: the first details the period from 1900 to 1938, and the second outlines the early years of the Second World War, from 1939 to 1942. Although King's experience with the "Oriental question" was, arguably, greater than that of any other Canadian politician of his time, he proved to be anything but an advocate for the Japanese, Chinese, and East Indian peoples of Canada.

Many clues suggest why King would ultimately decide early in 1942 to intern British Columbia's Japanese-Canadian population. In an effort to contextualize and explain how the internment policy was framed, this analysis focuses specifically on King's political activities leading up to 1942 as they pertain to the "Oriental question" by reviewing the policies and decisions that include his experiences with the 1907 Vancouver Riots and Asian immigration, among others.[4]

Mackenzie King was a political realist and an opportunist, but he was not a racist in his direction and handling of policies affecting Japanese Canadians. His attitudes toward Asians were very much in keeping with, and often more moderate than, general opinion of the day. While he may have shared some aspects of popular opinion against Japanese Canadians, he also recognized the need for diplomacy and balanced opinion. His balancing act, however, had some serious

Fears over Asian immigration and the opium trade fuelled the fires or racial tension, particularly in B.C., as this Samuel Hunter cartoon suggests."An Angry Dog – Little Nippon Decides to Keep Away," January 23, 1908. (National Archives of Canada C-038302)

consequences. Throughout King's political career, especially with regard to the "Oriental question," several examples, when taken together, establish a continuity, a constancy, of racially motivated – albeit diplomatically framed – actions that had adverse effects on the Chinese, Japanese, and East Indian populations of Canada. Beginning with King's appointment as commissioner for the 1907 Vancouver Riots and continuing with his 1907–08 investigations into "increased" Oriental immigration, the 1910 royal commission dealing with the opium traffic in Canada and the ensuing Opium Act of 1911, the "continuous journey rule," the 1923 Chinese Immigration Act, and the 1928 revisions of the "Gentleman's Agreement," a clear pattern emerges. Although these important and telling aspects of King's early political career are often neglected in explanations of his 1942 decision to intern Japanese Canadians, they show a pattern that proved not to be in the best interests of the Asian minorities of Canada. King had his own thoughts, but his deft gauging of popular opinion largely dictated the policies. His prior experiences, in addition to the special and difficult circumstances both immediately before the war and in its early years, help account for his decision in early 1942 to intern British Columbia's Japanese-Canadian population. In this case, however, political realism may have had as detrimental an effect on race relations as racism and racist governmental policies did.

The King historiography, consisting largely of political biographies and sensationalist publications, ignores the issue of race and the prejudices and beliefs that shaped Mackenzie King. The available works tend to focus on the politics and policies of the King government, especially during the Second World War and post-war reconstruction periods. There is a remarkable absence of scholarship dealing with King's early political career; indeed, historians have generally not been very kind to King. With the release of the King diaries to his authorized biographers in 1960, the broad outlines of his spiritualist interests were revealed, in addition to his extremely close relationship with his mother, his relations with women, and his fascination with the positioning of the hands of the clock when he was making important decisions. The "weird Willie" industry took off. In 1976 C.P. Stacey, Canada's most distinguished military historian, published *A Very Double Life: The Private World of Mackenzie King.*[5] Much of this attempt at a biography of King was coloured by Stacey's feelings of contempt for King's handling of the conscription crisis, resulting in the vulgarization of someone who was arguably one of Canada's most important political leaders.[6]

Some of King's defenders thought history should only concern itself with the public side of his life. H.S. Ferns and B. Ostry, in *The Age of Mackenzie King,*[7] though providing a largely critical account of the policies and politics of the King government, nevertheless conclude that King was a skilled political statesman who managed the country effectively in very difficult and unusual circumstances. J.L. Granatstein commented that King brought prime ministership to near-tactical perfection in an essay in the collection *Mackenzie King: Widening the Debate.*[8] More recently Michael Bliss attempted to resolve the public and private King in his book about the prime ministers of Canada, *Right Honourable Men.*[9] Bliss's portrait of King is a remarkable re-evaluation of a leader who not only stabilized the country through trying times but who introduced the modern welfare state to Canada. Included in this account is a more professional look at King's "after hours" activities. Perhaps as more time passes we may obtain more histories that move away from the profane toward the professional and King will no longer be judged in light of his idiosyncrasies.

Although historians and political biographers have found numerous perspectives from which to examine and analyze the public and private King, within these accounts there is a marked absence of any discussion of his dealings with Canada's population of Japanese descent or Asians in general. King's policies concerning Japanese Canadians are presented either as footnotes or are left out altogether. Only Ferns and Ostry critique King's political dealings with Asians, though they concentrate on his early career as deputy minister of labour and then as minister of labour in the Laurier government. They attribute the Liberal policy of limiting the labour market (specifically of Asian labour) to motives of racial discrimination and political expediency. Under King's leadership Canada moved more closely into the orbit of the United States both economically and politically. According to Ferns and Ostry, American and Canadian co-operation on Japanese exclusion was only one of the many ways in which the Liberals sought closer ties with the United States.[10]

Studies of Japanese Canadians are more numerous than are the available works on King and his political career.[11] Historians have generally explained the Japanese-Canadian community in Canada in the light of one major defining event – the wartime evacuation of the Japanese-Canadian population from the West Coast – and the focus is on the internment as a West Coast phenomenon. The emphasis has been either sociological–social, explaining the internment in light of the influence of West Coast public opinion on government policy, or political and elitist, focusing on the B.C. members of Parliament and their role in shaping government policy. The "real people" – the Japanese Canadians who were interned – are often portrayed as faceless victims who were helpless in the maze of government policies and politicians.

The image of the victim is a powerful one, often irresistible for many historians.[12] This is a valid interpretation of much of the research done on Japanese Canadians, who are usually presented as passive recipients of oppressive legislation enforced by a prejudiced government bureaucracy. While this type of literature does make a solid contribution in revealing that racism is a part of Canadian history, Japanese Canadians are shown as not being responsible for their own history. Where this method is not employed, the Japanese Canadians are lost in a sea of policy discussion; they are relegated to being mere bystanders.

A few studies have attempted to break away from the victim analysis. Keibo Oiwa, Audrey Kobayashi, and Peter Nunoda[13] each present, to varying degrees, a new approach to the study of the Japanese Canadians – as a diverse and effective *community*, as subjects of history rather than as mere objects. This is characterized by a focus on the empowerment of Japanese-Canadian history to effect a more "bottom-up" approach to their history. Each of these writers shows that the Japanese-Canadian community was not, and is not, passive and obedient. Oiwa shows that the Nikkei (the overseas population of Japanese origin) adopted the strategy of self-marginalization for biological, economic, and cultural survival, and not in an attempt at passivity and obedience. Through an examination of the redress movement, Kobayashi places the focus on the Japanese-Canadian community itself, specifically with respect to its transformation in the conclusions drawn from its past. Nunoda's work is an important revision of some of the oversights in the academic treatments of Japanese-Canadian history. Because of the tragic and unique ordeal endured by Japanese Canadians, researchers have sought to explain their experiences in terms of white–Asian relations, a generalization of ethnic solidarity that denies the fact that the Japanese-Canadian community, like its white Canadian counterpart, was stratified. Nunoda effectively argues that the history of the Japanese-Canadian community is not that of a classless, unified group who were universally successful in economic terms.

Each of the above authors demonstrates that ample room remains for further work, broader interpretations, and perhaps a changed emphasis in this area of research, not unlike that which is also required for the study of Mackenzie King. Historians need to look beyond 1942 in assessing government policy as it pertains to Japanese Canadians. By changing the focus to what happened *before* 1942, it can be seen that the internment policy was not simply an aberration but part of the long tradition of the legal, political, and social marginalization of Asians in Canadian history, a history in which King played a central role.

From his earlier career as the deputy minister of labour in the government of Sir Wilfrid Laurier to his eventual career as the prime minister of Canada, King probably accumulated more experience than any other Canadian politician in dealing with the "Oriental question." Yet with all of his exposure to the issues of Chinese immigration and the problems of opium, for example, King would prove to be anything but an advocate for Asian Canadians. In fact, many of his recommendations, while based on careful study and seemingly balanced consideration, actually restricted the rights and freedoms of all Asians in Canada.

Following the 1907 Vancouver Riots, King was appointed by Laurier to assess the damages sustained by the Japanese (and later, the Chinese) community. Out of this commission came two more investigations, one dealing with the opium

Damage done by the Asiatic Exclusion League to the store of K. Okada, 201 Powell Street, Vancouver, September 8-9, 1907. (National Archives of Canada C-023555)

trade and the other with the issue of increased Oriental immigration. Although they resulted from a systematic study of both issues, King's recommendations concerning each topic had serious consequences for the Chinese, Japanese, and East Indians of Canada. On the subject of the opium trade, King's report laid the foundations for the Opium Act, which, while not using language that singled out the Chinese community, nevertheless gave wide powers of search and seizure to the police, who then used these powers against the Chinese in Vancouver's Chinatown. With regard to King's investigations into increased Asian immigration, his recommendations would have far-reaching consequences, such as the 1928 revisions to the "Gentleman's Agreement" with Japan; the "continuous journey rule," which restricted the mobility rights of East Indians, legally British subjects; and the 1923 Chinese Immigration Act. King often claimed to be fair and tolerant in his dealings with Orientals, but the reality was much different. King was guided by the middle-class Victorian notions on race, which in turn permeated his government's policies concerning Asians, the climax of which was the 1942 internment of Japanese Canadians.

King was a product of the late Victorian age, and this was largely reflected in his beliefs concerning race. He could be many things to many people. He was both modern and traditional. He was very religious and prayed and read the Bible daily in the fashion of most of the Victorian middle class. He owned a radio and a car and had a chauffeur and a cook. While dismissing many of the ideologies that suffused the thoughts of North Americans and Europeans, in several ways King was more "modern" than many of his Canadian contemporaries. In an age that valued education, King certainly represented the new intellectualism. At university he chose an innovative field of study, industrial relations, and unlike most Canadians who undertook graduate work, King chose to attend Harvard instead of Oxford or Cambridge. This proved to be a wise choice because Canada's involvement in matters American was expanding. King developed contacts in academia and in business, both of which involved many people who were, like him, a blend of the modern and the Victorian.[14] However, although King had reached a kind of compromise with the secular and technological age, his views about race were decidedly rooted in the late nineteenth century.

Social Darwinist doctrines held that the "progressive" political, social, and industrial development of the Caucasian nations was proof of the manifest superiority of the Caucasian race. Caucasians' "natural" obligation to rule "inferior," less capable, non-white peoples only began to be questioned in the 1920s and 1930s. With respect to Asians (or "Orientals," the common term of the time), the prevailing view held that they were not savages but had previously been *so civilized that they had degenerated.*[15] King's sympathy with these doctrines is rather circumspect, though he did demonstrate Lamarckian, rather than Darwinian, views of evolution.[16] His opinions nevertheless demonstrate the sharp divisions concerning "race" in Victorian and post-Victorian Canadian society:

> We cannot but feel that the future of the white races will depend largely on the extent to which the black and yellow races become educated and prove their capacity for education. The part played by physiology in brain development, transmission of acquired characteristics, etc., etc. My feeling is that we should face the problem squarely and give every race a chance and let the fittest survive.[17]

King believed that acquired traits could be passed on to future generations. It was important, therefore, to pass special legislation to control the work of women of child-bearing age so as to prevent any negative peculiarities that might arise from the nervous strain of the new white-collar occupations:

> What physical and mental overstrain, and underpay and underfeeding are doing for the race in occasioning infant mortality, a low birthrate, and race degeneration, in increasing nervous disorders and furthering a general predisposition to disease, is appalling.[18]

Although King shared some of the automatic responses of middle-class Canadians on the subject of race, there is no evidence of racial bigotry in the literary products of his student days. In fact, his early writings as a student reporter in the 1890s give evidence of liberal ideas on racial matters. One of the main points of contention in his study of Toronto's slums, for example, is his revulsion of the treatment of black people in Toronto. Additionally, throughout his lifetime, King's personal dealings with non-whites and non-Anglos were reportedly free of condescension and marked by personal sympathy.[19] In his formative years at the family home of Woodside in Kitchener (then Berlin), Ontario, King learned by example to fit in well with both the English and the German populations of Berlin. His father, John King, though an ardent anglophile, was flexible enough to respect the values and cultures of his German friends and neighbours. Family friends also had an impact on the world view of the King family. The Reverend Winchester, who taught German to the King children, was appointed minister to a Chinese colony in British Columbia. It was this close-knit interaction with the Reverend that helped to stimulate King's interest in Canada's Asian population.[20] This was particularly true with regard to the Japanese.[21]

King's political experience with West Coast hostility toward Asians was longer and more intimate than that of any other federal politician in the immediate pre–Second World War period. The Vancouver Riots of 1907 were the culmination of anti-Asian hostility on the West Coast that reached its peak in the mob actions on September 7.[22] The main issue was Chinese and Japanese immigration. Following the riots Prime Minister Laurier sent King, then the deputy minister of labour, to Vancouver to investigate the causes of the riot, assess the damages to Japanese property, and arrange compensation. After a series of hearings King awarded

Japanese riot victims a total of $9,175 in compensation. Although both Japanese and Chinese residents faced losses in the wake of the riot, Laurier initially felt compelled to reimburse only Japanese claims. It is likely that China's lack of international prestige, its less aggressive efforts to protect the welfare of its citizens overseas, and its more distant relations with Canada and the Empire led Laurier to conclude that the Chinese could be treated with less regard. It is also likely that his own prejudices against the Chinese were a factor in his decision. According to Laurier, the Chinese were not a nation but "a mere aggregation of peoples" and simply "a coolie race subject to head tax."[23] It was only after two entreaties from Imperial officials (who had hoped to settle claims for Britons in China) the following year that King was requested to assess Chinese losses as well. King himself was also responsible for persuading Laurier to recognize the claims of the Chinese equally with those of the Japanese.[24]

During the inquiry into the Vancouver Riots, King was one of the few non-Asians concerned in the matter who kept his temper and preserved his open-mindedness. Indeed, even the Imperial Japanese Majesty's Consul, in a letter acknowledging receipt of a letter from King briefly detailing his actions as commissioner, complimented King on "the great skill, unvarying patience and urbanity" that marked his conduct of the commission.[25] As usual, his comments on the problem were extremely circumspect. He concluded that the roots of West Coast tensions were "consequent upon an increase in numbers ... rather than particular peoples or any characteristics of those peoples," and he envisaged their satisfactory resolution through negotiation with Asian nations to seek mutually acceptable immigration levels.[26] This explanation of the cause of the Vancouver Riots is illustrative because it demonstrates that King avoided, in his language, the conventional wisdom that spoke of antagonism between the races. King's conclusion suggests that economics and racism are mutually exclusive factors whereas, in fact, they are really quite compatible. Yet it would prove to be easier for governments to speak in the language of economics, within which they could couch their racial beliefs.

What is perhaps most astonishing about King's role as commissioner is how broadly based his responsibilities proved to be. King's initial task to examine the cause of the riot and assess its losses was eventually extended to include an examination of Japanese immigration, the "inducement" of Oriental labourers to emigrate to Canada, immigration from India, and the abuses of opium. Few seemed to question King's role and influence in these matters, save for Howard Duncan, counsel for the Japanese government during the riot inquiry, who objected to King proceeding with an inquiry into labour inducement, contending that this point was beyond the scope of the commission.[27] The initial commission to assess the losses faced by the Japanese as a result of the Vancouver Riots proved to be a very fruitful position for King, from which he could launch into other examinations of the "Oriental question."

The Chinese opium fiend and opium den were popular images of Oriental degeneracy that had already been the target of organized reformism when King went to Vancouver in 1908 to investigate Chinese losses from the riot of 1907. Two Chinese opium merchants submitted claims of six hundred dollars for damaged stocks and loss of business, alerting King to the extent of their traffic. Upon questioning the merchants further, King learned that the majority of their customers were white people. Generally, the use of opium was not a great concern in Canada because it was widely used for the treatment of such ailments as coughs and nerves, epilepsy, and diarrhea. The "indiscriminate" (or recreational) use of opium, however, had long been associated in the public eye with the "Chinaman" in Chinatown, but King's revelation provided documentary evidence that the practice was seeping out into the white population. With the support of the "better class" of Chinese merchants in Vancouver, King announced that "we will get some good out of this riot yet" and launched a special inquiry into the West Coast opium industry. In July 1908 he submitted his report, *The Need for the Suppression of the Opium Traffic in Canada*, in which he recommended that the importation or manufacture of opium be outlawed "save in so far as may be necessary for medicinal purposes." Shortly thereafter Canada became the first western nation to prohibit the production and sale of opium for recreational purposes. Opium dens across the country were thus subject to police raids.[28]

Now recognized as Canada's resident expert on opium, Mackenzie King was selected as the national representative at an international convention on opium in Shanghai in 1909. There his fervour to halt the opium trade was reaffirmed by knowledge gained of the international dimensions and implications of moral degeneracy. Prompted by a popular outcry from the Canadian West for even stricter enforcement, King urged the federal government to appoint a royal commission to investigate the opium phenomenon more fully. From the fruits of these intensified labours came the Opium and Drug Act, which King introduced in 1911. It made opium possession a criminal offence and increased police powers of search and seizure. Included in the legislation was a "reverse onus" provision, which relieved the state of the necessity of proving that an accused was knowingly in possession of opium. Police were allegedly tempted by this provision to plant evidence during Chinatown raids; further, that the Chinese were the intended objects of punishment was explicitly mentioned in the House of Commons, and even the form for reporting convictions was divided into columns for "Chinese" and "Others." The benefits of the riot were now beginning to take shape.[29]

The events in Vancouver in 1907 and the continuing prospect of large-scale Asian immigration prompted a more careful articulation of what constituted desirability. King's several reports, prepared in the wake of the riot, contributed much in this way. Immediately after settling Japanese claims, King was instructed to examine the origins of the Oriental influx. His report, which dwelt at length on Japanese immigration, attributed the riot largely to "a matter begotten of alarm occasioned in consequence of the increased immigration from the Orient generally" and "was not directed against the Japanese personally.[30] These conclusions, cleverly avoiding the issue of "race" by singling out the Japanese, were based on documents King seized from many immigration companies as well as on the testimony of several Asian witnesses. While exonerating the government of Japan from any major responsibility for the problem of Asian immigration, King singled out high immigration from Hawaii and the unscrupulous activities of Canadian immigration companies as the principal issues. The most satisfactory way to solve the problem, he concluded, was to prohibit immigration from and through Hawaii, to forbid the practice of importing contract labour, and to limit carefully the remaining number of Japanese arrivals. King himself believed that the information and recommendations that he provided in turn assisted in effecting the "Gentleman's Agreement" (more officially known as the Lemieux agreement) with Japan, negotiated in 1907–08 by Rodolphe Lemieux, postmaster general and minister of labour. After a month of negotiations Japan and Canada concluded an agreement whereby Japan would "voluntarily" restrict emigration to four hundred people per year. Lemieux justified the need for restriction by adopting the stance of the West Coast exclusionists, arguing that differences between the two cultures precluded the assimilation of Japanese people into British society, especially that of British Columbia.[31]

King made no recommendations concerning Chinese immigration to Canada, but he did suggest that East Indians had often been lured to Canada by inducements from steamship companies, ticket agencies, and other individuals who gained (financially) from their plight. He also believed that the friends and relatives of these East Indian émigrés were responsible for painting a misleading picture of Canada as a land of great wealth for all. According to King, their time in British Columbia resulted not only in their own personal hardship but also caused internal strife within the province. He recommended that immigration from India be discouraged.[32]

Since India was part of the British Empire and its citizens legally British subjects, the suggestion that immigration from this country to other parts of the Empire should be curtailed presented certain complications. But because the issue of East Indian immigration was a pressing one, King went to London and then to India in early 1908 to devise an acceptable method to exclude Indians. Based on his discussion with various Imperial officials, King reported that

> the native of India is not a person suited to this country, that, accustomed as many of them are to the conditions of a tropical climate, and possessing manners and customs so unlike those of our own people, their inability to readily adapt themselves to surroundings entirely different could not do other than entail an amount of privation and suffering which render a discontinuance of such immigration most desirable *in the interests of the Indians themselves.* [emphasis added]

To facilitate the possibility of Indian exclusion, King recommended a campaign of negative publicity throughout India regarding emigration to Canada, to press steamship companies against carrying Indian emigrants to Canada, to require immigrants to possess a certain amount of money before entering Canada, and to propose a "continuous journey" rule. All of these recommendations were forwarded to effect the desirability of keeping "India for the Indians and Canada for the Canadians."[33]

Soon after these proposals were made, the Laurier government passed orders-in-council in 1908 requiring all "Asiatic" immigrants (except those covered by other regulations) to possess at least two hundred dollars before setting foot in Canada,[34] and all immigrants were prohibited from entering Canada unless they came from the country of their birth or citizenship by "a continuous journey and on through tickets" purchased in their home country.[35] Although Indians were never *specifically* named in the regulations, because separate immigration provisions existed for Chinese and Japanese, Indians were the only "Asiatics" affected by the $200 levy. Although the order applied indiscriminately to all immigrants to Canada, it was really intended for East Indians because there were no means available to make a continuous journey from India to Canada.

The results of the orders-in-council were immediate: Canadian immigration from India declined from thousands to a mere trickle after 1908. Mackenzie King's detailed reports virtually eliminated all Indian immigration, providing effective restriction while avoiding the increasingly unacceptable practice of indicating the undesirability of immigrants on the basis of their race or nationality. Thus the "continuous journey" clause, together with the "Gentleman's Agreement" and the Chinese Immigration Act, formed the new foundations of the Liberal government's Oriental immigration restriction policy.

The issue of Oriental immigration was one that occupied a good deal of King's early political career, and he recognized the importance of his handling of such a delicate issue to his potential political longevity. It would have been very simple for King, in seeking to be a popular politician, secure in the Canadian political arena, to declare openly his belief in the advisability of complete Oriental exclusion. But it was the duty of a statesman, he believed, to "look above matters of popularity to the issue in its larger bearings."[36] Since King had informed the Chinese government of the necessity of immigration restriction during his mission to China in late 1908, China could hardly object to the enactment of tougher restriction laws if this condition were not met. Thus, when the issue of Chinese immigration again obtained centre stage in Canadian politics in the early 1920s due to increased numbers of Chinese immigrants, there was renewed pressure on the federal government to find another measure to exclude Chinese immigration.

During the inquiry into the Vancouver Riots, King rationalized the problems he encountered and presented them to the Japanese government through a general ethical proposition related to what he believed to be the facts of political economy. This general proposition he defined as "The Law of Competing Standards":

Assuming there is indifference in the matter of choice between competing commodities or services, but that in the case of such commodities or services the labour standards involved vary, the inferior standards, if brought in this manner into competition with a higher standard, will drive it out, or drag the higher down to its level.[37]

On the surface there is nothing startling about this law; it is simply a postulation about competition framed by classical political economists. Only in its application to the policy of Asian exclusion from Canadian labour markets warrants special attention. This policy had the advantage of providing a scientific and ethical justification for what popular opinion in British Columbia desired regarding Asian immigration. The usefulness of the Law of Competing Standards was not in the discovery of a policy for Canada but as a means of persuading the Japanese government (and then the Indian government) to accept the Canadian government's decision regarding the exclusion of Japanese and Indian immigrants. These rationalizations provided King not only with ethical and scientific justifications for the 1907 mob actions, but also with political justifications that enabled him to push aside his humanitarian beliefs for political ambition. By the time King dealt with the question of Chinese immigration in the 1920s, his rationalizations were even more cleverly articulated. In 1922 Prime Minister King drew an analogy to "Gresham's law of the precious metals": "where two kinds of metals were in circulation as coinage, if one was of finer quality than the other, the baser metal tended to drive the finer metal out of circulation." The same premise could be applied to the mingling of "races," for according to King, "sooner or later, the particular civilization that has a lower standard will … bring the higher standard down to its level."[38]

That lower standard was viewed by many Canadians and Canadian politicians, including King, as having many deleterious effects on the future of Canada, not the least of which was Canada's economic situation. It was a common belief that Orientals, especially the Chinese, threatened the economic status of the white working man. The apparent willingness of the Chinese labourer to accept lower wages than his white counterparts would threaten the livelihood of white wage earners. The Chinese economic threat was also alleged to deter the immigration of other groups. More "suitable" white immigrants would hardly wish to move to a country populated with scores of Orientals. This threat did not extend to Chinese students, merchants, and diplomats, which were classes that were considered temporary in nature; they would return to China once their business in Canada was concluded. Again, King's allusion to Gresham's law during the debate in the

House of Commons over the question of "Oriental Aliens" is particularly illustra-tive here: "The people from the Orient when they come to our shores do not have like standards to maintain. The result is that unless our labour is protected against this competition, sooner or later it is brought down to the economic level of the race that is competing against it." This was not solely the fault of the Oriental, however, for King laid the blame squarely with unscrupulous capitalists who showed little concern for the virtues of organized (and presumably homogene-ous) society.[39]

In 1923 the King government enacted the Chinese Immigration Act, which abolished the head tax but excluded all Chinese from entering Canada except stu-dents, merchants, diplomats, and Canadian-born returnees.[40] The exclusion policy worked: Chinese immigration was virtually stopped until after the Second World War, when the act was repealed in 1947. King had succeeded in delicately balancing the desire for complete Chinese exclusion with the political necessity of avoiding the language of restriction. But what is equally interesting about the Chinese Immigration Act is not simply that it indicates many historical circum-stances underlying its basic principles, such as economic interests, culture, and regional isolation. In approving this act explicitly, King and his government were supporting the new ideology of race. Far beyond economic or moral distinctions was the notion that a person's "race" was indelible and permanent and that if the higher races were not protected, the lower races would, through increased immi-gration and miscegenation, weaken the superior strain. A biological worldview, once part of King's casual musings, now formed the core of Canadian immigra-tion policy.

From the mid-1920s onward, West Coast extremists continued to urge their case in Ottawa. For his part King, sensitive to this pressure and sympathetic to its aims, resumed discussions with Japan on the subject of immigration in April 1925.[41] Canada demanded a further revision to the Gentleman's Agreement. Af-ter a series of protracted negotiations and debates the Japanese government yielded late in May 1928 to the stiff resolve of the King government and agreed to limit the number of emigrants destined for Canada to 150 per year and to end the migration of "picture brides."[42] Japanese immigration, though not completely stopped, was slowed to a mere trickle. It was not until the late 1930s that the is-sues of Japanese emigration to Canada and people of Japanese descent in Canada were again central concerns in Canadian politics.

Japanese militarism in the late 1930s, especially Japan's invasion of China in the summer of 1937, combined with the long-standing belief in Asian inassimilability, exacerbated West Coast residents' growing fear of increased and illegal Japanese immigration, as well the fear of Japanese fifth column activities in British Columbia. Newspapers like the Vancouver *Province* were warning that "some of our hot resentment … must inevitably recoil on the Japanese who are living in this country."[43] Other nationally circulated magazines bore such titles as "The Rising Sun's Dark Shadow Over Canada" and "The Japanese Invasion of Canada."[44] A wave of anti-Asian sentiment swept across the West Coast once again. In early 1938 King promised a public inquiry into rumours of illegal Japanese entrants. Subjected to countervailing pressures, King was anxious not to embarrass British interests in Asia by taking any initiative that might provoke the ire of the Japanese government, but he could not ignore British Columbia's popular opinion.[45]

Although King was prepared to follow the apparent consensus in racial matters, others actually defined that consensus. One was B.C. member of Parliament Ian Alistair Mackenzie, the minister of pensions and health in 1941 and the only West Coast representative in cabinet. Throughout his career Mackenzie was known for his anti-Asian posture, commonly adopting an anti-Asian stance in his election campaigns. While this stance was not unique in B.C. provincial politics – it was in the tradition of paying lip-service to organized interest groups such as labour – Mackenzie's adherence to the issue long after it was politically necessary attests to the virulence of his sentiments. In his view Asians were a political, economic, and strategic threat to British Columbia. He also maintained that the success of politicians who did not represent the Co-operative Commonwealth Federation (CCF) depended on their taking an anti-Asian stance in order to reduce CCF support in British Columbia.[46]

Mackenzie's lesser, but just as vocal, ally from British Columbia was Angus Neill, member of Parliament for Comox–Alberni. Neill voiced his concerns on several occasions in the House of Commons, and his views, though representing the extreme, nevertheless are a blunt indication of white attitudes toward Asians. Neill thought that a "firm hand" was necessary in dealing with the Japanese, for (quoting Kipling): "you cannot breed a white man in a brown or yellow hide."[47] Here the widespread beliefs in inassimilability and white superiority were used in an effort to influence federal policy.

At the core of the Asian exclusion policy lay a single central belief: the idea of peaceful penetration. This implied, in the words of historian Peter Ward, "the quiet, relentless, and insidious infiltration of Japanese immigrants into west coast society."[48] Coupled with the various widely held stereotyped traits so often attributed to the Japanese,[49] the idea of peaceful penetration created an overwhelming impression that immigrants from Japan (and the rest of Asia) severely threatened white British Columbia. It could lead King to conclude, following a conversation with U.S. president Franklin D. Roosevelt, that "this Oriental Immigration question is the greatest one this continent has ever been face to face with."[50] Indeed, when asked by the acting president of Waiwupu, China, why all foreigners were not excluded, King replied that Canada admitted people with similar standards of living and that restrictions were becoming increasingly great against those who "tended to undermine the existing standards." The implication was that the Asiatic standard was different from (or less desirable than) that of other countries.[51]

In comparison with his peers, then, King's views of Asians were generally "moderate" for his time: he usually attributed conflict between Asians and whites to economic competition rather than inherent hostility. Nonetheless his opinions reflected the contemporary belief that Asians posed a threat to the very fabric of white society. King's handling of issues pertaining to such sensitive and potentially inflammatory issues as Asian immigration showed a careful, and carefully crafted, consideration of all possible courses of action. Despite his confidence in the policies of his government, he would nevertheless modify these policies to meet local problems. Generally his actions were not based on any ideological grounds to which he strictly adhered. Rather these ideologies informed, but did not define, his dealings with Asians in Canada. Thus, at the time the question of internment was presented to the King government, there was already a long-established pattern in place that influenced not only how the federal government would act, but also how King himself would respond while considering the plight of nearly 23,000 Japanese Canadians and Japanese nationals. The examples thus far presented that establish such a pattern include King's political responsibilities with the 1907 Vancouver Riots, the Opium Act, and the recurring questions of Asian immigration (which in King's time included Chinese, Japanese, and East Indians under the eurocentric term "Oriental"), all of which were variously affected by his Lamarckian views of race and his long-established beliefs about social justice. Although King did not acquiesce to the demands of the more extreme

The Japanese-Canadian internment camp at Hope, B.C. (National Archives of Canada C-047393)

elements, in each of these cases this "balancing act" nevertheless had very serious implications, specifically concerning the personal freedoms of Asians in Canada. From an extended perspective, King's vacillations almost completely prevented any further immigration of Asians to Canada until the late 1940s. Given this pattern it is inaccurate to consider the decision to intern Japanese Canadians as a phenomenon of 1942. The manner in which this decision was made by King and his government had a long history.

The decision to intern Japanese Canadians was not taken in Vancouver or in Victoria, where anti-Japanese traditions and war hysteria were strongest, but in Ottawa, where officials opposed the radical demands of most of British Columbia's elected representatives. Additionally, the government that made this decision was not a minority government clinging to power and needing to acquiesce in every shade of public opinion. Rather, King's wartime government was a sophisticated political machine capable of circumventing strong national public opinion when it felt the demands of the public to be unwise, as was amply demonstrated in the conscription crisis of the same year.[52]

The above factors suggest that other considerations prompted the federal government, more specifically Prime Minister King, to support the demands of British Columbia's political representatives in a manner contrary to all the liberal principles for which Canada was supposedly fighting. With the Japanese attack on Pearl Harbor on December 7, 1941, and the outbreak of the Pacific War, British Columbia extremists agitated for the complete removal of Canadians of Japanese descent from the coastal region – an area where the Japanese army and navy were expected to land at any time. In the week following Pearl Harbor some Japanese in Vancouver were the victims of sporadic acts of vandalism. Publicly King appealed for calm and told the nation in a radio address on December 8 that "the competent authorities are satisfied that the security situation is well in hand. They are confident of the loyal and correct behaviour of Canadian residents of Japanese origin."[53]

Privately King felt that the likelihood of violent anti-Japanese demonstrations in British Columbia was very real and thought that Japanese Canadians might again become victims of vigilante action from their neighbours. Foremost in the deep recesses of his thoughts was his experience with the 1907 Vancouver Riots, and he did not wish to have them repeated under his government.[54] Certainly King feared that unless proper security precautions were taken and the Japanese Canadians and Japanese nationals were protected from white provocation, the Japanese government might use a racial disturbance as a *casus belli*. King's fears were confirmed by F.J. Hume, chairman of the Standing Committee on Orientals in British Columbia, who warned:

> In British Columbia particularly, the successes of the Japanese to date in the Pacific have to a great extent inflamed public opinion against the local Japanese. People here are in a very excited condition and it would require a very small local incident to bring about most unfortunate conditions between the white and Japanese.[55]

The idea of total evacuation was finally considered after a succession of policies, each one aimed at further restricting the civil liberties of British Columbia's Japanese-Canadian citizens. For example, in an additional step to quell the extreme anxiety on the West Coast, King announced a policy of registering, which included thumb-printing, all Japanese Canadians in British Columbia. Those who failed to comply with these latest measures would be taken into custody.[56] Such incremental policy-making was the manner in which King customarily formulated his decisions. The question of Japanese immigration illustrates this approach. Actions beginning in 1908 with the "Gentleman's Agreement" and ending in 1928 with further amendments to that document represented a series of modifications that King and his colleagues undertook to use diplomatic means to meet the needs of British Columbia while not offending the sensibilities of Japan.

King was mindful of the safety of the Japanese residents of British Columbia, and he shared many British Columbians' concerns about the security of the West Coast. He thought the vulnerability of the West Coast to Japanese attack was a very real threat, and he was often at odds with the heads of Canada's military forces over this issue; they were skeptical of claims that Canada's Japanese minority posed a threat to national security. Both the police and the military were quite assured of the contrary, both before and after the attack on Pearl Harbor. Of the probable forms and scales of attack on the West Coast, the military consensus was that any offensives would likely be taken against sea-borne trade and would bring shore bombardments only.[57] But while King did not completely share the anxieties of West Coast residents, he accepted the possibility of a Japanese invasion of British Columbia. Afraid of "leaving the back door open for the Japs to come in" and concerned about the instability of West Coast opinion and the threat to public order it posed, King had few options in 1942.[58] He may have felt that he was faced with a choice of evils: the internment of a minority group or the possibility of mob action. For King, internment was the only choice that would quell the fears that threatened to consume the residents of the West Coast. Whether any alternative policies could have been formulated is a moot point.

Tied into the anxiety about civil disorder and the vulnerability of the West Coast was the fear of rousing "Japanese ire." What this ultimately meant was a concern for the welfare of Canadians in Japan. There is no evidence, however, that the Japanese government related the issue of Canada's treatment of Japanese Canadians to that of Japan's treatment of the Canadian merchants and missionaries in that country. Meetings between King and Baron Tomii, the Japanese Minister to Canada, held at various times before war with Japan was declared, indicated the Japanese minister's concern with the many restrictive policies.[59] Even after the surrender of the Canadian troops in Hong Kong in late 1941, there is no evidence that an official linkage was made by Japanese authorities between the potential for reciprocal action against Canadian POWs and the treatment of the Japanese Canadians. The cause of this pressure for King, then, was internal rather than external.

On January 14, 1942, the King government announced a partial evacuation policy that aimed to calm British Columbians' fears as well as address the concern for the safety of Canadian prisoners in Japanese hands. Yet the news from Hong Kong (where 1,600 Canadian troops had been taken prisoner), particularly the reports of Japanese treatment of prisoners, aggravated the unrest and the hostility toward Japanese Canadians in British Columbia. By mid-January Japanese troops had taken much of Malaya, the Philippines, Burma, and British North Borneo. Thailand was occupied, Britain's most modern battleship was sunk, and late in January the Japanese military laid siege to the island of Singapore. News of this swift succession of decisive victories revived the old notion of the Yellow Peril in a new and disturbing light. On February 19 King recorded his own fear that it would be "a very great problem to move the Japanese and particularly to deal with the ones who are naturalized Canadians and Canadian born." Despite that fear he felt action was essential because "there is every possibility of riots. Once that occurs, there will be repercussions in the Far East against our own prisoners." The situation was awkward, he recognized, because "public prejudice is so strong in B.C. that it is going to be difficult to control."[60]

At about the same time, officials in the United States were also formulating policy with regard to Japanese-American populations in several U.S. states. It is possible that the diplomatic consideration of synchronizing policy with the United States – of attempting to ensure a continental uniformity of policy regarding Japanese minorities – may have contributed to the decision for complete internment. Members of the War Cabinet Committee understood on February 26 that the Americans were planning not only a complete evacuation of their west coast Japanese-American populations, but that this would be carried out by the army. Likely such news would have had a great impact in convincing reluctant cabinet ministers of the desirability of total evacuation and would also explain this entry in King's diary, "I feel too we have been too slow in getting the Japanese population moved in B.C.," which otherwise seems out of place in the context in which it appears.[61] At the diplomatic level Canada's undersecretary of state for external affairs, Norman Robertson, and the American ambassador, Pierrepont Moffat, had already agreed to "the importance of our pursuing parallel policies as nearly as possible" and to keep each other informed of any intentions "to enlarge the numbers now interned on the Pacific Coast."[62]

Under heavy pressure, fearing riots on the West Coast and for the safety of Canadian POWs, and mindful of the American situation, the Canadian government took decisive action. On February 24 it approved an enabling measure that permitted total evacuation. It is interesting to note that the powers granted under order-in-council P.C. 1486 were almost identical to those outlined in the American Executive Order 9066. Three days later the announcement was made that all persons of Japanese "race" would have to leave the protected zones.[63]

From thumb-printing to internment, King and his government had succeeded in plotting a measured but effective course through the most delicate issue of the "Oriental question." The internment policy was based on a variety of reasons that were exclusive to the early years of the Second World War but that also had their origins in and similarities to decisions of the past. Throughout the war it was imperative to King that Canadian unity prevail: he did not want a repeat of the divisive political controversies of the First World War that ultimately brought down the Borden government. King and his government were determined to keep Canada unified throughout the war and to intervene in the life of the nation whenever and wherever necessary. Canadian unity was also tied into imperialism, though King was not an ardent imperialist. Thus West Coast strife had to be quelled so as not to take away from the appearance of a strong war effort, even if it was to the detriment of the Japanese Canadians. Nevertheless King did not wish to rouse "Japanese ire," especially when it became known in December 1941 that many Canadian POWs were in Japanese hands; so the Canadian situation had to be handled carefully. Finally, the internment of the Japanese minority was not only a Canadian phenomenon; it was a continental occurrence. Public opinion on the U.S. West Coast was one factor among many in the American decision to intern Japanese Americans.[64]

Taken together, these explanations point toward King's ability to appraise the most politically expedient course of action. It is, however, not as simple as blaming King's dishonesty and his desire to be all things to all people, as some have charged.[65] The internment of Japanese Canadians, then, is linked to the non-disruption of the government's wartime program, external issues of foreign affairs, and King's retentive push for national unity. Japanese Canadians thus became entangled in a web of wartime preparations, complications, and restrictions that were designed to maintain unity in Canada during a most chaotic time.⁶⁶ In a larger historical sense, the internment decision can also be seen as another example of restrictive, punitive, and incremental measures designed to balance the extreme with perceived necessity and to achieve this balance in as diplomatic a process as possible.

Perhaps in an age when millions were sent off to extermination camps, the injustice done to Japanese Canadians might not seem to have been very great. But this injustice was committed in Canada and consequently should be judged by Canadian standards, not those of Nazi Germany or Imperial Japan. King was faced with many dilemmas as federal government policy dealing with the Japanese-Canadian situation was constantly being formulated and revised in the early stages of the Second World War. Often caught between two extremes, King, in keeping with the entire course of his political career, chose the middle ground – but not because he lacked any answers or because he desired to be all things to all people. On the contrary, in his conception of what politics was about, King understood what worked. He was more of a realist and more disciplined in his basic ideas about politics than were many of his sophisticated contemporaries whose theoretical assumptions had little regard for historical forces.

Certainly King *did* share some of the racist ideas of his times. He held some views of Asians that today would be considered racist (and possibly some of King's contemporaries, especially members of the CCF, would have thought him a racist) but that were temperate in the context of the intense anti-Asian sentiments in Canada. Yet when British Columbians' demands for internment grew ever louder and more insistent, it was not simply those demands that influenced King's consideration of the issue. Knowing first-hand what the force of those demands could do if they went unchecked, King believed that the possibility of civil disorder on the West Coast was very great. He did not wish a repeat of the 1907 Vancouver Riots. It would not only exacerbate the fragile situation on the West Coast but would disrupt the overall unity of a Canada that was already under considerable wartime strains. Thus the decision leading to the internment of Canada's Japanese-Canadian population was very closely linked with the concept of implementing total war machinery, like other wartime measures, such as press censorship, that few Canadians expected would be continued after the war.

Despite King's confidence in the policies of his government, he would modify them to meet local problems. Nevertheless, although he shared certain popular opinions, he did not completely conform to them. Rather, he harnessed popular opinion to suit his own political needs, such as obtaining complete party obedience and, often, parliamentary support for his schemes. In 1928, for example, King could satisfy the cries of exclusionists without resorting to the specific language of exclusion by limiting Japanese immigration to a very select group of "temporary" classes. In 1908, as deputy minister of labour, King made several recommendations regarding "Oriental" immigration that had the effect of severely curtailing the numbers of these immigrants but that also managed to avoid presenting Canadian immigration policy in an outwardly negative light. Even the Opium Act of 1911, ostensibly designed to curtail the drug trade in Canada, was for all intents and purposes designed to harass Chinese merchants across the country.

What happened to Japanese Canadians in 1942 was not simply based on the series of circumstances that surround the early years of the Second World War. Rather, the internment should be seen as part of a long-standing pattern of incremental policy-making in the history of the Oriental question. It is the final point, as well as the focal point, in the King tradition of seeking a consensus on issues relating to the marginalization of Asian Canadians and immigration from China, Japan, and India that ultimately proved to have major consequences both for Asians in Canada and for those wishing to emigrate to Canada.

Racism was not the prime minister's sole motivation for the policies that would result in the internment of Japanese Canadians. But King *did* participate in the racist ideologies of his times. He believed in the idea of "race" and in the separation of races, among other concepts. But these beliefs could be moderated according to the political circumstances, which is scarcely surprising in this moderate and middling man. Nevertheless, King and his government upheld values that we think of today as not very admirable. Although he was following the morality of the day and was able to check the more extreme elements, his actions and policies gave credibility to the racists' accusations. The impact of the "Oriental question" and King's handling of this issue demonstrate that sometimes political realism can have as deleterious an effect on race relations as racism can.

8

No Need to Send an Army Across the Pacific:

Mackenzie King and the Pacific Conflict,

1939-45

Galen Roger Perras

On January 5, 1944, Prime Minister William Lyon Mackenzie King and C.G. Power, his minister of national defence for air, discussed Canada's contribution to the final invasion of Japan. Power wanted to send sixty Royal Canadian Air Force (RCAF) squadrons, but King, recalling the bitter loss of Canadian soldiers at Hong Kong in December 1941 and the controversial use of draftees in the Aleutian Islands in 1943, worried that most Canadians would be unenthusiastic about such a role. Certain "that there was really no place for sending any army over the Pacific" and that Canada would "get little credit" from its allies "for anything" it might do, the war-weary leader also believed that Canada had "an obligation to share" in Japan's defeat.[1] Therefore, by 1944's end Canada was preparing sizable contingents for the penultimate assault upon Japan. The process would be bumpy. Obsessed with domestic unity, mostly indifferent to the Pacific conflict, determined to avoid mistakes like Hong Kong, unhappy with previous military advice and initiatives, but feeling pressured to play a major part in Japan's defeat, King would only permit such a role under strict governmental scrutiny. Most importantly, he would employ Canadian forces to achieve Canadian strategic goals.

King never gloried in his role as national warlord, as Winston Churchill and Franklin D. Roosevelt certainly did. Though C.P. Stacey has argued that King's martial disinterest was so marked that he "would have understood those Chinese intellectuals, who, we are told, regard soldiers as an inferior race whose proceedings deserve only the contempt of civilized men," more recent scholarship asserts that King supported rearmament after 1935 to protect Canada against American encroachment.[2] Such concerns had emerged early in King's political career. In 1908 King was recruited by President Theodore Roosevelt to tell the British that he favoured Anglo-American co-operation to restrain Japan. Having allied itself with Japan in 1904, Britain had little time for Roosevelt's notion, but Sir Edward Grey reassured King that America would invoke the Monroe Doctrine if Japan ever threatened Canada. Then, when Wilfrid Laurier created the Royal Canadian Navy (RCN) in 1910 to deflect demands for a Canadian contribution to the Royal Navy (RN), King noted that while ships on the West Coast "would be best from the point of real efficiency to the Empire," they would "be unpopular in Quebec & the East." Ten years later, when Admiral Viscount Jellicoe suggested fielding fifteen Canadian warships in the Pacific, King, in opposition, thought Canada should "recognize an obligation to coast defence, & to the British Navy." But after coming to power, in the wake of the Anglo–Japanese alliance's replacement by multinational agreements limiting Pacific naval armaments in 1922, King cut the navy to just two destroyers.[3]

When King nervously attended his first imperial conference in 1923, British attempts to centralize foreign and defence policies made little headway. King greatly distrusted imperialists, and his minority government rested on a shaky concord between isolationist French Canadians and anti-militarist Progressives. Arguing that Canada had never brought the Empire into a conflict and that it was unlikely to do so given its geographical isolation and good relations with America, King won the hard-fought concession that each Dominion's primary military responsibility was home defence, despite vehement Australian opposition.[4] He told Parliament in 1936 that with "respect to all the great issues that come up," Canada's first duty to the Empire and the League of Nations was "to keep this country united." After 1937, though King knew that Canada would support Britain against Germany, he would not commit for fear that Britain would adopt a harder line that might bring on conflict. When he approved rearmament in 1936–37, King was less interested in Europe than he was in securing British Columbia in the wake of Franklin D. Roosevelt's comments that America might intervene if

Canada could not rebuff Japanese aggression, a concern shared by some Canadian academics and military officers.[5]

In September 1939 King desired a war of limited liability that emphasized air power and economic production. Those hopes vanished when Germany crushed France in 1940, leaving Canada as Britain's ranking ally. But when Canada's military advocated an expeditionary force in 1939, O.D. Skelton bitterly complained that the generals had been insincere regarding home defence. As undersecretary of state of external affairs (USEA), Skelton emphasized home defence, arguing "that we cannot in this war ignore the Pacific as we did in the last." However, he also opposed a hard line policy toward Japan because a Pacific war "would almost certainly mean German victory in Europe and elsewhere."[6]

General H.D.G. Crerar, chief of the general staff (CGS), believed that any effort in the Pacific might lose the European war. Intent on building a formidable Canadian army that would play a major role in destroying Germany, Crerar had told defence minister J.L. Ralston in July 1940 that the risk of a Japanese attack was quite low and that since Canada could rely on American intervention, it did not need substantial home forces. King's accession in August 1940 to Roosevelt's suggestion of a Canadian–American Permanent Joint Board on Defence (PJBD) to coordinate continental defence only enhanced the "big army" drive in Britain. As negotiations between America and Japan stalled in late 1941, Canada had just six battalions, twenty-five warplanes, and three minesweepers in British Columbia.[7]

King had informed Japan's minister in September 1940 that Canadians were "prepared to fight in any quarter of the globe where the British Empire was threatened." But in August 1940 he also had said that Canada might remain neutral in an Anglo–Japanese war so as not to injure Anglo–American relations, adding that Canada's Pacific coast was "wholly undefended." Then in October, when invited to participate in a Singapore-based conference about defence co-operation in the southwest Pacific, King, against Skelton's desires, had sent an observer to the meeting though he had agreed with Skelton that Canada should not send military forces to the region.[8]

Japan's December 1941 offensive changed much. First, nearly two thousand Canadian troops sent to Hong Kong in November 1941 were lost when Japan captured the colony. Exactly why Canada despatched those soldiers remains unclear. We know that Major General A.E. Grasett, Hong Kong's Canadian-born former commander, had told Crerar in August that two additional battalions would al-

The arrival of Canadian troops in Hong Kong, November 16, 1941. (DND Col. / National Archives of Canada C-049743)

low Hong Kong "to withstand for an extensive period of siege an attack by such forces as the Japanese could bring to bear against it." Still, Crerar denied that his former classmate had asked for Canadian troops, an assertion that even Crerar's sympathetic biographer has found difficult to accept, especially as Grasett immediately suggested upon arriving in London that Canada "might be agreeable to send one or two battalions" to Hong Kong.[9] We also know that Canadian and Australian criticism regarding Canadian military inactivity had grated upon Crerar, particularly a highly critical Toronto *Globe and Mail* series in the summer of 1941 that Crerar believed was a politically motivated attempt to embarrass the army.[10]

But why did King agree? No doubt he had felt the sting of criticism about army inactivity. Most importantly, King felt shut out of the burgeoning Anglo–American relationship. When Franklin D. Roosevelt created Lend-Lease in early 1941 to funnel military aid to Britain, King had to go hat in hand to Roosevelt to secure Britain's right to "spend" Lend-Lease dollars in Canada. When Anglo–American staff talks began in early 1941, Canada had only observer status and was excluded from America's negotiations with Japan, much to King's displeasure.[11] After learning that Churchill and Roosevelt had not invited him to their Newfoundland meeting in August 1941, an enraged King, having declined to visit Britain since the war's start, suddenly flew to London in late August. There King, reminded by Ralston that Canadian troops had been "robbed" of opportunities to fight four times by Britain, asked Churchill whether Canada could do more. On September 19 Britain formally requested a Canadian brigade for Hong Kong.[12] Conditionally approved on September 24 by Canada's powerful Cabinet War Committee (CWC) without much discussion when Crerar saw no military reason to object, final sanction was given on October 2; King's sole concern centred on ensuring that the initiative would not lead to conscription for overseas service.[13]

A royal commission cleared Canada's government in 1942 of any substantial wrongdoing for the Hong Kong defeat, but the controversy convinced King that war was far too serious a matter to be left to his generals. Despite military assurances that British Columbia faced the prospect of only minor Japanese raids, cabinet minister T.A. Crerar had told journalist Grant Dexter on December 8, 1941, that King wanted two divisions in British Columbia, a move that threatened the army's British plans. King had noted on December 9 and 11 that as an invasion of British Columbia "seemed wholly probable," Canadians would not want any more soldiers sent overseas.[14] This set the stage for a bitter battle that pitted a prime minister intent upon shoring up home defence against an army determined to emphasize its British program. Canada's Chiefs of Staff (COS) advised that while Allied defeats had adversely altered the Pacific's strategic balance, since Germany constituted the greatest threat it remained "vitally important to ensure that attention is not unduly diverted from the Atlantic." The army offered only eleven anti-aircraft guns to British Columbia, while the RCAF promised 120 fighter planes. Anything more, army chief Kenneth Stuart argued, played "into the hands of our enemies."[15] But after Singapore's stunning loss in mid-February, and with the Vancouver *Sun* demanding that the flow of Canadian soldiers to Europe stop while "the war moves towards Canada across the Pacific," King seems to have regarded Canada's generals as his greatest foe. Telling Dexter and Bruce Hutchison on February 27 that Japan soon would attack Alaska and British Columbia, King complained about army ambitions and advised them "to keep banging away at the generals" about home defence. The row finally abated in mid-March when Stuart, claiming that his job was in jeopardy, created three new home defence divisions.[16]

Lieutenant General Kenneth Stuart inspecting personnel of the Cameron Highlands of Ottawa in England, January 29, 1943. (National Archives of Canada PA-138350)

Home defence figured prominently in a request for aid to Australia. King must share much of the blame for the ensuing political disaster for making Victor Odlum Canada's high commissioner to Australia in late 1941. Recently removed from a divisional command in Britain, the supremely self-confident Odlum, who once admitted that he had "learned to see things, not as they are, but as they ought to be, or, rather, as my fancy would like them to be," arrived in Australia in early January 1942. With Australians fearing an imminent Japanese assault, Odlum promised a Canadian division, prompting Australia to request troops, warships, and RCAF planes.[17] To King's credit, he had told Odlum on January 12 that only the CWC was competent to determine force dispositions, but then eight days later he said that "consideration" would be given to Odlum's suggestions. Further, Australian high commissioner William Glasgow came away from a January 17 meeting convinced that King was "favourably disposed" to helping Australia.[18]

Glasgow may not have erred, for King often resorted to ambiguous phrasing to hide his real meaning. Moreover, Ottawa did not know what to do. When the CWC discussed aid to Australia on January 14, Power described it as, "to say the least, premature." Two weeks later the Canadian services advised sending nothing more than a few air crews and six minesweepers to the Antipodes, yet an indecisive CWC tried to pass the buck to the newly formed Anglo–American Combined Chiefs of Staff. But by mid-February Ralston was considering dispatching a brigade against the wishes of Canada's COS, who insisted that home defence, Britain, and the general war effort had to come first.[19]

But Singapore's fall and a devastating Japanese air raid on Darwin on February 19 convinced Australians that invasion was possible by May. Certain that Australia "had one month to live,"[20] Australia's minister of external affairs, H.V. Evatt, flew to North America in late March to get Canadian troops. Evatt had reason to be confident for at the inaugural meeting of the Pacific War Council (PWC) in Washington, D.C., on April 1 he heard Roosevelt state that Canada should be doing more in the Pacific.[21] King dreaded Evatt's arrival because Odlum's predecessor had described Evatt as "quite insincere" and willing to "sacrifice anything and anybody to satisfy his own ambition."[22] Glasgow also had warned USEA Norman Robertson in late March that Evatt had complained rather violently that "Canada was not rallying to Australia's aid in a way that Australia had a right to expect." Additionally, Evatt's introductory letter struck King as revealing some "sort of inferior complex, an over-sensitiveness and touchiness," but to his surprise King found Evatt "sincere and a fine type of man." Most importantly, though King explained how extensive Canada's existing military commitments were, the CWC, swayed by Evatt's case, seemed to promise some munitions and possibly a brigade to Australia.[23]

Sympathy's shelf-life is frequently short, and the next day King told the CWC that Evatt had suggested privately that despatching a small radar unit would suffice. Evatt, however, had cabled home that Canada was preparing a contribution "in the form of certain equipment other than aircraft," and upon hearing of Canada's change of mind he entreated King to save the situation. But when King and Evatt attended the PWC on April 15, while expressing sympathy for Australia's position, King explained that Canada's military commitments and domestic problems "had made it increasingly difficult" to meet Evatt's requests. Then on April 28, the day after Canadians had voted to release him from a pledge not to use draftees overseas, King, facing the fact that Quebecers had voted 73 percent against the change, gave an unequivocal answer; Canada would not send troops to Australia, and King fervently hoped that Australia "could be trusted to deprecate the criticism of the amount of Canadian aid."[24]

King's victory came with a cost; Australian–Canadian relations would remain tense for years.[25] Resisting America's siren call proved far more problematic. During 1940–41 PJBD planning discussions, Canada's military had encountered American demands that Canada's army should defend Alaska in a crisis and that Canadian forces at home should submit to American strategic control. By the summer of 1941 the army had overturned a September 1940 PJBD agreement that committed Canadian army, air force, and navy resources to Alaskan defence on the grounds that "the political need" for Canada to promise some measure of assistance to America in the dark days of 1940 no longer applied in 1941. Therefore, when Ottawa and Washington approved joint plan ABC–22 in July 1941, while the RCN and RCAF remained committed to Alaska, the army was saddled with no such obligation.[26]

The command issue took longer to settle. Canada had been willing to relinquish strategic control if Britain fell, but even then PJBD Canadian section head O.M. Biggar, worrying that America would then be "Canada's sole as well as her overwhelmingly stronger ally," had recommended such control only over certain specified areas at sea, a limitation the CWC had affirmed in April 1941. Though Roosevelt wanted strategic control, given "that in actual defense nine-tenths of the total effort will fall on the United States," he had much bigger fish to fry, and without his active interest the Americans did not prevail. After some bitter discussions, deciding that Canadian co-operation "would come about almost automati-

Mackenzie King in 1941. (National Film Board / National Archives of Canada C-013225)

cally" in a crisis, the Americans had agreed that command unity could be implemented when Canadian and American military chiefs or their designated local commanders agreed to do so.[27]

But this truce unravelled with America's entry into the war. On December 15 Brigadier General L.T. Gerow, viewing the earlier agreement as "defective" and operating within a military milieu that now regarded command unity as vital to combat perceived axis superiority, approved an assessment that western North America should have a unified command system.[28] But Canada's military worried that accepting American demands would undermine its argument that Japan posed no serious threat to North America (and questioned American steadiness), whereas Robertson and H.L. Keenleyside viewed command unity as evidence of an "unblushedly imperialist attitude." Therefore on January 20, 1942, the PJBD abandoned the debate, though the Americans insisted the lack of unified command would subject the West Coast "to an unnecessary hazard."[29]

Certainly Canadian military and political unity had played a role in resisting the American demands, but American disunity and strategic circumstances ranked higher. Roosevelt never thought that the issue was important enough to warrant his personal intervention, perhaps because, as historian Fred Pollack has claimed, Roosevelt created the PJBD only to ensure that he would get the Royal Navy if Britain collapsed; when Britain survived, Roosevelt's interest in the PJBD faded. Had Roosevelt made the case directly to King, one doubts that King would have rebuffed him. The American army's case also was weakened badly by the United States Navy's (USN) condemnation of command unity as a pointless slogan that did not account for the vast differences between land and sea operations.[30] Additionally, as the initial crisis faded and it became clear that Japan was concentrating in southeast Asia and the southwest Pacific, the Americans realized that substantial national force disparities had given them de facto operational control over British Columbia. Canada could refuse formal command unity, knowing that circumstance and geography dictated that America would safeguard British Columbia. This was a dishonest position, but one entirely consistent with Canada's historical practice of depending upon a more powerful patron for protection.

In June 1942 the Imperial Japanese Navy (IJN) fell into an ambush at Midway Island and lost four aircraft carriers. Japan's sole success in the overly complex scheme lay in the Aleutian Islands, where it had occupied the islands of Attu and Kiska. Midway's victory can be attributed in part to the fact that USN crypto-analysts had broken the IJN's secret codes and knew Japan's plan. But the mad scramble to meet the Japanese threat revealed just how few resources Alaska had. Uncertain whether the air force could reinforce Alaska in time, Lieutenant General John DeWitt of Western Defense Command (WDC), which encompassed Alaska and the western continental United States, asked Canada's Pacific Command to send two RCAF squadrons to Yakutat, near Anchorage, within twenty-four hours.[31] DeWitt had good reason to expect assistance. ABC–22 bound the RCAF to aid Alaska in an emergency, while on April 27, 1942, the PJBD had agreed to let local commanders determine the redistribution of West Coast air strength. Moreover, A.F. Stevenson, British Columbia's senior RCAF officer, had begun planning to transfer planes to Alaska as early as May 5. But the RCAF, which had objected to the PJBD's April decision on the grounds that it seemed "to place upon Canada the onus of providing re-enforcement [*sic*] in the event on an attack upon Alaska," had convinced the CWC on May 14 to restrict warplane transfers to the Alaska panhandle. Therefore when DeWitt's request came, Power and his staff ruled that RCAF squadrons would only go to Annette Island, near Prince Rupert, where they sat pending a possible move to Yakutat.[32]

With substantial Japanese forces converging upon the Aleutians, DeWitt appealed Canada's decision. Stuart advised standing firm, and Power told King that because the warplane dispatch would threaten Canadian security, the squadrons should stay at Annette until the "situation developed further and [the] purpose of reported enemy concentrations more clearly indicated."[33] Switching tactics, DeWitt called upon PJBD member General S.D. Embick to intervene. Embick revealed the scope of the Japanese offensive to Major General Maurice Pope, the senior Canadian PJDB member, who while doubting that the situation was as dire as Embick thought, counselled the American to speak to Air Commodore H.V. Heakes. Making a pointed reference to ABC–22, Embick told Heakes that the planes likely would be held at Yakutat only until June 8. Four hours later Heakes cabled that the squadrons would soon be on their way to Alaska.[34]

The RCAF's official history has argued that these "complicated and occasionally irascible negotiations" might have been avoided had Canada been kept "fully in the intelligence picture." This greatly overstates the case. Certainly America had not revealed all that it knew about Japan's intentions, but between May 18 and 30 it had sent Canada four messages outlining enemy plans. The problem was not a shortage of timely information but that Canadian officers did not believe the

Mackenzie King, Winston Churchill and Franklin Roosevelt at the Quadrant Conference, Quebec City, August 11-24, 1943. (NFB / National Archives of Canada PA-210089)

Americans. On May 28 Pope had raised doubts about American steadiness and intelligence-gathering abilities, concurring in a British assertion that the USN was overly anxious about the Pacific.[35] In the wake of its command unity victory, Canada's military confidently had expected that its new home defence emphasis would defeat DeWitt's request. But King tellingly declined to support his military. Often accused of deferring excessively to Roosevelt, in this case King had reasons for taking America's side. First, on April 1 Roosevelt had indicated that the Aleutians would be a vital bridge if the Soviets allowed American bombers to use Siberian bases to attack Japan. But as American forces were heavily engaged elsewhere, Roosevelt had noted then that he "might have to look to Canada for assistance in securing Alaska and the Aleutians." Then on April 15, when Roosevelt had accentuated Alaska's vulnerability, an impressed King had replied he might send forces to Alaska "later on."[36] Moreover, Robertson, who had told King in March that not every Allied nation had to make its major military effort against Germany, thought that a visible Canadian troop presence in Alaska might balance a growing American military and civilian presence in Canada's northwest on projects like the Alaska Highway.[37] Writing to a friend, King argued that as Canada might require assistance to defend British Columbia:

> Not to be able to send planes and ships into American territory, as for ex-
> ample Alaska, and islands that lie beyond, is to risk much in the way of
> additional co-operation by the United States in the defence of our country,
> as well as their own, and to convey to American citizens generally a wholly
> erroneous impression, especially, where, as of present, they are sending
> troops and ships and men to the United Kingdom, to Australia, New Zea-
> land and India. This is a very serious ground of misunderstanding to per-
> mit to continue for any length of time.[38]

King likely thought that Canada's contribution to Alaska likely would be small and short. But as Japan consolidated its Aleutian foothold, by September 1942 Canadian planes were in the western Aleutians raiding Kiska and Attu, and they would not leave until September 1943. Moreover Canada's Aleutian contribution was expanding. In August 1942 the RCN allocated five small ships to the Aleu-tians, telling naval minister Angus Macdonald only as the vessels were about to sail. Although two Canadian military assessments contended that Japan might move against continental Alaska and the Queen Charlotte Islands to strike a psy-chological blow against North American morale, the Chiefs of Staff advised against any north Pacific counter-offensive that might draw resources away from Germany. Though he released the vessels, an indignant Macdonald limited their tactical independence and informed a disappointed USN that no additional ships would be forthcoming. No less angry, King complained that Canadian officers had no right to make such commitments without prior CWC permission. King did not object to providing modest assistance to Alaska; indeed, on September 4 his government sent three small anti-aircraft units to Alaska. What he wanted the military to understand was that the CWC had to be provided with the full details of all operations "in which Canadian assistance had been requested."[39]

King's demand for full and timely disclosure figured most prominently when Aleutian operations came up again in May 1943. The American services had en-gaged in often pointed arguments among themselves and with the British about future Pacific operational prospects, with Admiral Ernest King demanding more aggressive action against Japan. The argument reached the boiling point when the

Combined Chiefs met at Casablanca in January 1943. Convinced that his own officers were overestimating Japan's capabilities and that plans to use the Aleutians to assault the Kurile Islands might delay an invasion of Europe, General George C. Marshall watered down a proposal to retake the western Aleutians as soon as possible in favour of "operations to make the Aleutians as secure as possible."[40]

Marshall's restrictions and USN concerns about the size of Alaska's garrison was a major problem for DeWitt. Though Alaska's garrison had an authorized ceiling of 110,000 soldiers, many were support and air corps personnel unsuitable for offensive action. Though the Joint Chiefs had ruled that the ceiling could be exceeded for offensive operations, on April 19, 1943, the American army told DeWitt that he could gather only two additional regiments for Aleutian action. DeWitt thus looked north of the 49th Parallel. Visiting Major General George Pearkes in Vancouver on April 19, DeWitt relayed that Attu's invasion was imminent and that an operation against Kiska was likely. Pearkes, removed from a divisional command in Britain in 1942, suggested enthusiastically that Canada might desire a role at Kiska and offered an observer team for Attu. Pleased, DeWitt promised his full cooperation in any shared future action.[41]

But Stuart did not act until after Pope reported that State Department official John Hickerson had lobbied him on May 8 for a token Canadian army role in the Aleutians, with Hickerson telling Embick that "my guess is that such an invitation would be gratefully accepted." Hickerson was right. As the Canadian army's sole combat role since Hong Kong had been the spectacularly catastrophic Dieppe raid in August 1942, Stuart was most eager to do something in the Pacific. So when Pearkes reported back on May 25 that DeWitt had suggested either a battalion-sized garrison force for the western Aleutians or a brigade group ready by August 1 for an amphibious landing, on May 26 Stuart presented five reasons for accepting both suggestions: troops would gain combat experience; army prestige and morale would be enhanced; using home defence conscripts in an active theatre would lessen hostile public opinion towards the so-called "Zombies"; removing enemy forces from American soil would improve relations with America; and participation coincided with PJBD plans.[42]

King greeted Stuart's proposal quietly on May 26, but he had realized quickly that Ralston knew nothing about the Aleutians. Having recently reminded the military again about delivering all important material to the CWC's attention, King angrily concluded that Stuart had initiated contact with DeWitt without

Ralston's authorization. Yet when the CWC reconvened the next day, much of King's anger had receded, thanks to Robertson. Still concerned by the American presence in Canada, Robertson thought that sending forces to the Aleutians would deflect Australian demands for a Canadian role in the south Pacific, enhance Canada's standing in America, and counter American activities on Canadian soil. Frequently quoting from Robertson's memorandum, King told the CWC that he conditionally supported an Aleutian role. Concerned though that another military failure could damage his government disproportionately while success might accrue too little credit, King, claiming no knowledge of Pacific planning, insisted that final approval would come only when the American government formally asked for Canadian participation, and if troops could be found without causing problems for Europe. Power, however, thought that the garrison option sounded dangerously like Hong Kong, and Stuart, fearful that everything was slipping away, averred that he had made no commitments with the Americans. The CWC then promised its consent only if Roosevelt or Secretary of War Henry Stimson personally invited Canada to send troops to the Aleutians.[43]

The matter was anything but settled. Directed to extract the American invitation, an appalled Pope did so but complained bitterly that it would be "more consonant with our self-interest to let the Americans know that we wanted to play our part in the expedition rather than to seek lamely the 'cover' of an invitation from them." Stimson sent the desired invitation on May 29 after insisting that planning had to be handled only through military channels. The American army also had to overcome the USN objections that Canadian participation was an obvious attempt to subvert Alaska's garrison ceiling that lacked any apparent "great political benefits."[44]

But King had misled the CWC about his knowledge of Allied planning. He had been present in Washington on May 20, when Roosevelt had discussed Attu (attacked by American forces on May 11) and had alluded to an operation against Kiska. Moreover, King had responded then that he welcomed "every measure to evict the Japanese from the Aleutian Area."[45] A charitable explanation might be that King did not recall that meeting, but more likely King had chosen to forget so as not to strengthen Stuart's position, a position King liked less and less after May 27. The prime minister reacted badly when told of Hickerson's approach to Pope, complaining that PJBD members should not intrude in operational strategic planning. Stuart and Pearkes were not off the hook either for their contacts with

DeWitt, but King was more concerned about faulty procedures than about the substance of those talks. All that changed on May 28, when a livid Ralston told King that journalists had informed him that Canadian troops were on Attu. That evening Ralston forced a browbeaten Stuart to explain to King that the troops were only observers, calming King's fears that the army had covertly initiated an operation. Stuart assured King that he would never again discuss military operations without obtaining political approval, blamed Pearkes for exceeding his instructions, and accepted that no further Aleutian troop transfers would occur without cabinet approval. The next morning King reconsidered sending soldiers to Kiska after reading accounts of Attu's bloody fighting. Yet he restrained himself, fearing that cancellation would compel Stuart's resignation and might damage his relationship with Roosevelt. Believing that the CWC was doing its best under very difficult circumstances, King consoled himself that participation in the Aleutians would prevent America from receiving all the credit for safeguarding the West Coast.[46]

King insisted, however, upon various restrictions for the Kiska-bound brigade (Greenlight Force). Stuart had dropped the garrison proposal as unworkable, but when Ralston accepted Stimson's Kiska invitation he insisted that the CWC's approval of the actual troop despatch would be "subject to the satisfactory completion" of the military plans. A horrified Pope again was instructed to obtain the formal American directive authorizing Kiska's invasion, but while the Joint Chiefs let Pope see the document, they declined to release it unless the CWC promised to severely restrict its circulation. The matter was resolved only when Ottawa relented after Pope attested that he had read the directive.[47]

Pope had been appalled by this tiresome "constant hunting for cover" that cast doubt upon American military competence.[48] But Pope was wrong. More concerned about Canadian military competence than American inefficiency, King was unwilling to let Stuart proceed unfettered. As the Hong Kong Royal Commission had noted that 120 soldiers had been dispatched to that doomed colony without adequate training, the government insisted that all Kiska-bound soldiers had to have six months' training by August 1, 1943, only to agree to four months when Pearkes insisted that rule would injure the brigade's formation.[49] Greenlight Force's administrative history admits that one third of every brigade unit (five thousand men strong) had to be replaced in a month thanks to an inadequate medical boarding system, too many over-age officers, and the army's policy of treating home defence formations as reinforcement pools rather than as proper units. Le Régiment de Hull, seven officers short when the process began, lost twenty-one more, including its commander. Prior to July 9 the army ordered Pearkes to confirm on three separate occasions that the remaining men were fit for combat, and still when the troops shipped out on July 12, twenty-six insufficiently trained men had to be left behind on the dock. One company nearly mutinied, numerous men were absent without leave, and some apprehended deserters had to be put aboard their transports at gunpoint.[50]

But the CWC would not authorize the final move to Kiska until Brigadier W.H.S. Macklin had found the brigade's readiness and the American tactical plan acceptable. DeWitt ruled that only Pearkes could see the tactical scheme but caved in after Major General J.C. Murchie, vice-chief of the Canadian General Staff, announced he was coming anyway. Murchie arrived on Adak Island on August 6 but informed Ottawa that all was fine only on the evening of 11 August, just hours before the expedition's departure. Owing to time zone differences and the need to decode Murchie's lengthy message before Ottawa could reply, Pearkes found himself in a most awkward position on August 12; some ships had already left for Kiska, and he had no authorization to let Greenlight go. Fortunately Ottawa's affirmative answer reached Pearkes before the first Canadians left.[51]

This final problem left a bitter taste. Pope opined that Murchie's inspection had been a travesty of military direction. Either Canada wanted to drive Japan from the Aleutians or it did not, and if it did then it should have accepted American direction. Pearkes complained that the authorization delay had put him in a "most unfair" position, though he would have sent the troops without authorization rather than risk the expedition to Kiska.[52] Certainly both generals had a point. King had put them in difficult positions, but it is hard to sympathize with Pearkes because he had secretly negotiated with DeWitt to force King to accept a *fait accompli.* One doubts that Ralston and King thought they could derail a major military endeavour at the very last moment, but that cannot be ruled out either. It certainly was not one of Canada's finer moments, and clearly illustrated that Canadian civil–military relations in 1943 were at a dangerously low ebb.

After risking considerable political capital by sending home defence conscripts to their first combat zone, King's mood did not improve when Greenlight and thirty thousand American soldiers landed on Kiska on August 15 only to find that Japan's garrison had been covertly withdrawn in July. Four Canadians and dozens of Americans died in the unopposed landing, the victims of friendly fire and mines, but this was far better than the projected 20 percent casualty rate had the Japanese remained. Though one adviser advocated saying nothing about what the army's official historian has labelled a "fiasco" and "a ridiculous anti-climax," King's radio address emphasized his commitment to British Columbia's security and claimed that Canada's Alaskan role aided "in the defence of Australia and New Zealand."[53]

Pearkes and Stuart possessed even more ambitious plans. On May 31 Stuart had initiated "Poppy," a study about employing Canadian troops in the Aleutians, mainland Asia, and the southwest Pacific. Furthermore, he demanded that the officers involved shun official communications channels and the official filing system,[54] truly extraordinary measures that cast doubt upon his judgment. Pearkes was no better. On July 5, after DeWitt had mentioned moving against the Kuriles, he and Pearkes had promised to keep talking about Canada's future role in the Pacific. Murchie cautioned Pearkes that such plans were a government matter, but that warning had no effect. Days later Pearkes told two officers that Kiska was the "first step to Tokyo and that Canada should be prepared to follow it up and stay with it to the end" and that Greenlight would "be the forerunner of larger expeditions from Pacific Command."[55]

By early August, Pearkes envisaged no less than three Canadian brigades for the Kuriles. Then he naively claimed that while he had not the slightest idea what King wanted, planning for the Kuriles had to begin immediately, a "frightfully difficult" task unless Ottawa quickly set its policy. To speed up the process, Pearkes suggested that Greenlight be kept in the Aleutians over the winter, its units then parcelled out through his planned force to train new recruits.[56] Intent on meeting those desires, on August 30 Stuart asked the CWC to retain three brigades in Pacific Command in case the Pacific conflict unexpectedly deteriorated and to serve as reinforcements pools for Europe. But Stuart made clear that Greenlight's fine performance at Kiska might prompt Washington to ask Canada for further assistance in the Pacific and, pointing out that it might take eight months to reform disbanded units, offered that such a delay might prove embarrassing.[57]

Stuart likely was confident because he had an unlikely group of strategic allies. Victor Odlum, now ambassador to China, wanted Canadian forces in China to cement a prominent place for Canada in China's post-war development. T.C. Davis, Odlum's successor in Australia, argued that a Canadian presence in the southwest Pacific would enhance Canada's prestige in Australia "and make for better feeling between Australia and Canada," while Roosevelt had noted in August that Germany's defeat would allow the Allies, including Canada, to transfer military resources to fight Japan. Even the RCN was contemplating Pacific operations that might get it cruisers, aircraft carriers, and a post-war blue water fleet status.[58] Keenleyside too advocated a Canadian role, having taken up Robertson's concerns about Canadian sovereignty after visiting Alaska and northwest Canada in 1943. A "northern nationalist" who believed that Canada's future "lay in the responsible development of the northern frontier," Keenleyside had been struck by the scale, intensity, and permanence of the American effort in the northwest. Worried that Canada's 46,000 static troops in the region could not balance the more dynamic and much larger American presence, Keenleyside wanted a visible part in north Pacific operations to demonstrate that Canada was an active participant in continental defence and desired a voice in determining Japan's postwar future.[59]

But King dispensed with the army's Kurile plans at two CWC meetings. On September 8, though he accepted the logic of keeping adequate reserves for unexpected eventualities and possible additional missions, King rebuked the military for seeking substantial commitments just in case America called when Canada already was heavily engaged in Europe. Then on October 12 the CWC decided to repatriate Greenlight as quickly as possible. When Ralston suggested leaving a small force behind to represent Canada's continued interest in the Aleutians, Stuart agreed with the ministerial majority that this would be a mistake. As Power put it, the period of active north Pacific operations was over and all the soldiers should come home.[60]

Greenlight returned to British Columbia in January 1944 to an insecure future. King too felt uncertain. Canadian forces were fighting in Italy, the Allies were preparing to assault Normandy in June 1944, the ghastly naval and airs wars with Germany were ongoing, and Canada's senior commander overseas, Lieutenant General Andrew McNaughton, had been relieved in December 1943. The Pacific was also on King's mind. He noted on December 1 that Roosevelt and Churchill had gone too far by announcing that Japan would be stripped of its colonies, leaving Japan little choice but to fight on, which might mean that Canada being brought "into the war against Japan on a larger scale than has been intended."[61] This was the context that produced King's January 1944 admission that Canada was obligated to play some part in bringing Japan down. The army's leadership certainly was aware of King's reservations. When an American officer queried Canada's intentions in February 1944, Brigadier R.B. Gibson responded that the army could only recommend deployment options to the cabinet, though he had asked permission to consult with Allied planners to weigh options. Only Pearkes was out of step. He wanted a brigade to fight in the central Pacific and had intended to arrange jungle warfare training courses in Hawaii until National Defence Headquarters (NDHQ) told him that the notion "would depend on future decisions of policy." Then in March NDHQ ordered Pacific Command's Sixth Division to transfer its general service personnel to reinforcement pools bound for Europe, adding that Pacific operations "will be correspondingly postponed."[62]

Britain, which wanted its Dominions to help recover lost Asian possessions, sought indications that such assistance might be forthcoming. But taking exception to Lord Halifax's advocacy of a united imperial foreign policy in late January, an irate King ordered Power, Robertson, and Privy Council clerk A.D.P. Heeney to draft a response. That document, ready by February 10 and vetted by King, insisted that Canada's commitment to the war with Japan would be determined by its status as a Pacific nation, its Commonwealth membership, a desire to defeat Japan, and its "close friendship and common interest with the United States," add-

King and colleagues at the Paris Peace Conference, August 1946. Left to right: Norman Robertson, Mackenzie King, Brooke Claxton, and Arnold Heeney. (National Archives of Canada C-031312)

ing that as a northwestern route across Canada to Japan might become more important, it might be "advisable for Canada to play her part in the Japanese war in very close cooperation with the United States, at any rate in certain operational areas."[63] Attempts to alter King's mind at a meeting of prime ministers in London in May 1944 failed. King discovered to his surprise that the British had not been able "to figure out just what was needed" to fight Japan, the result of a bitter battle within Britain's cabinet between advocates of a strong military effort against Japan and those wanting to rebuild Britain's battered civilian economy. Declining to support Australian prime minister John Curtin's demands for improved imperial consultative machinery for the Pacific war and the post-war period, King, noting that neither British nor Canadian plans had been finalized, refused to sign a statement that the Commonwealth had a common strategy to fight Germany and Japan.[64]

King informed the CWC that Canada should play its part in the Pacific war but "the form and extent of such participation should, however, receive careful consideration and should accord with Canada's special position and interests."[65] Determining those conditions fell to an ad hoc committee composed of the Chiefs of Staff, Robertson, and Heeney, but the military was anything but united. Seeking to repatriate Canadian crews serving in the Royal Air Force, the RCAF proposed forty-seven squadrons for the Pacific, only one less than it had in Europe. Having already agreed to provide Canadian sailors for British ships bound for the Pacific, the RCN wanted an extensive fleet for the Pacific and Indian Oceans. Stuart, writing from Britain, advised the committee to remember that army participation "against Japan could not be contemplated under the present system of service, until hostilities ceased in the European theatre," but after that it "might be logical to send Canadian force to serve with the British in South East Asia."[66] But neither Pope nor the army's chief Pacific planner saw it that way. While employing Canadian troops in the south Pacific was possible if "sanctioned by the political authorities," the notion struck Pope "as being quite fantastic." He therefore advised Colonel J.H. Jenkins that given American pre-war concerns about Canada's poor defences, Canadian interests would be served best by fighting with the Americans in the north Pacific. Jenkins took that advice to heart. Canada could either fight with Britain in Burma or Malaya, or it could operate with the Americans in China or Japan. But since Canadian troops lacked jungle warfare skills and because he feared that Americans would react badly if Canada's Pacific contribution was perceived as inadequate, Jenkins advocated having a division fight along-side the Americans in China or Japan.[67]

Army disunity hurt the pro-British cause within the ad hoc committee. The committee admitted that the simplest course would be to fight with British units in British theatres, especially since Britain expected Canadian assistance and America likely would not need Canadian help. But as the British apparently had "no particular long-term strategy for the assault upon Japan," the committee recommended that Canadian and Commonwealth interests "might be better served if the Canadian contribution to the war against Japan were made in an 'American' theatre, namely the North or West Pacific." After the CWC approved the recommendation, King cabled Britain on June 27 to say that Canada would make its military contribution in the north Pacific.[68]

King soon discovered that some people did not agree. On July 24 Britain's Joint Planning Staff (JPS) commented that while north Pacific operations were strategically acceptable, severe manpower constraints facing British services probably would not allow them to act prior to the summer of 1945. Therefore, contending that "there would be considerable advantages in concentrating the maximum British and Commonwealth forces either in South East Asia or in the South West Pacific," the JPS asked Canada for two divisions, forty-seven RCAF squadrons, and more than one hundred ships for southeast Asian operations. But while the RCN and RCAF had only minor quibbles with these requests, Murchie did not want to provide two divisions, while Gibson thought that Britain sought only to ease the strain upon itself without taking cognizance "of Canada's own strategic or political interests." Therefore the army pressed to participate in Japan's invasion to avenge Hong Kong and to restore its prestige in Asia. It proposed just one division, emphasizing that a division was "the minimum self-contained formation ... [which] would enable the Canadian contribution to be kept separate and not lost as an appendage to a United States or British force."[69]

The imbalance among the Canadian service proposals disturbed their political masters. With little knowledge of Allied intentions, Heeney worried that Canada's north Pacific desires might be frustrated by "*fait accompli*" that would see the RCN and RCAF "irrevocably committed" with the British in distant theatres. King therefore told his defence ministers on August 30 to balance military commitments and financial resources, and that the effort against Japan should meet the "requirements of the special Canadian position," take into account "other large external and domestic commitments," and "be one in which the form and extent of the participation of each of the Services is determined in relation to the plans of the other two." But despite Churchill's explanation that he did not expect Canada to fight in Burma, on August 31 the CWC ruled that no decisions could be made except by the full cabinet and then only after Canada had obtained additional information regarding Allied strategy.[70]

So when the services presented their recommendations to the full cabinet on September 6, the stage was set for a fight. The ministers liked the army's modest plan but looked askance upon more extensive RCN and RCAF schemes to operate in southeast Asia. Munitions minister C.D. Howe, noting that Canada lacked any Pacific territories, already had registered his opposition to sending forces to fight Japan "in combination with the United Kingdom," and he saw no reason to participate if Washington did not desire Canadian assistance. The CWC favoured slashing the naval and RCAF contributions – 50 percent in the RCN's case – and although various ministers proposed various options including aid to Australia, the CWC affirmed that Canada should take part "in the war against Japan in operational theatres of direct interest to Canada as a North American nation, for example on the North or Central Pacific rather than in remote areas as Southeast Asia." But the full cabinet also deferred a final decision until Allied plans, slated to be discussed at an approaching conference in Quebec City, became clear.[71]

The RCN was shaken by the rough treatment of its Pacific plans, a bitter blow for a service that had been in King's good graces, given its initially modest goals and early emphasis on home defence.[72] At August's end the navy had indicated that it could provide 114 warships plus crews for eight British vessels for RN-led north Pacific operations after Germany's defeat, but Macdonald had told the Cabinet on September 6 that the RCN could send forces also to southeast Asia. Thus, when King had argued that Canadians should not fight south of the equator because the climate there "was very unsuitable for our men," an incredulous Macdonald found such an arbitrary restriction "quite fantastic." But the real fireworks came on September 13. Maintaining that the "enemy must be fought wherever he was, regardless of geography," Macdonald's attempt to overturn King's restrictions sparked a bitter four-hour row. Senior RCAF and RCN officers and Minister of Finance James Ilsley supported Macdonald, while Murchie opposed sending any soldiers to southeast Asia. Convinced that the RCN was in bed with Britain's attempt to salvage its former Asian colonies, King counter-attacked. Insisting that no Canadian government could dispatch forces to southeast Asia "and hope to get through a general election successfully," King announced he would meet Churchill the next day to determine Allied plans. If the Allies intended to operate in the central and north Pacific, Canada's contribution "should be in that area and not in the South Pacific or in Southeast Asia." But if the CWC preferred Macdonald's option, then King stated that he would resign. Chastened by that threat, the CWC approved King's intentions.[73]

If King feared that Churchill might sabotage his victory, those worries were unfounded. Anxious to restore his nation's battered economy before facing British electors in 1945, Churchill already had decided to cut 700,000 military personnel after Germany's destruction. Not very eager to play a major part in the Pacific conflict, Churchill also told King that the Americans seemed intent on monopolizing the final offensive against Japan. Still, if the Commonwealth helped to bring Japan down, it would not be "appropriate or necessary to have Canadians serve" in southeast Asia. Instead, the RCN and RCAF should co-operate with British units in the north Pacific while the Canadian army could work with the Americans; Churchill added that the RCAF's forty-seven-squadron plan was "disproportionate." Very pleased that his argument had been "sustained," King ordered his military advisers to meet the American Joint Chiefs to work out Canada's exact role for the north Pacific. By September 16 Marshall and the Combined Chiefs had indicated that Canadian participation in operations against Japan itself was acceptable in principle.[74]

Macdonald, noting that Canada had declared war on Japan before America had and that Canada had no problem spending billions of dollars to fund allies and international relief efforts, demanded to know on September 22 why different rules were being applied to the RCN. His answer came in CWC meetings on October 5 and 11. When Macdonald tried to remove the geographic restrictions imposed upon the RCN, Justice Minister Louis St. Laurent accused the navy of being a British appendage, while King suggested keeping the RCN in home waters until the last thrust was made against Japan. Convinced that a less than frank King was putting electoral success and Quebec's interests ahead of war strategy, Macdonald had to endure the CWC's decision on October 11 to slash the RCN's proposed Pacific contribution by half and to prohibit the RCN from operating in the Indian Ocean. King's victory was complete when the cabinet ruled on November 14 that all Pacific-bound personnel, regardless of service affiliation, would

Churchill and the British Chiefs of Staff meet the Canadian War Cabinet, Quebec City, September 15, 1944. (National Archives of Canada C-026946)

have to volunteer expressly to fight Japan, a restriction that proved problematic for all the services.[75]

Just how the Canadian forces, especially the Canadian Army Pacific Force (CAPF), would be used remained a matter of concern. Concerned that it might not get the chance to fight, the army asked the Americans about their plans, only to be told in December 1944 that uncertainty about when Canadian troops might become available precluded any employment decisions. Only in late April 1945, after a considerable debate within the American military about general strategy, was Canada informed that the Joint Chiefs and General Douglas MacArthur had approved the CAPF's use in an invasion of Japan slated for 1946.[76] King, however, never relaxed his control over the process. When Roosevelt suggested deploying Canadian troops to China in March 1945, King indignantly complained that Roosevelt had proposed "anything of the kind." Then when the British asked Canada in August 1945 to allow the CAPF to serve in an imperial corps with British and Australian forces, the army, which had already begun equipping its troops with American weapons and adapting them to the American regimental system, declined. Finally, when Japan surrendered in mid-August, Canada summarily rejected two last British requests for the inclusion of Canadian units in the reoccupation of Hong Kong and for a Commonwealth occupation force for Japan.[77] Canada's Pacific war was over.

An assessment of King's handling of Canada's contribution to the Pacific war must offer mixed reviews. Though the prime minister obviously was rightly worried about the dangers of over-committing Canada to a massive global conflict, he vacillated. Having never made any real effort to get Canada a prominent place in allied decision-making during the conflict, King effectively had surrendered control over Canadian forces assigned to Europe. That may have been unavoidable, given that Britain and America wielded superior militaries, but for King a real voice in the war's direction would involve more responsibilities and likely many more casualties and domestic political complications. As King had told a British diplomat in 1938, "his experience of political life had taught him that any success that he had attained had been due far more to avoiding action rather than taking action."[78] And with America intent upon monopolizing the fight with Japan, King could treat the Pacific conflict as a discretionary war in which he could pick and choose national commitments.

Certainly he did not always choose wisely. C Force's dispatch to Hong Kong was a bad choice. Noted British strategist Basil H. Liddell Hart has maintained that strategy and common sense had been vainly sacrificed "for the sake of fanciful prestige," while Canadian historian George Stanley has argued that Canadian and British officials "displayed a political naiveté beyond comprehension" if they believed that two additional battalions would deter Japan. And though Carl Vincent has alleged that Britain deliberately "tricked" Canada into providing cannon fodder for an obviously indefensible position, one should see the reinforcement of Hong Kong as a noble and small part of a much larger Anglo–American effort to deter Japan from going to war.[79] Still, Crerar failed in his capacity as King's chief military adviser when he failed to fully explain the possible consequences of Hong Kong's reinforcement. Moreover, King too must share blame for approving the initiative in the hope of deflecting criticism of his government.

King's handling of the Australian issue also proved clumsy. He had not initiated the problem, but King had sent Odlum to Australia and he had taken too long to give an unequivocal answer. It is little wonder then that Evatt complained to a Canadian diplomat in late 1942 about King's "empty gestures to Australia" or that Curtin claimed that Australia was "almost the only Empire country doing anything."[80] But to offer a partial defence of King and the CWC, it seems that the

Canadian government, faced by so many demands and catastrophic Allied defeats, was paralyzed in early 1942. Just as importantly, the Canadian military, most particularly the army leadership, contributed to that paralysis through its unrelenting focus on Europe. Canada made the narrowly correct strategic decision by declining to send forces to Australia in 1942; Japanese intentions in the north Pacific remained unknown, and the logistical complications of sending Canadian troops across the vast Pacific would have been enormous.

But as the Aleutian problem in 1943 revealed most dramatically, the agreement between King and the military over Australia was the exception rather than the rule. In October 1939 King had told McNaughton that "nothing had been more distasteful or disgusting to me" than "the reference to conflicts between [British] civil and military authorities" in David Lloyd George's memoirs.[81] Yet King's victories over home defence and Alaska in 1942 obviously had not sensitized army leaders to prime ministerial concerns. Stuart and Pearkes had only their narrow service and personal interests at heart when they engineered Greenlight Force and were lucky not to be fired, though Pearkes was marginalized and Stuart went to Britain in late 1943 (ostensibly a promotion after McNaughton's removal). The Aleutian issue represented a dangerous breakdown in civil–military relations. Governments should not feel compelled to instruct their military experts about recruit suitability, training, or combat readiness; that the CWC did so speaks volumes about the perceived quality of the military advice it had been getting. In discussing the army's attempts to become the primary security adviser prior to 1939, historian Stephen Harris has concluded that such a process could succeed only when the

> army and government agree as to the nature of the job to be done, when politicians expect, as a matter of course that the best solution to the country's military problems will emerge from within the military's profession and when soldiers sense that the politicians will not pursue unrealistic military policies beyond the capabilities of the profession or exploit military policies and internal military affairs for political gain.[82]

The conditions for such success obviously were not present in 1943. Perhaps the problem could have been avoided by better communication, as the Chiefs of Staff attended only forty-five of the 167 CWC meetings after June 17, 1942. However, the military clearly had violated Samuel Huntington's dictum that officers had a duty to implement "state decisions with respect to military security even if it is a decision which runs violently counter to [their] military judgment."[83]

King had risked much by sending home defence conscripts to a combat zone more than a year before he would reluctantly despatch them to Europe in 1944–45, a controversial decision that led to Ralston's firing and Power's resignation from cabinet. Thus when Churchill told King in September 1944 that Canada could secure a place in future operations "along the Aleutian islands and the Kuriles," Canada's leader had responded acidly that he "did not wish our men assigned to any second Kiska role." If Canadian troops had to fight, then King wanted them to do so in more highly visible and important regions like Formosa, Japan, and even the Philippines.[84] To the army's credit, Pope and others had successfully adapted themselves to the new situation after Kiska. Their recommendations for future action were modest, they emphasized national goals rather than narrow service desires, and they rebuffed attempts to divert from King's dictated path. Having never withstood the governmental scrutiny endured by the army, the RCN stumbled into a confrontation with King over its overly ambitious plans in 1944, and King emerged the victor. The navy's contribution to the Pacific conflict, and by extensions its hopes for blue water fleet status in the post-war period, were severely curtailed. By 1945 Macdonald had left the Cabinet as well, but King, as always, remained.

One could argue that King had been mistaken when he told Power in January 1944 that Canadians would be unenthusiastic about playing a major part in Japan's defeat. An August 1944 government poll had revealed that just 15 percent of Canadians opposed making any contribution to the Pacific war, while 83 percent of British Columbians wanted a large contribution. But 19 percent of low-income earners, a group susceptible perhaps to the blandishments of the Co-operative Commonwealth Federation, opposed acting in the Pacific, as did 38 percent of Quebecers. And when Canadians went to the ballot boxes in June 1945, the government got just 37 percent of the military vote and saws its parliamentary seats fall from 178 to 127.[85] How much influence Canada's potential Pacific role played in that election remains unclear, but King's tenure as Canada's longest-serving prime minister owed something to his political skills and intuition. Perhaps King did not fully understand martial matters, but then again few generals and admirals fully understand politics.

9

Right and Honourable:

Mackenzie King, Canadian–American Bilateral Relations, and Canadian Sovereignty in the Northwest, 1943-48

P. Whitney Lackenbauer

The influx of massive numbers of American soldiers into the Canadian northwest during the Second World War aroused both political and public concerns. Ever since, historians have been divided in their assessments of the King government's role in either preserving or sacrificing the sovereignty of Canada's expansive northern territory. Those scholars who have most stridently criticized the administration for selling out Canadian sovereignty to the Americans in the name of security have neglected the context of the time, missed the essence of the negotiations, and failed to comprehend the achievements won by the King government. Prime Minister William Lyon Mackenzie King, the ever-cautious, careful, and compromising leader, took both sovereignty *and* security concerns to heart. Given the exigencies, uncertainties, and realities of his time, King steered a prudent course. Rather than promoting the demise of Canadian sovereignty over the north, his government oversaw developments in the early post-war period that secured the protection of Canada's northern approaches and American acknowledgement of Canada's ultimate sovereignty.

King's diary is particularly insightful in terms of the prime minister's thoughts on Canadian–American relations. At times his thoughts on American designs in the north verged on paranoia; he appeared convinced that the long-term American objective was to control the entire continent.[1] At other points King seems to appreciate the United States's own vested security interests in the Canadian north, without tying the southern neighbour's plans and activities to one form of manifest destiny or another, providing fodder for historians to interpret and debate.

One prominent historian suggests that during these years the King government made Canada a dependant or "satellite" of the Americans. Donald Creighton's *The Forked Road* casts the Liberal government as anglophobes who chose the American path and subjugated Canadian independence to the United States. In this view, the Americans, always the enemy to Canadian autonomy and the most pervasive threat to Canada's British heritage, lured the susceptible King government into a trap that undermined Canadian sovereignty. During the Second World War, Creighton argues, the Americans "forced Canadian consent, paid little heed to Canadian Sovereignty, and generally acted as if they had a right to be on Canadian soil as if it were a separate but tributary part of the Empire of the United States." In the Canadian north, he explains, the Americans "enjoyed the power of numbers and the authority of command" while the Canadian government displayed "an inexcusable lack of responsibility in its failure to protect the nation's greatest assets."[2] In short, King betrayed the Canadian dream by "selling out" to the Americans. Perhaps even worse, Creighton would argue, King recognized the malevolent American designs on Canada's north and acceded to them. For historians who saw the country emerge from the Second World War a mere satellite of the superpower to the south, the journey of King's Canada down the "forked road" and into the embrace of American security was both tragic and conclusive.[3]

Shelagh Grant's more recent study is based on a set of similar, although more moderate, notions of the American threat and the implications of the King government's decisions regarding sovereignty or security needs in the north. The United States became involved in the defence of Canada during the war, she suggests, an involvement that continued through the peace, but Canada was never involved in the development of American strategy. As a result, the United States achieved an unofficial "military occupation" of northern Canada. The inability of the King government to grasp the enormity of American development projects in the north, or their overall impact, jeopardized Canada's sovereignty. Although Canadians wanted the north "free from American domination and secure against enemy attack," the King government's relationship with Washington, and the latter's intractable behaviour, seriously threatened Canada's hold on the northwest.[4] While Grant never deliberately accuses the King government of "selling out" to the Americans, she does show it collaborating and corroborating with an inherently dangerous and conniving force.

Historians who have tended to be more supportive of King seldom explicitly deal with the complex issue of northern sovereignty and security. Proponents of the "middle ground" school suggest that the Canadian–American relationship must be viewed as one of both co-operation and conflict. These historians (J.L. Granatstein, C.P. Stacey, James Eayrs, Norman Hillmer) note the shortcomings, tensions, and irritations between Canada and the United States but stress the accommodations and successes of co-operation, and they assess King's actions especially during the Second World War in light of the total Allied war effort.[5] In this context King had little choice: the primacy of Canada's security concerns, coupled with Britain's weakness, "forced Canada into the arms of the United States."[6]

Even these authors tend to avoid directly praising King for his efforts to preserve northern sovereignty and to ensure Canadian security during the war and early post-war period. C.P. Stacey devotes nine pages to "problems" in northwestern Canada in his masterful *Arms, Men and Governments*, but apart from mentioning the appointment of a Canadian commissioner to oversee developments in the region he provides little indication of what the federal government did to effectively protect its sovereignty.[7] John Thompson and Stephen Randall recognize that Canada "ceremonially took control" of the Alaska Highway after the war. They also assert that its construction undermined Canadian sovereignty in the region, "but as with so many other aspects of the U.S.–Canada wartime relationship, the Canadian government had little option" but to comply with American demands.[8] Prime Minister King seems to have taken few meaningful steps to actively assert Canadian sovereignty.[9] Subsequent actions by the Liberal government, most notably in the early post-war period, however, did generate significant results for securing the recognition of Canadian sovereignty in the Arctic.

This article is an attempt to address misconceptions and revise the story of King and northern sovereignty. Rather than looking at bilateral relations over the

Canadian north as simply a choice between "sovereignty *or* security," the government was unwavering in its determination to have both sovereignty *and* security after 1943. Given the changing contexts and constraints of the time, the prime minister was much more successful in achieving that end than many historians have suggested.

The basic chronology of the Second World War and the changes in the Canadian–American relationship are well known and require little reiteration here. A few key points will suffice. The late 1930s found President Franklin D. Roosevelt and Prime Minister King exchanging joint commitments to defend the northern part of continent. With the creation of the Permanent Joint Board of Defence (PJBD) in 1940, proved that these commitments were not mere platitudes. The PJBD was a means of overcoming American impatience and occasional insensitivity, as well as Canadian hesitancy. The tightening of the important Canadian–American bilateral relationship, however, also laid bare the precarious balance between allied co-operation and Canadian sovereignty, especially in the Canadian north.

Canada's sovereignty claims in the north were perhaps questionable, but the absence of any incidents threatening sovereignty before the war meant that the issue aroused little or no interest in Ottawa.[10] When war broke out it was assumed that the Arctic was a natural defensive barrier. The Canadian military did not believe an Axis foothold in North America was a serious threat, and given the dire situation on the North Atlantic and in Europe after April 1940, the King government was reluctant to invest money in unnecessary domestic security projects. The Americans, by contrast, were concerned about the overland and air routes to Alaska, their northernmost state. In between lay Canada!

The Northwest Staging Route was the earliest, and least politically contentious, bilateral military endeavour undertaken during the Second World War. Even before 1939 Canada had planned to build a string of aerodromes along an air route from Edmonton over northwestern Canada and onward to Alaska. The exigencies of war pushed the project forward with two main purposes: first to supply American bases in Alaska, and second to facilitate the transfer of Lend-Lease aircraft to the Russians for use on the Eastern Front. In 1940 the Northwest Staging Route began to take form, and by 1941 it was usable in daylight. The string of airfields was a product of joint Canadian and American development and construction that utilized the proper government channels in both countries.[11]

A major military-industrial project in the northwest was more controversial. The Canol (an acronym for Canadian oil) project was initiated in 1942 to ensure a supply of oil to Alaska (should the maritime route be lost) and to fuel defence efforts along the projected Alaska Highway and the staging route. It meant an expansion of production of the Imperial Oil facility at Norman Wells, as well as the construction of a pipeline and a Whitehorse refinery. American military officials pushed for the project. A reluctant Canadian government accepted it on the grounds that the Canol pipeline and facilities would be controlled by the Americans during the war, but at war's end the Canadian government would be given the first option to purchase it. Although historians tend to focus on Canadian concerns about the project's potential impact on sovereignty in the region, it should also be highlighted that the project's exorbitant expense and dubious mili-

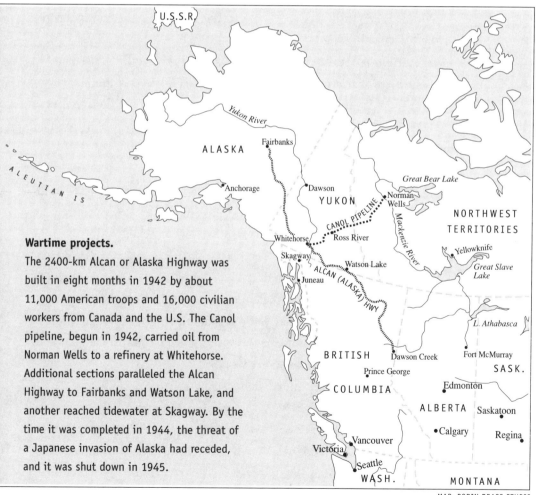

Wartime projects.

The 2400-km Alcan or Alaska Highway was built in eight months in 1942 by about 11,000 American troops and 16,000 civilian workers from Canada and the U.S. The Canol pipeline, begun in 1942, carried oil from Norman Wells to a refinery at Whitehorse. Additional sections paralleled the Alcan Highway to Fairbanks and Watson Lake, and another reached tidewater at Skagway. By the time it was completed in 1944, the threat of a Japanese invasion of Alaska had receded, and it was shut down in 1945.

MAP: ROBIN BRASS STUDIO

tary benefits generated significant political and military controversy in the United States.[12]

The Alaska (or Alcan) highway caused much less division. Beginning in the mid-1930s American politicians and diplomats lobbied Ottawa[13] for the construction of a highway through northwest Canada to Alaska. The King government, concerned about the financial costs and, more importantly, a loss of sovereignty, delayed attempts at serious discussion. Canadian officials similarly rejected approaches by American officials early in the war (and before the United States officially joined the Allied cause). It was not until February 1942, after the attack on Pearl Harbor and mounting fears of a Japanese invasion, that the Canadian government overcame its chronic nervousness and agreed to allow construction to begin – at American expense, and with the promise that at the end of the war the highway would become "an integral part of the Canadian highway system." A "pioneer road" from Dawson Creek to Big Delta, Alaska, linking the airports of the Northwest Staging Route, was built by U.S. Army engineers in an amazing eight months. At the end of 1943, a 2,451-kilometre-long, permanent, all-weather, surfaced road was opened for military use. It had cost the Americans nearly $150 million. It proved indispensable to transport thirty million tonnes of supplies and equipment to forces stationed in Alaska in 1944 before its military importance lapsed as the tide of the war in the Pacific turned.[14]

Historians Kenneth Coates, W.R. Morrison, Shelagh Grant, and others[15] have pointed out the local and national controversies that accompanied these northern projects. Between 1941 and 1943 the King government let American military officials in Canada's northern expanses operate virtually unchecked. By 1943 the government's "fit of absence of mind," to borrow Norman Robertson's apt characterization, was matched by Washington's equal ignorance of what was actually transpiring on the ground.[16] The Canadian government had indeed been oblivious to developments in the northwest, but once identified, the potential threat to Canadian sovereignty struck a resonant chord in the prime minister's politically sensitive mind, spurring his government to action.

The editors of King's diary noted that despite the prime minister's "close friendship with Roosevelt," he "was never without suspicions of the ultimate designs of the Americans."[17] As early as March 1942 King told the British high commissioner, Malcolm MacDonald, that the Alaska Highway "was less intended for protection against the Japanese than as one of the fingers of the hand which

America is placing more or less over the whole of the Western hemisphere."[18] At this stage, however, the prime minister did not deem the situation serious enough to take steps to assert Canadian control. The lack of information flowing back to Ottawa on activities of the fifteen thousand Americans in the northwest meant that King's profession of concern was rooted in intuition rather than in tangible indications or substantive evidence of a sinister American design.

As the war went on and trusted sources presented the prime minister with disturbing appraisals of the situation in the northwest, King became increasingly suspicious of American activities. In 1943 Vincent Massey and, more importantly, Malcolm MacDonald told King of ominous developments in the north that were seriously threatening Canadian sovereignty. The British high commissioner stirred the pot of Canadian concern to nearly a boil. Obviously paying heed to MacDonald's testimony, King replied that "we were going to have a hard time after the war to prevent the U.S. attempting control of some Canadian situations. [MacDonald] said already they spoke jokingly of their men as an army of occupation."[19]

This early period of ignorance and shock captured the attention of many historians. King's sporadic comments to his colleagues aside, the government had been woefully ignorant of American activities in the north and been rather oblivious to the apparent threat that this posed to Canadian sovereignty. For MacDonald's role in bringing the gravity of the issue to light (through his associations with the "northern nationalists" in Ottawa and his unusually close relationship with the prime minister), the high commissioner has been elevated to the status of a virtual saviour by some.[20] MacDonald, however, only had the power to raise concerns, not to do anything about them. This responsibility fell to King and his colleagues.

If historians can correctly conclude that the prime minister had taken few steps to counter the potentially damaging effects of the American "invasion" of the north to 1943, his government took an increasingly assertive course of action after Macdonald's presentation to cabinet that year. Sovereignty concerns led King to appoint a special commissioner for defence projects in the northwest, as the high commissioner had advised. The days of sad neglect were over. Brigadier (later Major General) W.W. Foster, based in Edmonton, became the eyes and ears of Canada in the northwest. And the new northern policies of the King government were more activist in nature. Future American initiatives to build more roads and air-staging routes were blocked, agreements were reached that the American troops would depart from the north after the war, and the Canadians made plans to buy back from the United States those facilities and installations that were already built or in progress in the north. The Americans agreed, or at least complied, with each of these requests.[21]

The American response, if one avoids the lure of the "conspiratorial view" of history, was not a cause for concern but cautious optimism. The American authorities saw Foster's appointment as an effort to improve and simplify Canadian–American liaison in the northwest, to centralize Canadian authority in the area, and to delegate authority from Ottawa. According to the American army historian, the American officials found Foster agreeable and co-operative and they were pleased to have a Canadian counterpart with wide powers. The Canadian government, for its part, saw this as an opportunity for more effective control over American activities and more effective protection of Canadian sovereignty. There were still occasions for Canadian concern after 1943, but the Cabinet War Committee now had a trusted representative in the field. American indiscretions would now be dealt with through high-level diplomatic channels.[22]

King, double-hatted as prime minister and secretary of state for external affairs, was ever-conscious of the impact that defence policy had on external policy and internal public opinion. Rhetoric aside, the prime minister's actions indicate that he did not feel that the threat to Canadian sovereignty spelled impending doom, but he worried that the appearance of the loss of sovereignty could endanger public support for these projects as well as for his government. Although King continued to allow the United States to work alone in the far north, in more densely settled areas he was adamant that Canadian labour and contractors be used. The Americans complied. The King government also insisted that the Americans use diplomatic channels and respect Canadian sensitivities. The cabinet was not always informed of American plans in timely fashion,[23] but its willingness to delegate authority to the special commissioner to deal with specific requests without reference to Ottawa[24] indicated that it did not feel a need to micro-manage the situation. For its part, the United States would have post-war interests in the region, most notably the airfields leading to Alaska, and it did not look forward to having to relinquish these sites. Nevertheless, they believed they had no choice but to comply with the King government's wishes that after the war the sites be placed under Canadian control. Senior American officials never seriously questioned Canada's *de jure* sovereignty in the northwest, nor did they assert that their money and troops represented *de facto* American sovereignty.

Despite King's persistent worries, Canada's claim to the northwest was more substantial at the end of the war than it was at the onset. Physical development had occurred, the ownership of permanent facilities passed into Canadian hands, and negotiations with the United States yielded various provisions indicating that Canada needed to be consulted and agreements reached before activities could be undertaken on or over its territory. Despite King's rhetorical displays of abject concern in cabinet and in his diary, there were no surreptitious violations of Canada's *de jure* sovereignty contrived by senior-level American officials. While *de facto* sovereignty had been less clear at times, the withdrawal of American troops at war's end meant that even this primary cause of concern was departing. King may not have realized it, but he had taken appropriate steps during the last half of the war to protect the multifaceted Canadian interests in the region.[25]

Historians have made too much of the Second World War as the catalyst of a new "golden age" in independent Canadian foreign policy-making. In reality there was more continuity than change in Canada's basic approach to external affairs.[26] Canada did not abandon its linchpin role, it continued in most cases to defer to British authority in international matters out of its direct realm of interest, and decision-makers remained ever conscious of the delicate domestic balance on which governance depended. King himself, the consummate worry-wart

Canadian delegates Louis St. Laurent and Mackenzie King at the United Nations Conference on International Organization, San Francisco, June 1945. (National Archives of Canada C-022720)

and cautious pragmatist, remained wary of the bureaucrats and the private sentiments he shared with his diary often harkened back to his pre-war quasi-isolation-
ist posturing rather than a new-found idealism. New realities dictated that, rather
than allowing Canada a more independent role in external affairs, the international
context may have constrained Canada's foreign policy more than ever before.

Events during the fall of 1945 caused King to be apprehensive about North
America's vulnerability to Soviet attack. The prime minister knew the wartime
alliance with Russia was falling apart, despite his lofty goals of keeping it together
through diplomatic and economic means. One must not, however, take this line
of argument too far. The Gouzenko affair did little to endear the prime minister
to the Soviet Union, but the potential military threat to the continent was not
deemed immediate. As Robert Bothwell suggested in a recent article, for Canadians the "Cold War" was yet to really heat up, and neither King nor his administration were having apocalyptic nightmares.[27] The prime minister remained uneasy
about the long-term impact of the United States on Canadian sovereignty and
feared unnecessarily provoking the Soviet Union.

According to King it was time to get Canada back to "the old Liberal principles
of economy, reduction of taxation, anti-militarism, etc."[28] The defence budget
was slashed, and the bloated wartime forces were cut down accordingly. Nevertheless, during the war the prime minister had often noted that the defence of the
Canadian north would be an important post-war issue. He had learned that, given
the vested strategic interests of Canada's southern neighbour in the northern
reaches of the continent, a passive approach to northern security and sovereignty
was unworkable. At the same time, the American influence had to be counterbal-
anced. Whatever he chose to do, King would remain deliberate and cautious.

In a twist of fate, the Arctic would now be the front line in any future world
war.[29] As David Bercuson has offered, this posed a series of important questions
for defence and foreign policy-makers:

> Did Canada have the resources to guard that front line to the satisfaction
> of its powerful ally, the United States? It was obvious, almost from the start,
> that it did not. But could Canada allow the United States to mount that
> "long polar watch" alone, from Canadian territory? Would this not be an
> admission that whatever sovereignty Canada claimed in the polar regions
> was weak at best and nonexistent at worst?[30]

Canada's resourcefulness in balancing the conflicting issues of northern sovereignty and continental security had to take into account the limited options that were available.

Donald Barry has identified "defence against help" as a key component in the King government's foreign policy. This response to Canada's curious security dilemma is based on the premise that the United States, in the process of guaranteeing Canada's safety, may itself become a security threat. If Canada was neither able nor willing to militarily defend the northern approaches to the United States, the Americans would be compelled to take whatever measures they required to ensure their own defence regardless of Canadian preferences. The *Final Report of the Advisory Committee on Post-Hostilities Problems* recognized this dilemma and that Canada could not retreat back to an isolationist posture. Canadian officials concluded that joint planning with the United States for peacetime defences in the northwest was the most viable option. The dilemma remained: how could Canada help protect the continent against the Soviet Union, something it could not do alone, while, at the same time, protecting the Canadian north against the United States?[31]

The study of northern sovereignty issues in the early post-war period is inextricably linked to negotiations for bilateral defence collaboration. Both countries had a vested interest in joint defence of the Arctic approaches to North America, and neither wanted to unnecessarily offend the other. King, like others at the time and several historians since, seemed to have misunderstood both the context and nature of the American requests. A grandiose plan for northern air defence proposed in early 1946 was not part of an overall strategic plan and certainly was not part of a senior level conspiracy to take over the Canadian Arctic. The nature of this partnership led senior U.S. officials to dismiss problems that were more serious from the Canadian point of view as "minor notes of discord."[32]

In fact, American officials did recognize Canadian insecurities about sovereignty in the north[33] and actually made the solution to Canada's dilemma somewhat less tedious than it might have been. The State Department knew that it had to respect and attempt to allay Canadian sensitivities, and although it occasionally acted too friendly and informally for Canadian tastes, it did not try to bully the Canadians when they were uncomfortable.[34] American military officials desired arrangements for bases in the North *if they were reasonably obtainable by negotiation,* but there was never any suggestion of moving unilaterally. Indiscretions by lower-level American officials (usually military) were always met by loud

Canadian protests,[35] and were not indicative of the regard for Canadian sovereignty among high-level U.S. decision-makers. American members of the PJBD wanted to preserve American access to specific Canadian sites but also were interested in "'signing Canada on' as a faithful postwar ally."[36]

Nevertheless, Canadian concerns persisted. In 1946 the Americans flooded Canada with requests for new projects and for the use of terrestrial and air space. King's concerns about sovereignty surfaced again – with a vengeance. If we are to take King's cabinet appeals seriously, the Americans, not the Russians, were Canada's most immediate security threat – they had a "conscious policy" to take over the hemisphere for protection. The prime minister decided to play the counterweight and linch-pin cards, ones he had often used to great effect when dealing with London. He stalled American attempts to conclude a basic plan for joint security until he had discussed matters with the British.[37] The United States was indeed a partner, but when it came to gathering intelligence the prime minister still held British opinion in the highest regard.

At a cabinet meeting in late June, having returned from Britain, King brought up the issue of U.S. weather stations in the north. While the prime minister was absent, the Cabinet had decided not to allow the Americans use of Canadian territory for protection of their own country. King was more realistic, although typically careful and apprehensive about moving too fast. The British had told him that they needed the United States if they were ever to hold their own against Russia. In this light, a bilateral agreement for Canadian–American defence co-operation would bolster Commonwealth security, not detract from it.[38] Accordingly King's message to the cabinet, once again, was to buy time and proceed with caution.

What Canada needed from the Americans was a guarantee that they would not try to protect the northern approaches by leaving Canada out of the picture. King had chosen a course of retraction in defence spending and troop levels, and Canada could not afford to secure its northern front alone. Sensational media coverage ensured that King would be conscious of domestic perceptions as he charted the road ahead.[39] It was not a choice between security or sovereignty. The solution had to offer both.

King's delay tactics worked wonders. The deluge of requests from the American military began to slow in the face of obvious reluctance. King also refused President Harry S. Truman's apparent attempts to extract commitments about the northwest when they met at the White House in October 1946 and mitigated serious concerns by working out an amendment to the proposed joint defence agreement designed to "safeguard the sovereignty and protect the interests of the country in whose territory joint exercises [were] undertaken." King realized, better than his cabinet colleagues, that Canada could not afford to undertake northern defence projects itself. The consummate politician, he also realized that while Canada agreed in principle to closer collaboration, deferring formal concurrence with PJBD recommendations could be used as leverage to get a better sense of the American strategic worldview.[40]

If the possibility of conflict was "inevitable," as King suggested it was, suitable bilateral arrangements still had to be worked out. When senior American and Canadian decision-makers met in late 1946, the U.S. representatives were much more open and flexible than the prime minister had anticipated. The Americans made no attempt to demand or insist upon specific Canadian commitments regarding the north. The idea of U.S. fighter bases in the far north was dropped, and the emphasis shifted to mapping and meteorology. The proposed projects were of the sort that the prime minister could sell to the public for civil purposes. King gloated that "the Americans had come around to his own way of thinking" and the United States was pleased to have Canada "sign on" to the general principle of joint defence co-operation, especially in the north.[41] In fact, the "safeguarding principles" on sovereignty desired by the Canadians were deemed "immaterial from the standpoint of United States interests" and in no way devalued the recommendation from an American perspective.[42] There was no secret American plot, and explicit guarantees of Canadian sovereignty were just around the corner.

In mid-February King announced in Parliament the general principles of U.S.–Canadian defence co-operation. If there had previously been a question of American intent, Canada's *de jure* sovereignty was now fully acknowledged: "As an underlying principle all co-operative arrangements will be without impairment of the control of either country over all activities in its territory." There was no mention of the sector principle[43] to which Canada had staked its northern sovereignty and to which the Americans remained noncommittal; the wording of the recommendation avoided such contentious language. Like every bilateral agreement relating to the Canadian north, it was a compromise that satisfied both parties. Despite all of King's concerns, the United States had never violated Canada's terrestrial sovereignty by legally claiming the northwest.[44] Canada now had official assurance that it would not do so in the future.

A worker at the Defence Industries Plant at Cherrier, Quebec, presents the 100,000th projectile manufactured there to C.D. Howe, minister of munitions and supply, September 1944. (NFB / National Archives of Canada PA-112908)

What remained was Canada's own action to preserve its *de facto* sovereignty. The construction of additional Arctic weather stations had been on the agenda for some time,[45] and the Canadian government was finally prepared to move ahead. Concerns about sovereignty, air rights, and expense meant that a joint project including provisions for Canadian personnel was preferred. External Affairs had suggested in 1946 that a formal request for sovereignty assurance should be avoided lest it indicate that Canada questioned the validity of its own claims in the Canadian Arctic.[46] In light of the February announcement, this was no longer a concern. In March 1947 C.D. Howe announced that nine arctic weather stations would be built over the next three years and that the co-operative undertaking was on Canadian terms. "Thus ended," one scholar has noted, "what was the last potential legal threat to Canadian sovereignty over its arctic *lands.*"[47]

If historians are correct that the media were preoccupied with a concern over sovereignty during the war and early into the peace, King's February 1947 statement to the House of Commons and the favourable arrangements regarding weather stations seemed to garner almost universal media support.[48] King still remained wary of getting too close to the Americans, but those around him were increasingly comfortable in the belief that American co-operation in the north was both popular and proper, now that a framework preserving both *de jure* and *de facto* sovereignty had been established.[49] Although the debate over sovereignty continued through 1947, this should not be taken to suggest that King had somehow failed to secure recognition of Canadian sovereignty. Rather, persistent concern indicated the depth of Canadian commitment and determination to preserve national sovereignty over northern lands. Fortunately, that battle, real or perceived, had been won.

David Bercuson has suggested that, by the end of 1947, Canada had established the principle of Arctic sovereignty and that the United States reaffirmed this principle each time a joint defence-related project was initiated as it sought permission for operations in Canada on a case-by-case basis. All told, Bercuson reasoned:

> Canada fared well in protecting its claim to the north in [the] early years of the Cold War. Through trial and error, Canada established the policies and procedures by which it safeguarded its interests and protected its sovereignty while still satisfying the defense needs of its superpower partner. In effect, Canadian control over the far north was systematically challenged for the first time since Canada had acquired the region, and, in effect, Canada's claim to the far north emerged stronger than ever. Given the stakes involved, it was a remarkable success.[50]

When King stepped down as prime minister in November 1948, his direct ability to conduct policy came to an end. His legacy lived on. From his retirement he would witness developments that made the course he had overseen in northern policy all the more meaningful. In 1947 the Soviet Union had developed an intercontinental bomber, and in 1948 Canadians realized that the need for air defences was more immediate than earlier studies had indicated. Louis St. Laurent continued to reassure Canadians that the government controlled the limited undertakings on Canadian soil, while at the same time calming American apprehensions over security. Canada, short of money and the trained personnel needed to run the network of stations in Canada, had to let the Americans back in. This time, it was on Canadian terms consistent with those established since 1943. Stations were under Canadian command, a majority of personnel were Canadian, and government approval for joint projects and activities was obligatory. The United States, following the precedent set by the weather station agreement of the previous year, agreed to a proviso that Canada's sovereignty was assured. In 1949 the Soviets exploded their first nuclear bomb, and the threat of a continental attack became more real and ominous than ever before. As King lay dying in

Ottawa, the Korean War began. The Cold War was now hot, and the potential threat of a war between the superpowers that seemed distant in 1945 was now increasingly real.

Where, then, should we situate King in this story? To the end, he remained wary of perceived American designs to annex Canada and the ability of the guarantees he had extracted to stand the test of time. How, then, should we take King's dire warnings about grand American intentions?

Above all, we need to remember that Mackenzie King's world had Canada at its centre. In this mindset, every action by another power had to be conscious, meticulously planned, and cognizant of Canadian concerns. In the northwest, however, he (and many historians[51]) missed the essence of what was transpiring. King never accepted what some of his government officials came to grasp – that senior American officials were consistently careful to avoid any infringement of Canadian sovereignty and that instances of disregard occurred at lower levels. This reality called for close monitoring of specific activities, not alarm about broad American intentions.[52] There was no grandiose American conspiracy at any senior level [53] – the reality was quite the opposite. Preoccupied with the war effort and then its new superpower role, the United States could at times appear aloof about Canadian concerns. This was not emblematic of malevolent intent – more of a friendship taken for granted. Joseph Jockel reminded us that the Americans' strategic agenda was full during these years, and there was no immediate military threat to North American security that would have demanded a high-level priority to Canadian issues.[54] With the two countries so similar in salient ways, it is understandable the individual Americans sometimes overlooked the distinctly Canadian concerns. As a whole, senior American officials, especially those in the State Department, did not. Thus, when Canadian officials confronted the Americans about sovereignty issues, the latter accommodated their northern neighbour's wishes. King could, and did, delay and shape American plans according to Canadian interests. The army of occupation may have bulldozed its way into the north up to 1943, but the King government's active intervention in continental defence matters afterwards bolstered Canada's sovereignty and continental security in the region.

Shelagh Grant asserted that "even more important than national security [in post-war Canada] would be renewed concern about the effects of co-operative defence on Arctic sovereignty."[55] If King's quixotic post-war mindscape is any indication, both sovereignty and security were inextricable issues that could not be dealt with as though they were mutually exclusive categories. During the Second World War the PJBD sought to balance all various theoretical factors (sovereignty, national security, domestic sensitivity) with the reality of war. Given Canada's overseas commitments, there was a need for bilateral continental defence co-operation if U.S. concerns were to be met. The effort was a success for Canada on several levels. First, northern development projects were completed on a scale that Canadians could not have achieved alone. For dismal failures like the Canol project, it was American resources that were wasted. Second, and most importantly, American compromises during the war demonstrated that the United States had no desire to legally challenge Canadian sovereignty. Although King at times seemed oblivious to what his government had accomplished and questioned the validity of American guarantees, there was a gradual emergence of meaningful Canadian sovereignty in the northwest by the end of the war. This gave the prime minister more reason to approach post-war bilateral negotiations with caution. He did not share the depth of concern about the Soviet threat that began to develop, almost immediately, south of the 49th Parallel. King did, however, recognize its existence, and he realized that a bilateral defence arrangement was favourable if not inevitable. So long as continental security arrangements did not require an abrogation of Commonwealth commitments or a loss of sovereignty, they were compatible with his vision of the world. King's careful approach to post-war joint defence agreements facilitated the emergence of official U.S. recognition of Canadian terrestrial sovereignty in the Arctic from 1946 onward. This recognition was also a product of American appreciation and acceptance of Canada's sovereignty concerns that the superpower to the south did not wish to aggravate.

Although King's pessimistic utterings to cabinet and in his diary seem to contradict the spirit of the agreements he reached and the proud public announcements he made celebrating the bilateral relationship, they should not detract from the successes he achieved in securing Canadian sovereignty over the north. These seemingly anti-American proclamations represent the workings of a mind that continuously searched out all possibilities and ensured that they were meaningfully discussed and pondered. Like the counterweights King used in his foreign policy, his expressions of concern to cabinet in the post-war period were a means of ensuring that his colleagues did not become too comfortable with the bilateral embrace, even when military officials were stressing expediency. King's concerns were rooted in elements of truth, remnants of the shocking realization of 1943 that the American presence in the northwest was nearly out of control. They should not, however, be taken too literally[56] or used to incriminate the prime minister himself. At the same time that King made these statements, he reminded cabinet that Canada needed to help with North American security and could not afford to go it alone in the north. Balance was the key. If cabinet needed to be reminded to "defend against help" from allies, King urged caution. If he sensed that the Americans were being too pushy he delayed key decisions, knowing they would not act unilaterally in the context of the time. Given the realities of the time, both countries got more or less what they wanted. There were compromises, of course, but King achieved, for the first time, a meaningful recognition of Canadian sovereignty over the north at the very moment he most feared it would be lost.

10

Unequal Citizenship:

The Residualist Legacy in the Canadian Welfare State

James Struthers

Living north of one of the least generous welfare states among advanced industrial nations has given Canadians a somewhat distorted image of their own political community.[1] Accustomed to defining their national identity by what they are not, Canadians take pride in pointing to the compassionate nature of their own society by drawing favourable comparisons between the generosity of the Canadian social safety net and America's more limited response to need, a contrast noted by Americans as well. According to novelist John Irving, writing in the pages of *Saturday Night*: "Compared to Canadians, Americans are isolated by their extreme selfishness, their personal avarice, their complete suspension of social conscience, not to mention their terror of the so-called welfare state; we simply don't accept our domestic obligation to care for those who can't take care of themselves."[2]

Although few Canadians would likely paint such a stark contrast (at least in public), the sense that a stronger commitment to caring and sharing makes them different from the United States is widely held among both academics and the general population. Assessing "The Canadian Welfare State at Century's End," political scientist Antonia Maioni argues that "a commitment to universality and equality in the provision of social benefits … distinguishes Canada from the …

'pure' liberalism in the United States and set the Canadian welfare state on a different course." Keith Banting points out that "the discourse of nation building creeps into even the most mundane corners of Canadian social policy" because "universal social programs ... represent one of the few spheres of shared experience for Canadians ... irrespective of language or region." For many Canadians, according to the editors of a recent anthology on Canadian social policy, the welfare state is "the heart of the nation, performing the dual function of establishing Canada's distinctiveness from our neighbours to the south and asserting a political commitment to public betterment."[3]

Among all social policies medicare is without question the most potent symbol of Canada's difference from the United States. Thanks to its universality in coverage and broad range of benefits "over the years, poll after poll has repeatedly demonstrated that health care is Canada's best loved social program." According to health economist Robert Evans, medicare has become "an important symbol of community, a concrete representation of mutual support and concern" demonstrating that "we really are a separate people with different political and cultural values."[4]

There is no question that important differences separate Canadian and American social policy, health care being the most notable example. According to the Office for Economic Co-operation and Development (OECD) statistics, Canada spends 3 to 4 percent more of its gross domestic product (GDP) on social expenditure than does the United States, a gap that has been growing over the past thirty years. During the painful economic restructuring of the 1980s and early 1990s, Canadian income transfer programs prevented the inequality of after-tax family incomes from widening, in marked contrast to a pattern of deepening economic polarization south of the border. At last count more than forty million Americans lacked any form of health insurance. As of 1997 over 18 percent of Americans were living below a rather conservative United Nations-defined poverty line, compared with 12 percent of Canadians. These are differences that matter.[5]

Their preoccupation with comparisons to the United States, however, does give Canadians a distorted mirror for seeing key aspects of their own social policy heritage. Viewed from a European vantage point, the Canadian welfare state is not so generous, comprehensive, or universal. It is, in fact, below average. According to the 1997 United Nations *Human Development Report*, for example, Canada ranked sixteenth of twenty-one OECD nations in terms of the percentage of its population living in poverty. As a 1997 OECD study also revealed, Canada ranked in the bottom third of twenty-six industrial nations in terms of public social expenditures as a percentage of GDP. As Swedish social policy analyst Gosta Esping-Andersen argues in his well-known typology of the "Three Worlds of Welfare Capitalism," when viewed against the full backdrop of western industrial nations, Canada is best described as a liberal, residualist, or means-tested welfare state. "The United States and Canada ... are the 'pure' cases of liberal hegemony," he writes, "virtually unchallenged by the paradigmatic alternatives of socialism or, for that matter, conservative reformism." Although recent critics note that Esping-Andersen's model tends to understate the comparative significance of Canadian health care spending, where universality is even more entrenched than in Europe, there is no disputing the extent to which Canada falls below European standards in most other areas of social provision.[6]

This article explores some of the origins of this "residualist" legacy in the Canadian welfare state by examining social policies for the unemployed, senior citizens, and mothers and children, the roots of which can be traced to the Mackenzie King era. In each instance, initial commitments to universality and broad rights of social citizenship were compromised by short-term demands of political expediency as well as by a longer-term quest to place firm limits on the extent of Ottawa's social welfare responsibilities. Moreover, in all three domains, residualist tendencies that were embedded in federal social policies at their inception and that remained muted during years of prosperity in the quarter century after 1945 returned in force during the tougher economic times of the 1990s. In the face of sharp program cutbacks, Canadians who previously enjoyed a social right to certain benefits found themselves suddenly disqualified from federal help. As a consequence, "unequal citizenship" became a theme of growing importance as Canada entered the twenty-first century.

Unemployment, more than any other social policy issue in this century, has posed the sharpest political challenge to the federal government. Medicare may be Canada's most popular social program, but unemployment insurance (UI) predates it by more than a quarter century and still remains the only example of the provinces agreeing unanimously to surrender exclusive constitutional authority to Ottawa. Understanding the development of Canada's welfare state after 1940 is also impossible without an appreciation of the trauma of mass unemployment that preceded it. The passage of Canada's Unemployment Insurance Act in 1940 thus provides a logical starting point for exploring the theme of "residualism" within the nation's social safety net.

The proportion of jobless in Canada who collect unemployment insurance dropped from 83 percent in 1989 to less than 42 percent in the year 2000. In Ontario the percentage was below 35 percent, at a time when the federal employment insurance (EI) fund was running a surplus of more than $23 billion. Most employees in Ontario in 2002 need the equivalent of twenty weeks of work rather than the eight weeks they required in 1971 to qualify for benefits, and the payments they receive dropped from a high of 66 percent to only 55 percent of insurable earnings as of 1996. Those making more than $49,000 a year must pay back 30 percent of their benefits to the government.[7]

This dramatic change in EI entitlement underscores the residualist core embedded in Mackenzie King's Unemployment Insurance Act of 1940. King's wartime legislation, much like Ottawa's recent reforms to EI in the 1990s, represented more of an attempt to limit federal responsibility for the jobless than it did the recognition of a new social right of citizenship.[8] Had Ottawa in 1940 actually taken over exclusive or even primary responsibility for Canadians thrown out of work, the perverse policy outcome we are witnessing today might have been far less likely.

Confusion over the political meaning of King's 1940 Unemployment Insurance Act is understandable given that the final reports of both the National Employment Commission (1938) and the Royal Commission on Dominion–Provincial Relations (the Rowell–Sirois Commission) (1940) argued precisely that Ottawa, not the provinces or Canada's municipalities, should have the primary obligation for coming to the aid of all those without work, not simply those who qualified for UI. Identical recommendations were contained within the Ottawa's Green Book Proposals presented at the 1945–46 Dominion–Provincial Conference on Reconstruction. All three documents stressed that a national scheme of unemployment assistance, administered and financed exclusively by the federal government, should accompany UI in order to provide a second tier of benefits to all the jobless who had either exhausted or were not eligible for social insurance. The memory of provincial and local bankruptcy through relief costs in the "Dirty Thirties," the growing influence of Keynesian macro-economic thinking within the Bank of Canada and the federal Department of Finance, and the administrative practicality of incorporating a national employment service, UI, and supplementary assistance to the jobless under one political authority provided compelling reasons for these recommendations.[9] If only Ottawa was responsible for those thrown out of work, then the unemployed's social right to assistance was clearly a function of national citizenship. There could be no passing the buck.

The key arguments for UI, however, did not rest on citizenship claims, Keynesian economics, or administrative logic. UI was, after all, a pre-Keynesian idea whose roots went back to Britain's early 1911 scheme. In Canada, detailed planning for Prime Minister R.B Bennett's UI bill began in 1933, the worst year of the Great Depression, when both his Conservative government and Mackenzie King's Liberal opposition still believed in trying to balance the budget. For Bennett the political attraction of UI lay precisely in its potential for limiting Ottawa's responsibility for the jobless only to those who actually worked steadily enough, during the bleak years of the Depression, to pay the necessary premiums in order to qualify. Through the passage of a UI bill, Bennett's key policy advisers pointed out, Ottawa could finally break off all its ties to direct relief and hand complete responsibility for that messy problem back to the provinces and local governments, where it surely belonged.[10]

Passed without the consent of the provinces, Bennett's 1935 UI bill was ruled unconstitutional. There is no doubt, however, that his successor, King, shared similar viewpoints concerning UI and Ottawa's connection to relief. When the National Employment Commission, which King appointed, recommended in 1938 that Ottawa should assume exclusive responsibility for the aid of all the jobless – not just those who might qualify for UI – King was appalled and did everything in his power first to change and then to bury their report. He expressed similar, although more muted reservations, concerning the identical arguments of the Rowell–Sirois Commission and the *Green Book* proposals on reconstruction. In public King blasted Ontario's Tory premier George Drew and Quebec's premier Maurice Duplessis for the failure of the 1945–46 Reconstruction Conference to agree to his government's *Green Book* proposals, arguing they had " made it a game of the most demagogic type of politics." In the privacy of his own diary, however, King confided that he too viewed his government's *Green Book* proposals as "setting forth far too much." As Alvin Finkel concludes, King was likely relieved when the premiers of Canada's wealthiest provinces rejected the surrender of taxing powers that Ottawa demanded as a precondition for assuming responsibility for its comprehensive package of social security reforms, including unemployment assistance (UA). As his Quebec lieutenant, Louis St. Laurent, told the premiers at the conference's end, "what the average Canadian wants and wants now is lower taxes. Specifically that means lower income taxes. … He wants a substantial tax cut effective right now." Finkel is surely right in concluding that going into the 1945–46 reconstruction conference, King was "more concerned about keeping taxes low than keeping his promises to introduce social reforms."[11]

King, unlike Bennett, had long been an advocate, at least in principle, of UI. "Insurance against unemployment recognizes that an isolated human being, not less than a machine, must be cared for when idle," he wrote in *Industry and Humanity* in 1918. "Where idleness is the fault of the social order, rather than the individual … the onus [is] on the State to safeguard its own assets, not more in the interest of the individual than in the interest of social well-being."[12] Like Bennett, however, King also realized that the virtue of UI lay in actuarial formulas that promised to place precise limits on his government's financial obligations to those out of work, quite unlike the open-ended morass of unemployment relief during the Great Depression from which Ottawa consistently struggled to escape. Entitlement to UI, unlike UA, was based on a metaphor of insurance, not citizenship, and on the contributory principle, not family or personal need. Workers paying into the fund after 1940 could collect benefits if they lost their jobs at the war's end – a policy that accomplished two objectives, King told his cabinet. It helped to rapidly build up a huge UI surplus, against which the federal government could borrow throughout the war, and it would "save relief expenditure" once hostilities ended.[13] As soon as unemployment insurance came into effect, his government cut off all federal contributions to provincial and local direct relief. They would not be resumed until 1956.

King's basic thinking on this question was shaped by both his long-standing hostility toward fiscal transfers to the provinces, dating back to the 1920s, and his suspicion of centralizing tendencies in the federal bureaucracy after 1938. As Mary Sutherland, King's key confidant on the National Employment Commission, advised the prime minister in 1938:

No matter which government is responsible for and administers relief … there will be constant pressure to increase the benefits and to enlarge the basis of admittance to benefits. If responsibility is centralized in the Dominion Government, the counter-pressure from local tax-payers will be eased. The irksome, unwelcome, and hard check provided by necessity by municipal officials, harassed by mounting demands on diminishing revenues, will be removed.

This was "admirably the correct point of view," King replied.[14]

Ottawa's residual approach to the needs of the unemployed continued throughout most of the 1950s. Despite the 1940 constitutional amendment on UI and its *Green Book* reconstruction proposals, the Liberal government of Louis St. Laurent tried its best to keep a safe distance from the jobless. Repeated demands by provincial premiers that Ottawa provide UA for almost half the workforce not covered by UI were rebuffed. "Constitutional responsibility for relief and assistance of the unemployed rested with the local authorities," St. Laurent told the Ontario Association of Mayors in 1952. His government did prove willing to modestly liberalize UI benefits for seasonal workers, financed out of a huge $600 million UI surplus, but even here its principal motivation was to deflect arguments that it move back into the field of subsidizing UA or welfare for the able-bodied. Eventually, astute political pressure from provinces, municipalities, and the Canadian Welfare Council, along with the impact of rising unemployment, succeeded in persuading a reluctant Liberal government to resume federal contributions toward the cost of local welfare for the able-bodied through the passage of the Unemployment Assistance Act in 1956. But the half-hearted nature of this commitment only underscored the extent to which the legacy of residualist principles toward the unemployed, previously articulated by King, dominated federal thinking on this question until almost the end of the 1950s.[15]

Seen in this context, Ottawa's recent drastic tightening of eligibility within its newly renamed employment insurance (EI) program, combined with the 1995 abandonment of the Canada Assistance Plan, represents not so much a new policy departure as a return toward the earlier arm's-length relationship toward the unemployed that characterized the administrations of both King and St. Laurent. Were either prime minister alive today, he would undoubtedly approve of both initiatives.

The residualist legacy also powerfully shaped and constrained Ottawa's response to the needs of the elderly. Such a pattern was initially entrenched through Canada's first income-oriented old age pension (OAP) plan, first legislated by the

Louis St. Laurent in 1948. King manipulated the Liberal convention in 1948 that chose St. Laurent as his successor. (National Archives of Canada C-008099)

King government in 1927. Paying a maximum of only $20 a month to seniors aged seventy and over whose annual incomes (including the pension) were below $365, the early OAP was explicitly intended to provide the indigent aged with only the barest of subsistence. By the late 1940s, when more than 40 percent of Canadians aged seventy or over were collecting the pension, opposition to the indignity and intrusiveness of its means test was widespread. So too was the sense that Canada's seniors were "entitled" to an OAP simply as a right of citizenship in reward for their contributions in building up the nation. The combination of these sentiments fuelled a powerful public campaign during the second half of the 1940s, led by organized labour, to abolish the means test and provide pensions through a universal old age scheme, paid to Canadians regardless of their income, who reached the age of seventy. This objective was embodied in the Old Age Security Act, passed by the St. Laurent government in 1951.[16]

At first glance, the arrival of old age security (OAS) seems to represent a clear triumph of universality over residualism in Canadian social policy. How else could one interpret a program that abolished means testing in favour of a flat monthly pension paid to everyone who reached a certain age?

In fact, the residualist legacy was central to Ottawa's policy planning and long-term objectives for OAS. Given broad public disgust with the means test in the 1927 OAP program and the growing popularity of America's contributory social security scheme for the aged south of the border, the St. Laurent government's only realistic political options by 1950 were not whether or not means testing should be abolished but simply on what basis a new social right for pensions should be constructed.

Key federal officials and Liberal cabinet ministers, along with St. Laurent himself, opted for the narrowest interpretation possible.[17] As an influential Department of National Health and Welfare memo on OAS argued, "it would be a great mistake for Government even to appear to monopolize the [pension] field by undertaking a complex and ambitious insurance scheme which would be expected to provide adequate pensions on retirement for everyone." Instead, Ottawa should enact a "minimum security pension" that would provide individuals and their employers with "as much leeway as possible … to build on top of the Government pension a supplementary scheme … which will be regarded … as being adequate." Low and unindexed benefit levels of $40 a month and a high age threshold of seventy – "an admittedly inadequate government provision," federal officials confessed – would send a clear message to the public that "government is not wholly responsible for providing for the retirement needs of its aged people." The alternative – a flat-rate pension that paid "reasonably adequate" benefits to the elderly in large cities, the parliamentary committee investigating old pensions pointed out, posed grave dangers to the work ethic in low-income regions because it would place the elderly "on a level of living superior to that prevailing in the locality as a whole." Instead, OAS benefits should be "set at such a level as to avoid so far as possible the social inequities of a situation in which the retired beneficiary group might find themselves in more favourable economic circumstances than those not yet retired who are still engaged in productive employment." As University of Toronto social work professor John Morgan quipped at the time: "The government has achieved the political minimum. The lowest sum per month at the highest age that they dared to suggest." In short, a minimalist, flat-rate, universal pension, rather than the more comprehensive retirement guarantee provided through America's contributory social security scheme, provided the

St. Laurent government with its best defence, in the political context of 1950, for asserting a residual responsibility for the well-being of the elderly.[18]

Further proof of the Liberals' minimalist approach toward pension policy came only six years later. Heading into a national election with a budget surplus of more than $258 million, Finance Minister Walter Harris agreed to only a six-dollar monthly increase for OAS pensioners, the first boost in their incomes since the plan came into effect in 1952, despite an 18 percent increase in the cost of living and an 80 percent increase in Canada's gross national product (GNP) since 1949. As Health and Welfare Minister Paul Martin lamented anonymously to a Windsor newspaper reporter, the pension increase was "cheese-paring, chiseling. We would have been better off to have left it alone than to come up with $6. It's psychologically cock-eyed because it looks and sounds mean." Conservative Opposition leader John Diefenbaker gleefully dubbed the Liberal finance minister with the nickname "Six Buck Harris." The label stuck and helped contribute to the Liberals' unexpected defeat in the 1957 election.[19]

The Liberals learned from their pension mistake. In plotting their road back to power during the Diefenbaker era, as Penny Bryden has clearly demonstrated, the Liberals under the guidance of David Croll, Tom Kent, Walter Gordon, and Maurice Lamontagne developed a comprehensive program of social security reform that included proposals for a new contributory old age scheme and universal health insurance.[20] However, despite the top priority assigned to pension reform during the Pearson government's first administration between 1963 and 1965, which resulted in the creation of the Canada Pension Plan (CPP) in 1965, the legacy of residualism lived on.

In did so in two ways, both of which have emerged as increasingly important within social policy debates of the 1990s. The first pertains to the limited scope of the CPP, which provided a pension benefit pegged at only 25 percent of the average industrial wage, far below the wage replacement value of most European public pensions and significantly below American social security retirement benefits, even factoring in the flat-rate benefits provided through OAS. The low benefit level of the CPP was a deliberate compromise, federal officials conceded, designed to leave "the private sector the scope that it needed" for continued expansion in the domain of financing an adequate retirement wage. As Health and Welfare Minister Judy LaMarsh told Parliament in 1963, in a statement reminiscent of her department's 1950 position on OAS, "the Canada Pension Plan is *not* intended to be comprehensive. ... [I]t is not designed to provide all the retirement income which many Canadians wish to have. This is a matter of individual choice and, in the government's view, should properly be left to personal savings and to private pension plans."[21] Given the Ontario government's close ties with the insurance industry, which fought strongly against the CPP, and Premier John Robarts's desire for an even more residualist national pension strategy, the CPP's modest scope was likely all that was attainable for the Pearson government in the context of the 1960s.[22]

The clear expectation of federal policy-makers was that over the next two decades the steady expansion of occupational pensions would fill in the gap between the minimum social provision provided for old age through OAS and CPP and basic income adequacy for Canadian workers facing retirement. This did not happen. By 1983, a federal government study discovered, only 40 percent of Canada's elderly were receiving any private pension benefits at all. Occupational pension coverage peaked in the late 1970s, at less than half of the workforce, and then began to decline. As a result organized labour, seniors' groups, women's organizations, the New Democratic Party (NDP), and even sections of the federal government itself, through the leadership of Health and Welfare Minister Monique Begin, began pushing for a doubling of CPP benefit coverage to at least 50 percent of the average industrial wage.

This "Great Pension Debate," which lasted between 1976 and 1984, in the end produced little of substance because the Ontario government, which retained a veto over any changes to the CPP, and key officials in the federal finance department were opposed to any substantial liberalization of public pensions. True to a residualist perspective on the issue dating back to the late 1940s, finance department officials argued that the quest for improving retirement income should come from expanding private pension coverage and through wider tax incentives provided through registered retirement savings plans (RRSPs). The Ontario government's position on the CPP throughout the 1970s and 1980s, according to Keith Banting, simply did not change: "The CPP should not be a tool of income redistribution, and the private sector should be the primary vehicle of retirement saving."[23] As a result Canadians facing old age at the end of the century could not look toward broadly based public pension entitlements such as either OAS or CPP to guarantee an adequate retirement income.

The gap was partially filled by the Guaranteed Income Supplement (GIS), the second major legacy of residualism emerging out of the pension debates of the 1960s. Launched in 1967, the idea for the GIS came from the 1966 *Report of the Senate Committee on Aging*, chaired by a Liberal senator, David Croll. Initially intended as merely a temporary program to bridge the ten-year gap until 1975, when the CPP began paying out its maximum benefits to seniors, the GIS has instead become a permanent and increasingly influential component of federal social policy. It became a favoured policy instrument during the inflationary decade of the 1970s because it provided an effective tool for containing expenditure on the aged by allowing the federal government to target its spending directly to the elderly in need, rather than being pressured into paying out far more expensive basic increases to all the elderly aged sixty-five and over through OAS.[24]

The GIS introduced two new key departures in the Canadian welfare state. The first was the concept of paying regular benefits on the basis of an income, rather than a needs or means test. Administered simply on the basis of a senior's self-declared income derived through his or her annual tax returns for the previous year, the GIS bridges the gap between a retiree's total annual income, inclusive of OAS and any other small amount of earnings, and a minimum income guarantee for the aged. Initially the non-taxable GIS was fixed at 40 percent of the monthly OAS payment, reduced by one dollar for every two dollars of other income. As of 1999 the maximum monthly GIS payment was worth approximately 120 percent of OAS and provided a single elderly person with a guaranteed annual income (including OAS) of eleven thousand dollars, a sum equal to 54 percent of the median income for single households and 59 percent for couples. Over time it cut the poverty rate of Canada's elderly in half, to only 7 percent of the sixty-five-and-over population, compared with a poverty rate of 22 percent for Americans in the same age category.[25] The GIS also inserted Ottawa directly into the administration of selective benefits based on the concept of needs rather than rights – a domain of social welfare, apart from veterans, that had previously been the exclusive responsibility of provincial and local governments.

The ongoing tension between targeting and universalism in federal social policy is clearly embedded within the complex evolution of OAS and GIS since 1967. At different points in the 1970s, 1980s, and 1990s successive federal governments attempted to scale down, de-index, claw back, and, most recently, abolish OAS altogether. Each attack on the program has been fraught with political danger. Conservative finance minister Michael Wilson's unsuccessful attempt in 1985 to de-index OAS from the cost of living produced the most concerted and successful mobilization of the elderly in Canada's history. His Liberal successor, Paul Martin, abandoned legislation designed to replace OAS and the GIS with a single Seniors' Benefit, targeted to family income, for fear of a similar political backlash. The "stealth" method of gradually clawing back OAS payments for seniors with individual incomes between $53,000 and $73,000, combined with the elimination of indexing for inflation below 3 percent annually, proved to be far less politically explosive. If left unchanged, however, it appeared that the clawback would soon transform OAS into a largely residualist program.[26]

Income transfers to mothers with children are the final policy area to be explored in this discussion of Canada's residualist social policy legacy. Here the precedents go back to the First World War era and the creation of provincial mothers' allowances for needy widows. From 1916 onward these programs, which represent Canada's earliest experiments in providing income security, created an imperfect right of social citizenship for women in a certain category. Justified on the basis that motherhood was a form of "service to the state," monthly allowances (or "pensions," as they were sometimes called) were paid by provinces to needy widows and deserted wives so that they could raise their children at home, on the condition that the women were judged to be "fit and proper persons." Mothers' allowances, in other words, constituted a hybrid form of entitlement governed by a strict code of state moral regulation that continued to distinguish between deserving and undeserving families.[27]

During the Second World War the King government introduced family allowances, Canada's first universal social program, which paid monthly benefits ranging from five to eight dollars per child to every Canadian mother; almost no conditions were attached, save that the children be attending school. Family allowances truly constituted a new form of social citizenship that emerged out of the unique political conditions of wartime Canada.

> I told the caucus that this thing [family allowances] went down to the very roots of one's convictions and beliefs. That my Liberalism was based on the belief that, in the sight of God, every soul was precious. My Liberalism was based on getting for men equality of opportunity. I had written *Industry and Humanity* ... [and] set out therein the doctrine of the national mini-

mum of living. … [M]y belief in public life had been to help all I could for the improvement of the lot of the people in my day and generation. … [I]f equality of opportunity meant anything, it meant that every man, every child, should have his chance.[28]

When he introduced the bill in Parliament in 1944, King was equally passionate in arguing that family allowances represented a fundamental new departure in Canadian social policy: "Charity has become a nauseating thing. The new order is not going to have things done as charity. What is to be done will be done as a matter of right."[29] Justified through the assertion of a new federal authority, the "spending power," the "baby bonus" (as it came to be called) staked out new territory for the federal government in the domain of Canadian social policy. Because they went automatically to every child, family allowances did not violate the province's primary constitutional jurisdiction over charity and social welfare. Instead, Ottawa claimed, they were well within the federal government's prerogative to make payments directly to its citizens. Family allowances were "not charity," Louis St. Laurent argued in Parliament, "because the payments [were] of right. … One is not 'entitled' to charity. … [This] is simply a gift by this parliament to some section of its taxpayers."[30]

As St. Laurent's "gift" metaphor suggests, however, the precise basis of the social right underpinning Ottawa's decision to create this ambitious scheme was never altogether clear. In hindsight it is possible to argue that family allowances could have been justified, much like mothers' allowances, as a reward to women for their "service to the state" or in recognition of the work of mothering. Had this been the case, women so entitled might have developed an effective political constituency in defence of the economic value of their labour within the home. Instead, discussion in Parliament focused on guaranteeing equal opportunity for children, compensating fathers for low income, and winning the support of men for defending their country. To the extent that women figured at all in the debate, it was mainly in the context of being trusted to use the money wisely in the interests of their children or in being encouraged, through family allowances, to vacate the workforce quickly at the war's end in order to produce babies and to free up jobs for returning veterans.[31]

As most historians who have studied the origins of this program agree, family allowances in Canada emerged, almost *sui generis*, in 1943–44 as a state-centred initiative to avoid inflationary wage increases, to stave off a growing electoral threat from the socialist left, to justify Ottawa's retention of taxing authority in post-war bargaining with the provinces, and to prevent a post-war depression without spending massive sums on public works.[32] The program was not a response to a grass-roots campaign by Canadian women for a new social right of citizenship.[33]

As a result, when the immediate political context that justified the creation of family allowances faded away, Ottawa quickly lost interest in the program. Between 1945 and 1972 the "baby bonus" was never increased, in marked contrast to OAS, so its economic value to Canadian families was allowed to atrophy into insignificance. Although the program still expressed the principle of universality, in practice it became increasingly residual by default. Between 1970 and 1973, officials in National Health and Welfare, inspired by the success of the GIS, began arguing that family allowances should be replaced altogether by an income-tested Family Income Supplement Plan (FISP) targeted only to low-income households. Because of strong opposition from the NDP during a period of minority government the idea was shelved, but the appeal of moving from universality to selectivity within family income transfer policy never disappeared within the federal bureaucracy.[34] It would re-emerge in force during the Mulroney years through the de-indexation, the clawback, and ultimately the abolition of family allowances altogether between 1985 and 1992.[35] Significantly, and in marked contrast to the steadfast support of OAS by Canadian seniors, by the late 1980s middle-class beneficiaries of family allowances were unable to mount an effective political defence of their universal entitlement in the program.

In 1998, out of the ashes of family allowances emerged the National Child Benefit Supplement (NCBS), Canada's "first new national social program in thirty years." It is a purely residualist, income-tested program built on the GIS model. The NCBS was Ottawa's most significant response to revelations that with 15 percent of its families and 21 percent of its children living below the low-income cut-off line, Canada ranked "among the worst of all major Western countries in rates of child poverty." Combined with the already existing Canada Child Tax Benefit, the NCBS, as of 2002, provides maximum annual benefits of up to $2,444 for the first child and $2,238 for each additional child per year to almost 2.5 million children. Maximum benefits are paid to families with net incomes below $22,397 and disappear for families with net incomes above $79,000.[36]

It is too soon to say whether or not this new targeted social policy, like its counterpart, the GIS for seniors, will have a major impact on reducing Canada's shockingly high level of child poverty, which jumped 47 percent between 1989 and 1996.[37] As of 1998 Ottawa's level of spending on the program remained almost $1 billion less (in constant dollars) than its 1984 total for family allowances, the child tax credit, and the child tax exemption. This outcome does not suggest that a significant investment of new federal resources, thus far, has been directed toward Canadian children. It is true that between 1996 and 2002 Canada's child poverty rate dropped from 20.4 percent to 17.2 percent of all families with children, but as even federal officials concede, this decline was "mostly due to the strong economic performance in the 1990s" rather than because of the implementation of the NCBS.[38]

One feature of the new NCBS program represents a particularly disturbing throwback to earlier moralizing distinctions between the "deserving" and the "undeserving" poor that characterized the first provincial mothers' allowances schemes. The additional $850 million in new spending on this program between 1998 and 2000 was only available as a monthly cash benefit for children in families of the working poor, a distinction which remains in place as of 2002. Families on social assistance in most Canadian provinces have seen the entire amount of this extra funding clawed back from their existing welfare allowances through separately negotiated federal-provincial agreements. Ostensibly, the goal of this new selectivity in federal social policy in distinguishing between children of the welfare and the working poor was to break down the "welfare wall" that deters their parents from leaving social assistance to seek out low-wage employment.

In practice, critics argued, it constituted a harsh denial of resources to poor children on the basis of the employment status of their parents. This policy also legitimized the glaring inadequacy of existing rates of social assistance across Canada, which in many cases are already pegged at less than half of the Statistics Canada poverty line and which in Ontario were cut back by 21.6 percent just before the NCBS was introduced. Unlike the Guaranteed Income Supplement for the elderly, this new exercise in targeting aimed at poor children also failed to channel additional federal money directly to its neediest clients – those living with single mothers on social assistance. Nor did it acknowledge that caring for children is work.[39] Jean Chrétien's government's return to the principles of "less eligibility" and unequal citizenship in mounting an attack on child poverty was nothing short of breathtaking. More than any other single policy initiative in recent memory, it also confirmed the lasting impact of residualism in the liberal Canadian welfare state.

Mackenzie King's ambiguous legacy continues to shape debates over the future direction of national social policy. His residualist approach to national responsibility for the jobless lives on within federal government reforms to UI and social assistance throughout the 1990s. The impact of broad-ranging federal cutbacks to EI combined with the abolition of the Canada Assistance Plan in 1996 resulted in a major downloading of the burden of coping with economic readjustment and the consequences of globalization upon provinces, municipalities, and the families of Canada's jobless. Ottawa's minimalist approach to dealing with the rights of the elderly, begun with the launching of Canada's first means-tested OAP scheme by Mackenzie King in 1927 and reaffirmed through the low benefit levels established through OAS in 1951, also continued to shape the pattern of inconsistent federal decision-making regarding the future of OAS. Since the launching of OAS, successive federal governments have only half-heartedly embraced and more recently attempted to shed the principle of universality as a starting point for the making of Canadian social policy concerning the elderly.

In the field of children's rights, however, King's policy record does contain the potential for more far-reaching reforms. In 1944, in the midst of total war and massive public debt, King embraced the idea of giving every Canadian child "an equal start in the battle of life" through the creation of universal family allowances. Although his motivations, as always, sprang out of a complex set of political calculations, the sheer scope and cost of the scheme blazed a bold and pioneering course for the national government in attacking the problem of child poverty in post-war Canada. Although much of this policy legacy was squandered by subsequent federal governments, it remains unique in North America. More than half a century later, one of every five Canadian children still live in poverty. The time is long overdue for King's Liberal successors to abandon residualism and rediscover the political will to combat this national disgrace.

Sociology for a New Century:
Mackenzie King's First Career

Kenneth Westhues

There are four important things to know about William Lyon Mackenzie King. Three are common knowledge. This essay is about the fourth. The main thing is that he was prime minister of Canada for twenty-two of the years between 1921 and 1948 and was arguably the most important figure in Canadian political history. Mackenzie King's political career is a window on the emergence of an independent Canada during the first half of the twentieth century: its gradual separation from Britain, the growth of its mixed economy, its accommodation of English and French, and its part in the Second World War.

The second mark of distinction is that even before becoming Liberal leader and prime minister, King shaped relations between capital and labour in North America. He was Canada's first deputy minister of labour in 1900. Elected to Parliament from North Waterloo in 1908, he was minister of labour in Wilfrid Laurier's government. From 1914 to 1919 he was on the payroll of the Rockefeller Foundation, as a confidant to John D. Rockefeller, Jr., and a troubleshooter for disputes with organized labour. In all these posts King pressed for compromise. In some sense the inventor of the company union, King forestalled proletarian revolt and helped lay the foundation of the welfare state.

The third noteworthy thing about King came to light after his death in 1950. Publication of the diaries he kept throughout his life revealed in his later years an exotic spiritualism beneath his bland, reasoned, unemotive exterior. The bachelor prime minister attended seances, communicated with spirits, read signs sent from beyond the grave, and sought advice from his deceased mother and dog. King's diaries are evidence of how complex and full of contradiction a human being can be.

From political, economic, and psychological viewpoints, King is of obvious historical importance. What few people know is that the same is true from a sociological viewpoint. The first career King embarked on after his graduation from the University of Toronto in 1895 was as a sociologist. Sociology was what he studied at the University of Chicago in 1896–97. It is the field in which he wrote his thesis there and earned his M.A. degree. Since sociology at the time had gained barely a toehold in universities, King may well have been the first Canadian to earn an advanced degree in it. By a wide margin, he is still the most prominent.

What led the young Willie King to embrace sociology at twenty-one years of age? How did he understand the field? What meaning did he think it had? By what methods was it done? What advantage did he see in sociology over the fields of journalism and law, which he rejected in its favour? How, in his view, did sociology relate to practical affairs? What use might it have?

King's temporary love affair with sociology is especially worth studying today, a century later, for the perspective it offers on the current crisis in this discipline. In North America sociology's heyday was the late 1960s and early 1970s. Since that time it has fragmented into factions defined by theoretical, methodological, and political orientation.[1] Over the past thirty years undergraduate enrolment in sociology has declined by about half.[2] The urgency of the discipline's problems in this dawn of the twenty-first century recommends careful study of why and how it attracted a bright youth like Willie King just before the dawn of the twentieth.

The French philosopher Auguste Comte coined the term *sociology* in 1838, joining the Latin word for *social* with the Greek word for *knowledge.* Comte's project was to discover social laws, counterparts to the laws of motion in physics, and thereby to create a natural science of society. Comte took a deterministic view, rejecting faith and free will. His goal, equally as undemocratic as Plato's two millennia before, was that society be ruled by a class of priests well schooled in the natural social laws.

The most famous nineteenth-century sociologist, Herbert Spencer, also modelled his work on natural science, drawing on Charles Darwin's laws of evolution for his foundational book, *The Study of Sociology,* in 1873. Spencer's concept of "survival of the fittest" held enormous appeal to those who had risen to the top of the laissez-faire capitalist economy. Through its popularity among captains of industry like Andrew Carnegie, Spencer's sociology found its way into American universities. William Graham Sumner, an ardent Spencerian professor at Yale, there taught the first sociology course on this side of the Atlantic in 1875.[3]

Yet the sociology that attracted young Willie King was distinct from what Comte, Spencer, or Sumner had in mind. There is no hint in King's diaries that he aspired to be a "scientist of society," that he believed social action is determined by natural social laws, or that he wished to study it the way physicists study non-human phenomena. On the contrary, King appears to have taken for granted the basic distinction between the human and the natural worlds. The student of human affairs might borrow from natural science methods like empirical observation and logical rigour, not to develop a detached, neutral science but instead to gain such understanding as might permit the building of a better society. Sociology was the study not of a given, inalterable social reality, a *thing* or *res* independent of human volition, but of a *status quo* that might be improved through willpower and skilled intervention.

Sociology in the last quarter of the nineteenth century was similar to what computer science has been in the last quarter of the twentieth: it was bursting with new ideas and was not yet pinned down to academic curricula. People learned it mainly on their own, by observing life, reading books, conversing with friends, and joining debating clubs. No university in Canada offered a degree specifically in sociology, but this was beside the point. What mattered was the ability to write critical, empirical social analyses, just as what counted in the computer industry in the 1970s and 1980s was not so much a degree as the ability to write code. Sociology in King's time was a popular movement, not just an academic discipline.

Buxton and Turner put it this way: "For us, 'sociology' is a body of knowledge that, incidentally, is taught; for them it was a public teaching that, incidentally, was a body of knowledge."[4]

Nearly all the prominent sociologists of the nineteenth and early twentieth centuries defined the field as communicating to the public at large knowledge about how society works. One prominent Canadian example was Colin McKay, who set forth his analyses in about one thousand newspaper and magazine articles between 1890 and 1930.[5] McKay was not doctrinaire; he drew upon scholars as disparate as Herbert Spencer and Karl Marx, Georg Hegel and Lester Ward. He did not defend the regnant economic system, but championed democratic reform. He identified with ordinary working people and aimed to produce knowledge that would enable social and economic change.

The single book that best illustrates what sociology meant in Canada when King was growing up was the first work of Canadian sociology. It appeared in 1897, the same year King was studying at the Univesity of Chicago. Its author was not a professor but a young, wealthy businessman in Montreal named Herbert Brown Ames.[6] He was the son of American parents. Travel and study in his youth had given him a perspective uncommonly broad among children of privilege and a keen sense of human solidarity. His goal was not only to keep the family shoe business afloat but to reform municipal politics in Montreal, thereby to build a more just, prosperous, and democratic city. In the early 1890s he helped found the Volunteer Electoral League, a kind of citizens' action committee for fair elections and responsible government. Ames was elected to the Montreal City Council in 1898 and held a seat in Parliament from 1904 to 1920.

The first step toward improving things, Ames reasoned, is a shared factual understanding of how things currently are. That is why he undertook his systematic study and published it. His book was not an academic exercise or pleasant hobby, not knowledge for its own sake. Nor was it aimed at some circle of literati cultivating trendy thoughts. It was directed to his fellow citizens, the Montreal public, sharply divided at the time between the well-off living on the hill, and the poor living below the hill:

> Most of the residents of the upper city know little and at times seem to care less regarding their fellow-men in the city below. To many of the former the condition of the latter is as little known as that of natives in Central Africa. … To pass from one to the other only well-ordered thoroughfares are travelled. From this beaten track they seldom wander and of other regions they possess little or no knowledge. At this time in the world's history, when careful observers and honest thinkers in every land are coming more and more to realize what is meant by the interdependence of society, when those who study city life are each day more fully persuaded that ordinary urban conditions are demoralizing and that no portion of the community can be allowed to deteriorate without danger to the whole, when it is being proven over and over again by enlightened municipalities that the public health can be conserved, morals improved and lives saved by a right

knowledge of local conditions and the proper use of measures for their amelioration, it is opportune that the citizens of Montreal should, for a time, cease discussing the slums of London, the beggars of Paris, and the tenement house evils of New York and endeavor to learn something about themselves and to understand more perfectly the conditions present in their very midst.[7]

The foundation of sociology, as this quote from Ames suggests, was first of all a consciousness or attitude: awareness that even if divided by class, manners, and living conditions, all members of a society are bound into a whole, and that with commitment and work this collective whole can be improved.

More than that, sociology was detailed empirical knowledge of precisely how the varied members of society are connected and how they lead their lives. It was not mere exhortation, the preaching of brotherly love. It was the gathering and analysis of social *data*, the information given to our senses by the way people live. The research reported in Ames's book was a house-to-house canvas of one of the poorer districts of Montreal. Information was gathered on employment, housing, sanitation, family size, incomes, nationality, and religion. Ames presented results of the survey broken down by neighbourhood so that readers could see precisely where incomes were lowest or indoor plumbing least available. Maps were included showing population density, overcrowding, death rates, and so on, neighbourhood by neighbourhood.

The title of Ames's book, *The City below the Hill*, points not only to its particular subject matter (a part of Montreal lying at low elevation) but to the focus of sociology as a whole. An old and powerful metaphor in western civilization is from Matthew 5:14: "You are the light of the world. A city built upon a hill cannot be hidden." Many political leaders over the centuries have seized upon this flattering image, this metaphor of excellence and superiority, for their own societies. John Winthrop, governor of the Massachusetts Bay Colony, described Puritan New England as a city on a hill. John F. Kennedy used the phrase to describe the United States of America. During the 1997 mayoral election campaign in Toronto, candidate Barbara Hall called that metropolis a city on a hill. It is an idealization of the way things are, a proud, righteous conception of the society at hand.

Ames's title captured the sharply contrasting emphasis of sociology: not flattery but empirical truth. Sociology would not gloss over problems. It would seek facts, all of them. Against idealized images, sociology would counter pose some-times harsh realities. In this way it would not nourish pride in the status quo so much as awareness of its faults and of the desirability and possibility of change. Sociology's home was in *The City below the Hill*. Spencer, Sumner, and their aca-demic colleagues notwithstanding, most of sociology was cold comfort to elites. It was a mirror of the way things are, warts and all. It was social knowledge with-out rose-coloured glasses. It showed how the lives of rich and poor, powerful and powerless, intersect, and how those intersections could be reshaped. Democratic values and sociological research tended to go hand in hand.

What kind of youth might be drawn to sociology of the kind just described? One whose life had contradictions in it, conflicting identities and experiences that gave distance from the social order at hand and raised questions about it, a back-ground that quickened a certain fascination with the human variety. Mackenzie King clearly felt that fascination by the time he was a Toronto undergraduate:

> I felt in a very philosophical mood tonight, especially while walking along Queen St. I was trying to understand the different types of faces, what peo-ple were thinking about, whither were they treading. I always feel that the fact of there being such great inequalities in the happiness and lots of dif-ferent people, is almost evident proof of a better world to come when we shall all have been made equal in the sight of God. [March 23, 1895]

King was just twenty years old when he wrote these lines, obviously already bitten by the sociological bug. A fellow student might have taken the same walk and been captivated by the stars in the sky, the design of buildings along the street, the traffic of motor cars and carriages, the goods in storefront windows, or the trees along the boulevard. What held King's attention, what he puzzled over, was the people passing by.

This fascination undoubtedly grew out of contradictions he felt during his first eighteen years of life, which he spent in Berlin, Ontario, a town later renamed Kitchener on account of anti-German sentiment during the First World War. He was born in a house on Benton Street, near the town centre, in 1874. Later his family moved to a modest estate named Woodside on the eastern outskirts, al-most in the country. Now restored as a national historic site, Woodside symbol-ized the King family's apartness from the local mainstream.[8]

Had King been raised in Toronto, a thoroughly British city at that time, his family's Scottish Presbyterian identity would have placed him squarely in the majority culture. Not so in Berlin. According to the 1881 census, 75 percent of the four thousand inhabitants, including most leading businessmen and politicians, were of German origin. German was the language of commerce in the stores along King Street and of worship in the Lutheran and Roman Catholic churches to which most residents belonged.[9]

Berlin's German character did not make the King family an outcast. The Anglo–German hostility that would come with the two world wars was still decades away. Especially in a county named for the Battle of Waterloo, Canadians of German and British heritage celebrated the common cause their ancestors had made on that occasion, to defeat a French tyrant. Loyalty to Queen Victoria was not thought to conflict with respect for her cousin, Kaiser Wilhelm.

Willie's father, John King, moreover, enjoyed respect as a lawyer, was involved in local politics, and kept his family at an above-average level of living. Willie attended public elementary schools, played sports, and acted in school plays during his high school years, at what is now Kitchener Collegiate Institute. By all accounts he got along well with his mostly German Lutheran classmates. Yet he would have been conscious day in and day out that they were different from him in ethnicity, language, and religion.

A further contradiction in young Willie's life was between the values of his maternal grandfather, for whom he was named, and the values in his immediate family.

William Lyon Mackenzie (1795–1861) was a champion of democracy in pre-Confederation British North America. He was the kind of man who might have become a sociologist had the field been invented earlier. Mackenzie ran newspapers and was Toronto's first mayor and a member of the provincial parliament. Fiery and principled, he opposed the oligarchy, the "family compact," that ruled Upper Canada in the 1820s and 1830s. In 1837 he led an armed revolt against the colonial government. The rebellion failed and Mackenzie fled to the United States, where he worked as a journalist and biographer. Pardoned in 1849, he returned to Toronto and was re-elected to the provincial parliament.

Although this grandfather was long dead by the time Willie was born, the boy revered him. Mackenzie was his most famous ancestor, and Willie carried his very name. He wrote in his diary:

Last night I read more of Mackenzie's life and felt more deeply inspired. I could not get to sleep for an hour or two after going to bed. [June 19, 1895]

And again:

Reading the life of my dear grandfather, I have become a greater admirer of his than ever. ... I have greater desire to carry on the work he endeavored to perform, to better the condition of the poor, denounce corruption, the tyranny of abused power and uphold right and honourable principles. [June 22, 1895]

On the other hand were Willie's parents, who thought more of Mackenzie's fame than of his principles. Isabel Mackenzie King, Willie's mother, had been born during the period of exile in New York. Money was tight throughout her upbringing. She was eighteen when her father died, leaving little wealth, so that she, her mother, and her sisters had to give music and dance lessons to make ends meet. In marrying John King, Isabel looked for a life of refinement and security. She discouraged John from running for political office, saying that her father had already given her enough politics for a lifetime. She was eager that Willie, the eldest of her four children, stay out of trouble and achieve such prominence and respectability as would vindicate the family name.

John King came from a conservative, intellectual family and was accepted in the Ontario elite, but he never managed to make enough money to keep his wife in the style she wished. The family never owned Woodside, only rented it, and sometimes it had to skimp on groceries to pay the servants. It was a close family whose lofty conception of itself outstripped its financial means. Thus Willie had to work his way through university with part-time jobs. His father pressured him relentlessly to make economic security his top priority: to become a lawyer and get himself established in Toronto, where he enrolled in university in 1891 and where the whole family moved in 1893.

That same autumn, as he began his third year of undergraduate study, still just nineteen years old, Willie King began his diary. Its pages document the varied intellectual paths he tried, first one and then another, that would lead, three years later, to his plunge into sociology at Chicago. More broadly, the entries chronicle an ambitious young man's interests, frustrations, preoccupations, and worries in the process of growing up. Most of what was on Willie King's mind a century ago resembled what is on university students' minds today.

Attending church is one example: Willie's parents attached more importance to it than he did. Willie – or Rex, as his friends called him – preferred to sleep late, sometimes observing that he had missed the Sunday service on that account. At other times he acquiesced to his parents' wishes, as on Thanksgiving Day, November 21, 1895: "This morning I wanted to sleep but mother and father were anxious for me to go to church, so with much reluctance I went, did not enjoy the sermon very much."

Finances, too, were on Rex's mind. He sold textbooks he no longer needed, announced on a bulletin board his availability to do tutoring in political science (October 14, 1895), and repaid "50 cents I owed Robinson from last year" (March 10, 1896). He could expect little financial help from his father, who at times came to him for short-term loans. Willie lectured himself: "I must also learn to save money and not let it fall through my hands" (November 23, 1895).

It was an era when premarital sexual activity was off limits for upper-middle-class youth. Sexual attraction was not to be admitted so freely as today. Even so, a boy could legitimately enjoy the company of girls in recreation. Rex liked swimming, boating, and tennis, the more so if one or another "young lady" was joining in the fun. It was also acceptable to have extended conversations with a girl on philosophic and religious subjects, and on plans for the future. The diary for August of 1895 records at length Rex's talks with a girl named Kitty, who seemed to encourage his ambition to achieve some position of influence. "As yet I do not know where it is to be, I believe it may be a professor of Political Economy, an earnest student of social questions. Or it may be in public life, parliament perhaps what if it might be both?" (August 27, 1895).

Like most students then and now, Willie sometimes got bogged down in his studies. "Tried to read Darwin on the Species but only covered a chapter or so" (July 5, 1895). He sometimes had writer's block: "I feel a great desire to write and yet find difficulty in expressing my thoughts, which come and go rapidly, pass unexpressed" (December 25, 1895). Because he would need a fellowship to pursue postgraduate studies, he worried about getting low marks: "very frightened of today's papers, did fairly well this morning but this afternoon went all to pieces. … Today will pull down my average terribly" (April 25, 1896).

Rex held many of his professors in low esteem and did not hesitate to write in his diary what he thought of them: "Again, our university has on its lists of professors and teachers a number of men for whom I have little or no respect they are many of them very uncultured, narrow-minded, and bigoted, and are far from being congenial company" (June 14, 1896). James Mavor, who held the chair of political economy and was King's main teacher, came in for particularly harsh comments. Rex wrote of a "very unsatisfactory talk" with Mavor and described him as ungrateful, inconsiderate, and selfish (May 7, 1896). On another occasion he set down a friend's "excellent description" of Mavor: "His presumption is limitless, his ability is practically nil, and his power for irritating humanity is egregious" (July 18, 1896).

Amidst the concerns most students share, Rex King had particular interests pointing toward a career in sociology, even though the word does not appear in his diary during his undergraduate years. There was at the time no separate department of sociology at the University of Toronto; none would be established until well after the Second World War. Toronto was a small university in King's time, having only about a thousand students. King described his interest as political economy, economics, social science, or political science, all of which referred to essentially the same kind of social analysis.

What strikes the reader of his diary is King's voracious appetite for learning about the society surrounding him, not just from books, but from direct observation of human experience. There was no corner of Toronto he did not want to see with his own eyes. After a day when his duties as a reporter had taken him to an especially broad assortment of events, he wrote: "Look at this for the phases of life I have seen today: criminal and pauper, political, religious, death, academic, theatrical. Have been in five different worlds. What a training for a student of Social Science" (November 14, 1895).

More than through course selection, King shaped his education by searching out off-campus opportunities to learn. His diaries report that he "talked with labour agitator, read pamphlet on conditions of labour" (October 7, 1895); that he visited the St. John's Mission, the children's hospital, a prison, a meeting of the Socialist Labour Party, and a county jail (September 9, 1895); that he took part in the St. Andrew's Club discussion of anarchism and social reform (December 9, 1895); that he learned about the "sweating system" in Toronto's factories (October 23, 1895); and that he had long talks with his "working friends" (July 25, 1895).

Rex purposely exposed himself to parts of society far removed from the life he had known at Woodside and in Berlin's Presbyterian church. He "went for a drive with Salvation Army people to visit their social institution" (June 4, 1896). He reported himself "much interested in the Catholic service, though I do not care for so much in an unknown tongue" (May 10, 1896).

The result was extraordinary tolerance for diverse ways of life and abhorrence of intolerance, even in the Protestant majority he belonged to. The Orange Lodges were at the height of their power in Canada while King was growing up, and he watched Toronto's Orange parade on July 11, 1896: "It did not seem right to me to see one class of society celebrating the defeat of another and keeping up a difference which long ago should have died out." Two days later he gave this reaction to an Orangeman's sermon: "I must say I was thoroughly disgusted. The narrow unchristian bigotry was more than any I have heard from Roman Catholics."

Rex's intellectual interests, his need for money, the example of several ancestors, and probably his father's political connections joined on October 25, 1895, to land him a job as reporter for the Toronto *News*. It paid five dollars a week, and lasted exactly that long. His assignments that week were for articles on the Princess Theatre, a missing old man, and a smothered baby.

On November 2, 1895, Rex moved to the Toronto *Globe*, which he described as a less sensational newspaper, at a salary of seven dollars a week. Assigned to cover Toronto's police court, he stayed in the job for ten months. His personal agenda was clear from the start: "I fully intend to make academic work my profession and am taking Journalism as an extra year of practical experience in the great school of life" (November 5, 1895). Reporting, he said, would be excellent experience, "especially to a student of social science," a department in which he expected to "do some practical good" (November 9, 1895).

The job more than met his expectations. He was sent to inspect the drowned body of an old sailor for description in the paper. He covered a druggists' convention and a meeting of the Women's Christian Temperance Union. Mainly, King observed proceedings in court, which nourished a certain cynicism about established institutions that is a hallmark of sociology. "I am much impressed with the farcical administration of justice we see exhibited here at times," he wrote on November 25, 1895. On December 31 he observed: "Saw the sublime and the ridiculous at the police court this morning." On January 23, 1896: "I must say I felt a sort of contempt for the politicians so sly and everything for themselves and power."

Mackenzie King (centre) with Archie Dennison (left) and John D. Rockefeller, Jr. while studying industrial relations under the auspices of the Rockefeller Foundation. Frederick, Colorado, 1915. (National Archives of Canada C-029350)

On June 20, 1896, after seeing a man sentenced to be hanged: "What an inhuman business law is! Victory in such a field I do not crave. How much higher Economics, which seeks the prevention of crime rather than its punishment, the restoration to society of the criminal rather than his extinction."

King's cynicism extended to the propertied classes, an attitude on which he must have looked back with a smile twenty years later, when he was being paid $230 a week to advise John D. Rockefeller, Jr. Sent on May 25, 1896, to cover the Woodbine races for the Associated Press, King wrote that evening that he had not enjoyed the occasion. He referred to "the society set" as "poor, feeble-minded creatures whose only pleasure is to be looked at and to look at others." He added that the men did not impress him either.

King trained his critical faculties also on his employer. When a member of the paper's board of directors nixed his application for a raise, he called it "an example of the meanness of a grit politician, also of large corporations. If I were at all independent I would leave the concern. But I will use these men as a means to my end meanwhile" (March 2, 1896). A later entry expressed his wish to see "a newspaper for the poor" (June 17, 1896).

King's heart had not been in journalism from the start. Just two months into the job he wrote, "I long to be connected with a University as a professor of Political Economy or Social Science" (December 31, 1895). Six months into the job he was bored: "I sicken sometimes at the thought of four more months of it, but it is a good experience I suppose" (May 19, 1896). He fantasized steadily about an academic career, setting down his aspiration to become president of the University of Toronto: "a high ambition but I think a noble one" (August 27, 1896). His last day at police court was September 3: "I had the schools and missions for my afternoon assignment, thus ending where I began on the News. I fear this is too often the case in Journalism. No progress, everlasting routine, it is one reason why I am glad to get out of it."

Rex King's stint as a reporter not only broadened his experience but gave him time to complete his law degree in June 1896 and to investigate alternatives for the academic studies he would resume that fall. His fellowship applications to Columbia, Johns Hopkins, Yale, Harvard, and Wisconsin yielded nothing promising. In the end, his options came down to two: remaining at Toronto to study constitutional history (in preparation for a career in law), or going to Chicago for sociology.

The first option, strongly favoured by his parents, led him to apply on June 11, 1896, for a fellowship at Toronto. Three days later, the independent-minded young man withdrew the application, explaining that he had submitted it only on account of

my father's and mother's very strong desire to have me do so. Father would be so proud if I held a position here, he feels he needs me as a companion and he longs for me to be with him. Mother certainly hates the thought of my leaving home. Father's desires expressed themselves in more than words. He used his persuasive powers strongly and being induced largely, almost entirely, by them, I wrote out on Tuesday night all my claims to success. This he, with pleasure, received, revised, had typewritten copies made, and corrected, punctuated, and all but signed, he even addressed the envelope for me.

In fact, Rex King had already accepted a fellowship to Chicago one month earlier. His diary entry for May 11 had read: "So I mailed my acceptance to Chicago with the words 'God help me' uttered voluntarily and yet involuntarily as I put it in the office box." It was an event almost one year earlier that had sealed King's determination to leave Toronto for the metropolis of the American Midwest, the "city of the big shoulders," as Sandburg would call it. The most famous woman in Chicago had visited Toronto for the Pan-American Congress of Education and Religion, and Rex King had gone to hear her speak.

Her name was Jane Addams. She was thirty-five years old. With her friend, Ellen Starr, she had founded in 1889 a grassroots community institution called Hull House in a Chicago neighbourhood brimming with new arrivals to the American melting pot. Hull House was the most famous of a distinct kind of institution established in many cities about that time, what was called a *settlement*. It meant simply a home "in the poorer quarters of a city where educated men and women may live in daily personal contact with the working people."[10] In terms of the title of Herbert Ames's book, a settlement was where the City on the Hill and the City below the Hill would meet.

Addams was a charismatic figure, skilled at raising money from the rich to help the poor. She was brilliant, capably grounding the settlement project in Christian teaching, Tolstoy's philosophy, and the Fabian socialism of George Bernard Shaw and Sidney and Beatrice Webb. Addams was also a sociologist, one of about a hundred scholars who would join in founding the American Sociological Society in 1905. As a public intellectual she combined study, research, and writing, on the one hand, with social and political activism on the other on behalf of democracy, equality, universal suffrage, and human rights. Vilified for her pacifism during the First World War, Addams was awarded the Nobel Peace Prize in 1931, four years before her death.

Addams's talk in Toronto on July 20, 1895, was on "the settlement idea," an institution that would embody and promote solidarity among all citizens, even in the midst of sharp divisions on class and ethnic lines. Rex King was swept away: "I never listened to an address which I more thoroughly enjoyed. I sat at the reporters' table with the other reporters (most of whom I know) and took notes for my own pleasure." King went to visit Addams that evening and travelled with her the next day to hear her speak again, this time of the late Arnold Toynbee, a social reformer in Great Britain who had inspired the settlement movement there. "I love Toynbee and I love Miss Addams," King wrote that evening. "I love the work which the one was and the other is and which I hope soon to be, engaged in."

Fifteen months later, as King packed his bags for the trip by train to Chicago, it was not just to join the Hull House community. Nor was it only to enrol for graduate study at the new University of Chicago, which had been founded in 1891 with a donation from John D. Rockefeller. It was *both*. The work King hoped to engage in was sociology, which had its more activist expression in Hull House, where Addams was head resident, and its more academic expression in the university, where Albion Small had founded America's first department of sociology in 1892 and where he was the department head.

For us a century later, when sociology has become mainly a specialized academic discipline, the intermingling of thought and action that defined the field in Chicago, when King arrived in 1896, is hard to grasp. Addams did not work in isolation from the university. More than once Small offered her an appointment to his department but she declined it, preferring to keep Hull House her institutional home. She did, however, teach in the university's extension division, and published articles in the *American Journal of Sociology*, which Small had founded in 1895.[11]

University sociologists were an integral part of Hull House. Charles Zeublin lived there. Charles Henderson, Mackenzie King's thesis supervisor, established a department of practical sociology in the Chicago's divinity school, and regularly lectured in the adult-education classes at Hull House. These professors, along with George Mead, John Dewey, W. I. Thomas, and other luminaries at the university counted Addams their colleague and Hull House a complement to their classroom teaching. Indeed, University of Chicago President William Harper favoured incorporating Hull House within the university. The grounds on which Addams successfully opposed this move show how public and democratic was the conception of sociology she held:

> [Hull House's] individuality is the result of the work of a group of people, who have had all the perplexities and uncertainties of pioneers. This group is living in the 19th Ward, not as students, but as citizens, and their methods of work must differ from that of an institution established elsewhere, and following well defined lines. An absorption would be most unfair to them.[12]

Chicago's two main homes for sociology, one at the university and the other at Hull House, were nonetheless distinct and physically distant. The University of Chicago was on the south side at 59th Street, the Midway Plaisance where the 1892 world's fair was held; it was, metaphorically, in the City on the Hill. Hull

House was in the City below the Hill, a core-area neighbourhood already past its prime. The two were far enough apart that commuting between them daily was expensive in money and time.

Arriving in Chicago after holidays in Muskoka, Rex King was determined to keep one foot in both sides of sociology. He went first to the university, met with Albion Small on October 1, 1896, and reported enjoying his talk with him: "I told Professor Small I was prepared to go to the Settlement at once, his advice was however to wait for a short time till I saw it, etc." On October 3 King met Henderson, then went for a second visit with Small, on whom the young Canadian appears to have made quite a positive impression:

> This afternoon I called on Professor Small and had a long talk with him on his doorstep, during the course of our conversation which was very free and unreserved he said he would give me the $520 in Sociology next year if I decided to take his course for my Ph.D. degree. This I am thinking seriously of doing as the work in Sociology fits exactly with the line of work I find most congenial. I like Professor Small also very much.

King also met with a Professor Laughlin, who suggested he do his thesis on rates of interest in the U.S. economy.

By October 6 King was immersed in coursework. He attended four lectures that day: by Small on "the province of sociology," by Henderson on the family, by Hill on tariffs, and by Laughlin on money. From 4:00 to 6:00 p.m., he took part in Henderson's seminar, "which I enjoyed exceedingly, took up work along the line I most desire, institutions, etc." Later that evening, he talked with Hill about the "advisability of taking sociology next year and changing subject of thesis."

King's diary entry for October 8, 1896, shows that then as now, professors courted bright students: "Tonight I have been busy reading Small and Vincent's *Introduction to Sociology*, an interesting book which Professor Small lent me." The book had been published two years before and was to become a standard text in American universities for the next twenty years. George Vincent, the co-author, completed his Ph.D. under Small's supervision in 1896 and went on to become president of the Rockefeller Foundation, which had funded King's research on industrial relations in 1914–17.

On October 9, eight days after his first meeting with Small, King travelled to

Hull House, and for the next three months he divided his time between academic work and settlement work. October 13 found him organizing a club of thirteen-year-old Polish boys at a settlement run by the university. On October 16, "I went down town to do practical work in Sociology," visiting the Medical Mission, Salvation Army headquarters, and the American Volunteers. His entry for the next day reports reading two further chapters of Small and Vincent's book, then visiting yet another settlement house and hearing Jane Addams talk about her visit with Count Tolstoy.

King continued to enjoy Henderson's seminar, noting in particular the discussion on October 20 of "methods of dealing with homeless men and women." Of all King's teachers, Henderson best represented the engaged sort of sociology King was looking for. The responsibility of the sociologist, as Henderson saw it, was "to aid in forming a judicial public opinion, as distinguished from the public opinion of a class and its special pleaders."[13] Toward that end, his method of research was to collect factual data on the history and current status of whatever subject, analyze the data systematically, and draw from it practical guidelines for current public policy.

Henderson was like King, moreover, in preferring direct observation and involvement to second-hand reports. He did not keep the human subjects of his research at arm's length. At Henderson's funeral in 1915, Addams said in her eulogy:

> I had the impression of a man who was anxious to know the poor people at first hand. He was not willing to take his sociology from the various pieces of paper which his students had brought him after they had gone through a street with a paper in one hand and a pencil in the other, but he wished to understand the social factors lying at the bottom of his subject from firsthand informations. [14]

On October 31, 1896, King moved into Hull House, and for the next two months he took his meals in common with the other residents and performed various tasks as needed in the operation of the settlement's social and educational programs. He began to feel estranged from the university. He wrote on November 19: "This morning I missed the first lecture by sleeping over time." And on November 23: "This morning I missed the first lecture on purpose, having slept till nearly 8, had a bath as usual."

Life at Hull House had frustrations of its own, worsened undoubtedly by King's knowledge that his parents back in Toronto did not altogether approve of his living there. On November 30, for example, he reported an instance of what today might be called "tensions surrounding gender issues":

> While at dinner I was told Miss Addams was ill and I was asked to speak in her place at the Kirkland Street Settlement. I agreed to speak on the life of Toynbee. Shortly after I was told it was a women's meeting and that a woman must address them, then Miss Barrie said I should go anyway, and so we went together. I spoke on Toynbee, she spoke on Hull House.

King ended the day's entry by wondering if perhaps he should transfer to Oxford University in England.

The first two weeks of December, before he returned home for the Christmas holidays, were a tempestuous time for King as he puzzled over the direction his life should take. On December 2 he wrote: "I am feeling very dissatisfied with things at present. I really gain nothing from the teaching at the University. There is need of men who can inspire others all seem so narrow and selfish. I long for a place of wider culture and deeper thought." Laughlin's lectures on money especially disappointed him. He described one as "feeble" (December 10), another as "an hour wasted" (December 14).

The hormones of a twenty-two-year-old male undoubtedly added to King's frustrations, since neither at the university nor at Hull House was there approval of *any* sexual activity outside the marriage bond. Indeed, Henderson publicly condemned masturbation,[15] attributing to it a range of personal and social ills. On December 6, 1896, King reported in his diary a "fierce war of flesh and spirit all day. When will I subdue the evil in me?"

On December 16 Addams gave King her photo, and he bought a copy of her book published the previous year, *Hull-House Maps and Papers*. It was the collaborative work of ten Hull House residents and included chapters on the sweating system in Chicago, child labourers, the economic conditions of garment workers, the Chicago Jewish community, Bohemians, and Italians. Perhaps the chapter of most lasting significance was Ellen Starr's essay on the importance of art even in the midst of poverty. Addams's book was for Chicago a richer, more detailed version of what Ames's book was for Montreal.

If the spirit of William Lyon Mackenzie had been stronger in Mackenzie King's immediate family, the trip home for Christmas might have encouraged the young sociologist to involve himself further in Hull House, or even to befriend Eugene Debs and the other radicals trying at that time to secure for the Chicago working class the right to unionize and strike. The Pullman Strike of 1894 was still vivid in memory: it had been violently suppressed.

As it was, King returned to Chicago in the new year feeling torn between Hull House and the university. On January 7 he concluded that the journey of two hours a day from his residence at Hull House to his classes at the university was simply too long: "I have to consider my life's usefulness and at present the University seems my field of work. I ought above all to be faithful to it. I had hoped to combine both." At that point he moved out of Hull House and plunged into work on his thesis, a historical study of the International Typographical Union.

King's M.A. research resulted in two articles published in the *Journal of Political Economy*: "Trade-Union Organization in the United States" (March 1897) and "The International Typographical Union" (September 1897). The first traced the history of trade unions in general and argued strongly in their favour, as against the more radical and politicized industrial unions:

> In this age when there is a tendency, especially among large sections of workingmen, to seek for better conditions along new and somewhat radical lines, and a parallel tendency to "cry down" old and existing institutions, laborers will do well to consider what these older organizations have accomplished in the past, what their more perfect development promises for the future, and what are the reasons which should lead them at this particular time to accept or reject a plan of social and industrial betterment which never before has had more reasonable opportunities or better facilities for ultimate success. [16]

King's second article applied this general perspective to the typographical union but in a way that more easily engages the interest of today's reader, in view of its historical detail. King had closely examined the union's written records, minutes of meetings, publications, and so on, as well as relevant legislation in several states and statistical data on journeymen printers and apprentices gathered by the government of Minnesota. Two questions he addressed are hot issues still today, despite immense technological change in the printing industry.[17] First was whether and under what conditions the union had admitted women. King set forth a principle that still guides public policy:

> It was found that the only successful mode of dealing with this new factor in the labor market was to give it fair treatment to combine with it, and by organizing female labor and demanding for woman the same remuneration for time and service as was given to man, to prevent the underselling of the one by the other. [18]

The second question King investigated was what place Negroes had. Again, he came down on the side of human equality, but his empirical sense was keen enough to see that this ideal was rarely achieved: "So far then as nominal privileges are concerned, they are not denied by the Typographical Union to the negro; but as long as the old racial prejudice exists, it will be questionable to what degree they are real."

King was neither the first nor the last graduate student to become physically ill from the work of writing a thesis. He wrote on March 2, 1897: "Completed in a hasty manner paper on International Typographical Union, of which I am thoroughly sick." He was bogged down in coursework, too: "I had an examination by Professor Laughlin, only two questions and I knew very little of either. I was thoroughly ashamed and disgusted, the truth is I have not been keeping up with lectures as I ought to have done."

By March 8 King was in a Chicago hospital. Henderson visited him there, and Small diagnosed him as having typhoid fever. His illness and hospital stay had no lasting effects, except that he fell in love with one of the nurses. It was she, he thought, who would give him strength to carry on the ideals of his namesake. Their romance continued off and on for the next eighteen months, long after he left Chicago.

To King's disappointment, the nurse fit no better than Hull House with the designs his family had on him. His sister Jennie wrote to him:

> What we all did hope and believe was that you would make a name for yourself that would help us all. You will never know the sacrifices that have been made for you.

His mother twisted the knife:

> I have built castles without number for you. Are all these dreams but to end
> in dreams? I am getting old now Willie and disappointment wearies and
> the heart grows sick. Sometimes when I hear you talk so much what you
> would do for those that suffer I think charity begins at home.[19]

In the end, King did more than acquiesce. He repented of having strayed from his
mother's wishes. His emotional ties to her grew stronger.[20] He would never be so
romantically involved again.

Rex's final months at Chicago were brightened not only by the nurse but also
by Thorstein Veblen, a professor at that time forty years old, whose fame as an
intellectual thorn in the side of the capitalist class continues to the present day.
Veblen moved toward more specifically economic research in later decades, but
John Kenneth Galbraith has written that Veblen's "enduring achievement was not
in economics but in sociology":

> Never after the publication of *The Theory of the Leisure Class* [1900] could
> a rich man spend with ostentation, abandon and enjoyment without
> someone rising to ridicule it as Conspicuous Consumption.[21]

After hearing Veblen lecture on scientific versus state socialism on May 18
King wrote that he had dealt with it "in a very able manner." On June 9 he wrote:
"Tonight I called for Dr. Veblen and we went for a long walk together. Had a most
interesting talk with him on a number of subjects. I think his name will become
known e'er long, he is a great student." On June 11, 1897, as he prepared to leave
Chicago, King wrote in his diary: "I received a paper today by which I saw that I
and my thesis had been accepted and I am now a Master of Arts. In truth I am
somewhat ashamed of the thesis."

Given that King eventually rose to the highest political position in Canada and
held it for two decades, why is his brief initial career in sociology so little studied,
so little known? There are at least three reasons.

The simplest is that at Harvard, where he enrolled in 1898 for his doctoral
studies, sociology was not yet established as a distinct discipline. Ideas similar to
those King had heard at Chicago were taught at Harvard, but under the names of

political economy, economics, labour relations, and political science. As a result King came to be considered an economist by trade. Even so, his Ph.D. thesis at Harvard focused squarely on the City below the Hill; it was an analysis of the sweating system, especially in the clothing industry.

King himself had a good reason to play down his year in Chicago sociology. In the course of his life, he gradually abandoned what sociology had meant to him: the application of social analysis to democratic social action, the continuation of the work of William Lyon Mackenzie, the emulation of people like Addams, Ames, Henderson, and Veblen. When King moved out of Hull House, broke up with the nurse, and tightened his ties to his mother, he was taking the initial steps toward a basic shift in priorities: away from trying to transform the status quo, toward trying to acquire within the status quo a position of power, wealth, and respectability.

Rex King was self-aware enough to observe this shift taking place. He rationalized it initially, writing in his diary on February 28, 1899: "I can do more for the working classes in the end by establishing my position first, gaining knowledge, influence, and authority. This is what they need most on their side."

As years and then decades passed, establishing his position became more and more an end in itself, and it became harder to rationalize. King could see in his own behaviour that he had "sold out": he had become a lackey of the capitalist class he had once ridiculed, the Rockefeller family in particular. His retreat into the spirit world is probably best understood as his way of dealing with the failure he knew he had become, by the standards of the man for whom he was named.

F.R. Scott, the McGill professor who asserted throughout his life the values King gave up, damned King after his death with some of the most venomous lines in the poetry of Canada:

> Truly he will be remembered
> Wherever men honour ingenuity,
> Ambiguity, inactivity, and political
> longevity.
> Let us raise up a temple
> To the cult of mediocrity,
> Do nothing by halves
> Which can be done by quarters.[22]

W.L. Mackenzie King in 1945. (National Archives of Canada C-027645)

A third reason for ignoring King's brief career in sociology is that while he was selling his values for a position on the world stage, most sociologists were selling out in a different way and for a lower price. On the whole, the discipline retreated into the safety and security of the university, cutting its ties to social action of the kind represented by Hull House and other settlements.[23] Sociologists gradually gave up trying to address the public in their articles and books. They withdrew into conversation among themselves: lectures heard and articles read only within the academic profession.[24] The rationalization of the academic sociologists, not unlike King's, was that sociology had first to establish itself as a body of knowledge and only later venture outside the academy to recommend reform. It may be because students and the public have seen through this rationalization that sociology, by the end of the twentieth century, had fallen on hard times.

The sociology that drew King to Chicago is a hard vocation to sustain, especially given the antidemocratic trend toward concentration of power in large corporations and the state. As King learned from his own experience, keeping one foot in the City on the Hill and the other in the City below the Hill is an awkward posture. Trying to meld social thought and social action is a groping, enervating, elusive, quixotic struggle, and it ends in failure more often than success. Charles Henderson was said to have died a "premature death from exhaustion."[25] Jane Addams succeeded in keeping Hull House vibrant until her death, after which it fell apart; what is left is now a museum on the campus of the University of Illinois, Chicago Circle.[26]

Yet sociology, as King knew it in his youth, lives on. In 1982, in Kitchener, Ontario, one block from where King was born, two young graduates of the University of Waterloo, Joe and Stephanie Mancini, along with several friends, founded an institution called the Working Centre.[27] Its aim has been to understand, embody, and promote social solidarity in much the same way Hull House did. The Working Centre runs a self-help centre for the unemployed and a soup kitchen in a nearby church hall. In the storefront on Queen Street, citizens teach one another computer skills, sewing, art, and new ways to make a living in an economy more complex than King ever imagined. The centre is a meeting place for people of diverse social stations, a breeding ground for new ideas about community gardens, recycling, municipal politics, and much else.

About a dozen social science professors from the Waterloo universities have seen the Working Centre as a complement to their own academic work. Since

1991 the University of Waterloo has offered occasional credit courses in the evening at the Working Centre, both as a convenience to older, part-time students and as a way of drawing younger students away from campus to the realities of life in the urban core. Most of the courses have been in sociology, others in political science and philosophy. In this way the Working Centre is a current intersection between the City on the Hill and the City below the Hill. Jane Addams would approve.

By recalling what sociology meant to Mackenzie King at the turn of the twentieth century, this essay has sought to recapture some of that meaning at the turn of the twenty-first. Instead of doing as King did, we might better do as he said in his 1918 book, *Industry and Humanity*:

> Education has been far too generally restricted to mean a schooling in a few elementary subjects essential to the gaining of a livelihood. It has been commended because commercially profitable. Too often, so-called higher education has meant only the knowledge which will command higher rates of remuneration. The emphasis has been upon material considerations, rather than upon life as spiritually interpreted. Education ought to be valued chiefly as enabling human beings to realize their highest capacities, and to serve and conserve, rather than to dominate and destroy. [28]

William Lyon Mackenzie King, 1852-1974:
A Chronology

1852	– Berlin is chosen the county seat of Waterloo County.
1857	– John King comes to Waterloo County.
1869	– John King establishes a law practice in Berlin.
1874	– William Lyon is born on 17 December in Berlin (Kitchener), Ontario .
1869	– John King enters politics.
1871	– Celebrations of the end of the Franco-Prussian War and foundation of German Empire.
1893	– John King returns to Toronto for a better law practice.
1895	– Completed B.A. studies at the University of Toronto.
1896	– L.L.B. University of Toronto.
1896	– King accepts entrance into a M.A. in Sociology program at University of Chicago.
1896	– Starts graduate study in the autumn.
1897	– Erection of statue of German Kaiser Wilhelm II in Victoria Park Berlin.
	– June: M.A. University of Chicago.
	– King enrolls in a PhD at Harvard University.
1900	– Travelling scholarship to visit Berlin, capital of the German Empire.
1900	– Canada's first Deputy Minister of Labor.
1902	– Settles strike at Lippert's furniture factory in Berlin.
1904	– Arthur Doughty appointed Dominion Archivist.
1905	– Establishment of Victoria Park, Berlin.
1907	– Saw the *Industrial Disputes Investigation Act* through Parliament.
1907	– Vancouver Riots against Japanese and Chinese immigration. King sent to investigate.
1907	– Launch of the Champlain Society.
1908	– Submission of the report *The Need for the Suppression of Opium Traffic in Canada.*

1908	– King dispatches Doughty to London to speak on the need for a national history.
1908	– King campaigns in Victoria Park on September 24 with Sir Wilfrid Laurier.
1908	– Elected as Member of Parliament for Waterloo North.
1909	– Acclaimed in second contest when appointed Minister of Labour.
1909	– Receives Ph.D. from Harvard University.
1910	– Debate over Naval Bill.
1910	– May: Unveiling of Queen Victoria's Statue in Victoria Park.
1911	– King introduces Opium and Drug Act.
1911	– Liberals defeated by Tories; King loses Waterloo North.
1914	– Outbreak of War. King and Liberals supportive of Government.
1914-18	– Worked as a consultant and troubleshooter for J.D. Rockefeller.
1916	– Mid-war, Berlin has a name change and becomes Kitchener; John King dies.
1917	– King defeated in North York in general election; King's mother dies.
1919	– King elected leader of Liberal Party; becomes leader of the Opposition.
1921	– December: King becomes Prime Minister.
1922	– King visits Victoria Park.
1922	– Chanak Crisis.
1923	– King is appointed to the British Privy Council.
1923	– King introduces the *Chinese Immigration Act.*
1923	– Imperial Conference, London.
1923	– King moves into Laurier House.
1923	– King speaks about the value of Canadian Archives in London.
1925	– Defeated in North York riding.
1926	– King elected MP in Prince Albert, Saskatchewan.
1926	– Liberals defeated in House of Commons; King loses office.
1926	– Liberal election victory after King-Byng affair; King again Prime Minister.
1926	– Old Age Pensions.
1930	– Cairine Wilson appointed first woman senator.
1930-35	– Liberals defeated in federal election; King re-elected in Prince Albert and becomes Leader of the Opposition; R.B. Bennett is Prime Minister.
1935	– July 1: Regina Riots take place.
1935	– October: Liberal party and King re-elected; sworn in as Prime Minister.
1936	– Regina Riot Inquiry Commission Report on the Regina Riots exonerates the RCMP.

1937   – King visits Hitler in Berlin, Germany in June.

1937   – Established the Rowell-Sirois Commission on Dominion-Provincial Relations.

1937   – King, after a long delay, appoints a new Dominion Archivist: Gustave Lanctôt.

1939-45 – Second World War Prime Minister.

1940   – Liberal Party and King re-elected.

1940   – King sees the *National Resources Mobilization Act 1940* through Parliament.

1940   – Creation of the Permanent Joint Board of Defence.

1941   – December: Japanese attack Pearl Harbor, Hong Kong.

1941   – American forces begin to enter the Canadian North.

1942   – Japanese Canadian internment.

1942   – King calls a plebiscite on conscription.

1943   – British High Commissioner Malcolm MacDonald raises concerns about the Alaska Highway.

1944   – *Family Allowances Act* .

1945   – King attends conferences on the end of the Second World War and the establishment of the United Nations.

1945   – Liberal Party re-elected, but King loses Prince Albert seat; King re-elected in by election in Glengarry (Ontario).

1947   – King makes one of his last visits to Kitchener; Woodside to be preserved.

1948   – King becomes the longest serving Prime Minister in the history of the British Commonwealth.

1948   – King resigns as leader of Liberal Party in August, and then as Prime Minister in November.

1950   – July 22: King dies at Kingsmere, Quebec; buried in Mount Pleasant Cemetery, Toronto.

1974   – Centenary of King's birth.

1977   – Full ownership of the King papers transferred to the Public Archives of Canada.

Endnotes

1. Wilson: "One of the Closest and Truest of Friends I Have Ever Had": Mackenzie King, Arthur Doughty, and the Public Archives of Canada

1 Joy E. Esberey, *Knight of the Holy Spirit: A Study of William Lyon Mackenzie King* (Toronto: University of Toronto Press, 1980), 161.

2 This is not to suggest that cultural activity in Canada at the time was non-existent. For an excellent study of culture in English Canada in the first half of the twentieth century see Maria Tippett, *Making Culture: English-Canadian Institutions and the Arts before the Massey Commission* (Toronto: University of Toronto Press, 1990).

3 Quoted in Janet Trevelyan, *The Life of Mrs. Humphry Ward* (New York: Dodd, Mead, 1923), 216.

4 W.L.M. King, "Historical Records and Personalities," in *Message of the Carillon and Other Addresses* (Toronto: Macmillan, 1927), 125.

5 John Stuart Mill, *Considerations on Representative Government* (1861), edited with an introduction by C.V. Shields (Indianapolis: Bobbs-Merrill, 1975), 229.

6 Thomas D'Arcy McGee, *Speeches and Addresses Chiefly on the Subject of British-American Union* (London: Chapman, 1865), 94.

7 National Archives of Canada, WLM King Papers, MG 26, series J4, reel C-2477, vol. 57, file 366, 44713-44714; quotation from 44714. Hereafter cited as the King Papers.

8 *The Globe* (Toronto), editorial, "The Champlain Society," October 31, 1907.

9 *Report concerning Canadian Archives for the year 1904* (Ottawa: King's Printer, 1905), viii.

10 Ibid., ix.

11 National Archives of Canada, Wilfrid Laurier Papers, MG 26G, reel C-817, vol. 344, Laurier to W.W. Gregory, November 11, 1904, 92018.

12 William Lyon Mackenzie King, *Industry and Humanity* (1918), with an introduction by David Jay Bercuson (Toronto: University of Toronto Press, 1973), 313. I would like to thank Peter DeLottinville, National Archives, for bringing this to my attention.

13 W.D. LeSueur, "Presidential Address, History: Its Nature and Methods," Royal Society of Canada, *Transactions*, 1913, lxv–lxvi.

14 Ibid., lxxiii.

15 King Papers, WLMK Diary, February 26, 1898.

16 Quoted in R. MacGregor Dawson, *William Lyon Mackenzie King: A Political Biography, vol. 1, 1874–1923* (Toronto: University of Toronto Press, 1958), 400.

17 For LeSueur's biography of William Lyon Mackenzie and Prof. McKillop's examination of the legal battle with Mackenzie King and the Lindsey family see William D. LeSueur, *William Lyon Mackenzie: A Reinterpretation*, edited and with an introduction by A.B. McKillop (Toronto: Macmillan, 1979), Carleton Library No. 111.

18 National Archives of Canada, J.S. Willison Papers, MG 30, D14, vol. 49, pp. 18501–18501, LeSueur to Willison, May 28, 1908.

19 Archives of Ontario, Lindsey Collection, Box 9, George Morang to W.D. LeSueur, May 6, 1908.

20 King Papers, series J7, reel H-2259, vol. 15, King to George Lindsey, July 7, 1908.

21 Archives of Ontario, Lindsey Collection, box

9, George Morang to W.D. LeSueur, May 6, 1908.

22 King Papers, Diary, December 27, 1911.

23 Ibid., January 11, 1912. Emphasis in original.

24 The pageantry and meaning of the Quebec Tercentenary celebrations are the subject of an excellent book by H.V. Nelles, *The Art of Nation-Building: Pageantry and Spectacle at Quebec's Tercentenary* (Toronto: University of Toronto Press, 1999).

25 William Wood and Arthur Doughty, *The King's Book of Quebec, vol. 1* (Ottawa: Mortimer, 1911), 127.

26 "Quebec Battlefields, Earl Grey's Appeal" (Mass Meeting at the Russell Theatre, Ottawa, January 15, 1908), 2.

27 Quebec Battlefields Association, *The Quebec Battlefields, An Appeal* (Quebec: April 1908), 37.

28 King Papers, series J5, Speech Notes, Canadian Club, Calgary, Alberta, May 22, 1908, reel C-1985, p. D2561. Emphasis in original.

29 A. Shortt and A.G. Doughty, eds., *Canada and Its Provinces, vol. 1* (Toronto: Brook, 1914), editors' introduction, viii.

30 W.A. Mackintosh, "Adam Shortt, 1858–1931," *Canadian Journal of Political Science and Economics* 4(2) (May 1938), 173–74.

31 A.G. Doughty, "Canada's Record of the War," *University Magazine* 15 (December 1916), 473.

32 On Doughty's collecting activities during the First World War see Robert McIntosh, "The Great War, Archives, and Modern Memory," *Archivaria* 46 (Fall 1998), 11–14.

33 National Archives of Canada, Arthur Doughty Papers, MG 30, D26, vol. 8, Doughty diary, March 16, 1923. Hereafter cited as the Doughty papers.

34 A.L. Burt to his wife, July 9, 1926. Quoted in Lewis H. Thomas, *The Renaissance of Canadian History: A Biography of A.L. Burt* (Toronto: University of Toronto Press, 1975), 90.

35 Ibid., Burt to his wife, July 13, 1926; quoted in Thomas, *The Renaissance of Canadian History*, 92.

36 Order-in-Council, P.C. 748, May 12, 1926.

37 National Archives, Records of the National Archives of Canada, RG 37, vol. 143 (Doughty scrapbooks).

38 Arthur G. Doughty, *The Canadian Archives and Its Activities* (Ottawa: F.A. Acland, 1924), 41.

39 Charles Stacey, *A Very Double Life: The Private World of Mackenzie King* (Toronto: Macmillan, 1976), 171.

40 King Papers, Diary, December 1 and 3, 1936.

41 Doughty Papers, MG 30, D26, vol. 2, King to Lady Doughty, December 2, 1936.

42 WLMK Diary, December 2, 1936.

43 For a fascinating view of the history of the King papers see Jean E. Dryden, "The Mackenzie King Papers: An Archival Odyssey," *Archivaria* 6 (Summer 1978), 40–69.

2. Frisse: The Missing Link: Mackenzie King and Canada's "German Capital"

1 Bruce Hutchison, *The Incredible Canadian: A Candid Portrait of Mackenzie King: His Work, His Times, and His Nation* (New York, Toronto, London: Longmans Green, 1953), 1.

2 H. Blair Neatby, "The Political Ideas of William Lyon Mackenzie King" in Marcel Hamelin, ed., *Les Idées politiques des premiers ministres du Canada/The Political Ideas of the Prime Ministers of Canada* (Ottawa: L'Université d'Ottawa, 1969), 121, at 123.

3 Ibid., at 134.

4 For analyses of King's motives for his visit to Germany in 1937 see C.P. Stacey, "The Divine Mission: Mackenzie King and Hitler," *Canadian Historical Review* 61(4) (1980), 502–12; Angelika Sauer, "Goodwill and Profit: Mackenzie King and Canadian Appeasement," in Norman Hillmer et al., eds., *A Country of Limitations: Canada and the World in 1939/Un Pays dans la gene: le Canada et le Monde en 1939* (Ottawa: Canadian Committee for the History of the Second World War, 1996).

5 See Heinz Lehmann, *The German-Canadians 1750–1937: Immigration, Settlement and Culture*, translated, edited, and introduced by Gerhard P. Bassler (St. John's: Jesperson Press, 1986), 66–79.

6 Berlin's industrial growth has been described in detail by Elizabeth Bloomfield, *City-Building Processes in Berlin/Kitchener and Waterloo, 1870–1930* (unpublished Ph.D. thesis, University of Guelph, 1981).

7 For Berlin's cultural life see H. L. Staebler, "Random Notes on Music of Nineteenth-Cen-

tury Berlin, Ontario," *Waterloo Historical Society* 37 (1949), 14–18; and Gottlieb Leibbrandt, *100 Years Concordia. Centennial Issue* (Kitchener: Concordia Club, 1973).

8 See rych mills and the Victoria Park 100th Birthday Historical Committee, *Victoria Park. 100 Years of a Park and its People* (Kitchener: Twin City Dwyer Printing, 1996), 18–22. Also see John English and Kenneth McLaughlin, *Kitchener: An Illustrated History* (Toronto: Robin Brass Studio, 1996), 83.

9 *Census of Canada 1911*.

10 See R. MacGregor Dawson, *William Lyon Mackenzie King: A Political Biography* (Toronto: University of Toronto Press, 1958), 7.

11 "Nord Waterloo Reform-Association," *Berliner Journal*, January 17, 1878, 2.

12 "Nomination für Nord-Waterloo," *Berliner Journal*, August 15, 1872, 2. Also see "Die Nomination für Nord-Waterloo," *Berliner Journal*, January 14, 1875, 2.

13 The address has been reprinted in *Waterloo Historical Society* 54 (1966), 78–80.

14 "Das Sängerfest. Der erste Festtag," *Berliner Journal*, August 19, 1875, 2.

15 *Census of Canada 1871*.

16 Also see Elizabeth Bloomfield, "Lawyers as Members of Urban Business Elites in Southern Ontario, 1869 to 1920," in Carol Wilton, ed., *Essays in the History of Canadian Law. Beyond the Law: Lawyers and Businesses in Canada, 1830 to 1930*, vol. 4 (Toronto: Butterworths, 1990), 112–48.

17 Bowlby had established his ties to the county's leading German families through marriage to the daughter of one of the county's most prominent Germans, Jakob Hespeler. Bitzer played an important role in the cultural life of the community as long-time president of Berlin's main German cultural organization, the *Gesangsverein Concordia*.

18 See "Ein Wort über den Countyrath," *Berliner Journal*, April 4, 1861, 2. "Wer wird Registrator vom County Waterloo?" *Berliner Journal*, December 17, 1863, 2. For the Davidson case also see Geoffrey Hayes, *Waterloo County: An Illustrated History* (Waterloo: Waterloo Historical Society, 1997), 35–36.

19 "Die Registratur-Angelegenheit," *Berliner Journal*, October 15, 1891, 4–5.

20 "Zum Austrag durch die Faust," *Berliner Journal*, November 22, 1877, 2.

21 "Verläumdungsklage," *Berliner Journal*, April 22, 1880, 2.

22 *L.J. Breithaupt Diaries*, Breithaupt-Hewetson-Clark-Collection, Doris Lewis Rare Book Room, Porter Library, University of Waterloo [hereinafter UofW Special Collections], July 30, 1887; September 29, 1887; October 4, 1887.

23 Ibid., February 3, 1890.

24 See Murray W. Nicolson, *Woodside and the Victorian Family of John King. Studies in Archeology, Architecture and History* (Ottawa: National Historic Parks and Sites Branch of Parks/Environment Canada, 1984), 18.

25 Ibid., 10.

26 For King's Berlin visit in 1900 and his relations to the Weber family see Maureen Hoogenraad, "Mackenzie King in Berlin," *The Archivist* 20 (1994), 19–21.

27 For the relationship between King and Mathilde Grossert see C.P. Stacey, *A Very Double Life: The Private World of Mackenzie King* (Toronto: Macmillan, 1976), 49–66.

28 "Kurze Lokal-Notizen," *Berliner Journal*, March 20, 1902, 4; *Berliner Journal*, March 27, 1902, 4.

29 "4000 People Hear W.L. Mackenzie King; Labor Policy of Laurier Administration," *Berlin Daily Telegraph*, October 10, 1908.

30 *Berliner Journal*, October 14, 1908, at 7 (translation from German by the author).

31 "(Eingesandt.) Deutsche Rede des Hrn King bei der Versammlung am 24. Sept. im Viktoria-Park," *Berliner Journal*, September 30, 1908, 12 (translation from German by the author).

32 "Magnificent Ovation to Sir Wilfrid Laurier and Mr. King," *Daily Telegraph*, September 25, 1908.

33 The author is indebted to rych mills, Kitchener, for providing him with the material relating to the *Daily Telegraph*'s stand on this issue.

34 "Richard Reid as a German," *Berlin Daily Telegraph*, October 7, 1908.

35 *Berlin Daily Telegraph*, October 8, 1908.

36 "North Waterloo Is Redeemed," *Berlin Daily Telegraph*, October 27, 1908, 1.

37 "Das Wahlresultat in Nord-Waterloo," *Berliner Journal*, November 4, 1908, 12.

38 See "King By Acclamation. The Minister Of Labor Unopposed," *Berlin News Record*, June 21, 1909.

39 See *Louis Jakob Breithaupt Diaries*, UofW Special Collections, July 10, 1909.

40 "A Message of Peace from Waterloo County for the Entire World," *Berlin Daily Telegraph*, July 12, 1909.

41 For the Grand Trunk strike as an element in the 1911 campaign also see Terence A. Crowley, "Mackenzie King and the 1911 Election," *Ontario History* 61 (1969), 181–96.

42 Translation from German by the author from "(Anzeige.) An die Wähler von Nord-Waterloo," *Berliner Journal*, September 6, 1911, 7. For Waterloo County Conservatives' exploitation of the widespread fear of annexation during the campaign also see "Why Americans are for Reciprocity," *Berlin News Record*, July 18, 1911; and "Annexation the Outcome," *Berlin News Record*, August 16, 1911.

43 G. Debus to Mackenzie King, January 11, 1911, as quoted in Terence A. Crowley, "Mackenzie King and the 1911 Election," *Ontario History* 61 (1969), 181, 185.

44 Diary Transcripts (Microform), William Lyon Mackenzie King (Toronto: University of Toronto), January 18, 1911.

45 See "Editorielles," *Berliner Journal*, March 31, 1909, 2.

46 "Kurze Lokalnotizen," *Berliner Journal*, November 17, 1909, 6.

47 *Belleville Intelligencer*, August 30, 1911, as quoted by T.A. Crowley, "Mackenzie King and the 1911 Election," *Ontario History* 61 (1969), 181, 189.

48 See J. Murray Beck, *Pendulum of Power: Canada's Federal Elections* (Scarborough, ON: Prentice-Hall, 1968), 120–36.

49 Annamaria Tessaro, "Mackenzie King in North Waterloo," *Waterloo Historical Society* 66 (1978), 18 at 32–33. For the 1911 election also see John Carter, "The Reciprocity Election of 1911: Waterloo North, A Case Study," *Waterloo Historical Society* 62 (1974), 77–91.

50 *Official Report of the Debates of the House of Commons of the Dominion of Canada*, vol. 103 (First Session–Twelfth Parliament, 2 George V, 1911–12 (Ottawa: C.H. Parmelee, 1911–12), Session of November 27, 1911, at 402.

51 Ibid.

52 King Diaries (Transcripts), July 25, 1925.

53 King to C. Mortimer Bezeau, June 11 and July 26, 1932, Wilfrid Laurier University Archives (WLU), William Lyon Mackenzie King Collection, files 1.3.24 and 1.3.25.

54 King to L.O. Breithaupt, September 1944, as quoted in "Lived 8 Years at Woodside, King Corrects Statement," *Kitchener Record*, September 27, 1944.

55 English and McLaughlin, *Kitchener: An Illustrated History*, at 116–25; Barbara M. Wilson, ed., *Ontario and the First World War 1914–1918: A Collection of Documents* (Toronto: Champlain Society for the Government of Ontario, University of Toronto Press, 1977), LXXIV–LXXXIV.

56 See Geoffrey Hayes, "From Berlin to the Trek of the Conestoga: A Revisionist Approach to Waterloo County's German Identity," *Ontario History* 91(2) (Autumn 1999), 131–49.

57 For Sims see "Biography. Harvey J. Sims," *Waterloo Historical Society* 33 (1945), 41–42.

58 WLU, King Collection, file 1.3.23, King to C. Mortimer Bezeau, November 3, 1931.

59 King Diaries (Transcripts) October 1, 1936.

60 Ibid., June 27, 1937.

61 Ibid., June 29, 1937.

3. mills: "On the Hill Over Yonder … "

1 To Berliners Mackenzie King was known as Billy or Willie. Elsewhere he was Mackenzie. Sometimes the two collided. For a humorous anecdote see "Alex Schafer Played Hookey With King," *Kitchener-Waterloo Record*, July 26, 1950.

2 For the background history of Berlin/Kitchener, I am not noting points. See the bibliography for titles pertinent to the community's history; likewise, except in a few instances, for general information on the King family and Mackenzie King's career outside Berlin/Kitchener. King family life is preserved and displayed at Woodside National Historic Site, 528 Wellington Street North, Kitchener, N2H 5L5.

3 Joseph Schneider Haus, 466 Queen Street South, Kitchener, N2G 1W7.

4 rych mills, *Victoria Park: 100 Years of a Park and Its People* (Kitchener: Victoria Park His-

torical Committee,1996), 6–13. The book has many details on the development of the park. It was published before the patterns outlined in this paper emerged, so, alas, it has just four brief mentions of Mackenzie King: 25–8, 35.

5 "Toronto Heard From," *Berlin Daily Telegraph*, August 8, 1906.

6 Companion of the Order of St. Michael and St. George. Canadians were still entitled to receive British orders of chivalry in 1906.

7 "Toronto Heard From," *Berlin Daily Telegraph*, August 8, 1906.

8 "Greatest Celebration … Is Over," *Berlin Daily Telegraph*, August 9, 1906.

9 And *five* years hence! For a telling anecdote of a Tory voting King see H. L. Staebler, "Mackenzie King," *Waterloo Historical Society Annual Volume* 38 (1951), 10–13.

10 F.A. McGregor, *The Fall and Rise of Mackenzie King* (Toronto: Macmillan, 1962), 25–28; see also R. MacGregor Dawson, *William Lyon Mackenzie King: A Political Biography: Vol. 1, 1874–1923* (Toronto: University of Toronto Press,1958), 188–90.

11 "Postmaster-General … For Berlin," *Berlin Daily Telegraph*, July 5, 1907.

12 "Glad Hand Was Given … Victoria Park," *Berlin Daily Telegraph*, July 5, 1907.

13 "Postmaster-General … For Berlin," *Berlin Daily Telegraph*, July 5, 1907.

14 Ibid.

15 During the period covered by this essay the titles prime minister and premier were both used to describe the head of the Canadian government. To avoid confusion, only prime minister has been used here.

16 Charlotte Gray, *Mrs. King* (Toronto: Viking, 1997), 285.

17 McGregor, *The Fall and Rise*, 36. Also see Dawson, *William Lyon Mackenzie King*, 179–80.

18 Dawson, *William Lyon Mackenzie King*, 191. The grammar, punctuation, and spelling are King's. (All quotations in this paper are as they appear in source documents. Additions are indicated.)

19 King resigned as deputy minister the same day. See "W. L. Mackenzie King … For This Riding," *Berlin Daily Telegraph*, September 22, 1908.

20 "W.L.M. King Receives Nomination," *Berlin Daily Telegraph*, September 21, 1908. John Hostetler is called Henry in other articles listing Wellesley's Liberals. It may be two separate people, the same man, or an error. For example, see "Sir Wilfrid Entertained," *Berlin Daily Telegraph*, September 25, 1908.

21 "Richard Reid Is Nominated," *Berlin Daily Telegraph*, September 28, 1908. Among those declining were Seagram, J.R. Eden, C.H. Mills, H.L. Janzen, and W.V. Uttley. Over the next three years Uttley from his position as editor of the *Berlin News Record* would be a severe critic of King. Early in 1908 he had been Berlin's mayor for a month, losing a provincially ordered second election to Allen Huber.

22 "They Dined Together," *Berlin Daily Telegraph*, September 28, 1908. Also see "Alternating Currents" (column), *Berlin Daily Telegraph*, September 30, 1908.

23 "Editorial Notes," *Berlin Daily Telegraph*, September 23, 1908. Emphasis added.

24 Headline, *Berlin Daily Telegraph*, September 24, 1908. Emphasis added.

25 Allen Huber's story is chronicled in John English and Kenneth McLaughlin, *Kitchener: An Illustrated History* (Waterloo: Wilfrid Laurier University Press, 1983), 96–100.

26 Numerous articles cover the day's events in both papers: *Berlin Daily Telegraph*, September 24, 25, 26, 1908; *Berlin News Record*, September 24, 25, 26, 1908.

27 Gray, *Mrs. King*, 71, 302.

28 "A Picture of … King" (cartoon), *Berlin News Record*, October 24, 1908.

29 "Magnificent Ovation … Mr. King" under "Our Candidate," *Berlin Daily Telegraph*, September 25, 1908.

30 Ulrich Frisse kindly provided a translation of the German-language speech that King read to the crowd. The German text appeared in the *Berliner Journal*, September 30, 1908.

31 "Magnificent Ovation … Mr. King" under "Canada's Premier," *Berlin Daily Telegraph*, September 25, 1908.

32 "Magnificent Ovation … Mr. King" under "Want Mr. King," *Berlin Daily Telegraph*, September 25, 1908.

33 "Notes From the Toronto Star," *Berlin Daily Telegraph*, September 26, 1908.

34 "Big Crowds … No Great Enthusiasm," *Berlin News Record*, September 25, 1908.

35 "Professional Decorators," *Berlin News Record*, September 26, 1908.

36 "Conservative Organ's Prejudiced Guess," *Berlin Daily Telegraph*, September 28, 1908.

37 Photograph in *Berlin Daily Telegraph*, September 29, 1908, 1.

38 "Mayor Versus King," *Berlin News Record*, September 26, 1908. Like many in Berlin, the *Toronto Star's* staff correspondent fell under Allen Huber's spell. During the election campaign he wrote a delightful, tongue-in-cheek piece on the mayor's colourful personality. See reprint of the Star's article "Hottest Fight in Canada," *Berlin Daily Telegraph*, October 19, 1908.

39 Gray, *Mrs. King*, 308–09. The joy in the King household in Toronto amidst the city's overall celebration of a national Liberal victory is well described in Charlotte Gray's study of Isabel Mackenzie King..

40 House rented from Joseph Zuber, a Berlin hotelier. During the 1999 125th Mackenzie King Colloquium, each speaker was presented with a banister post. These were saved by Carl Totzke when 96 Queen was torn down in 1964 and donated thirty-five years later to the colloquium organizers. In the Kitchener Public Library the Hoffman/Heather Collection (MC 92 49b) contains a series of 1909 letters from C.E. Hoffman, 117 Queen North, to his wife, who was travelling in Europe. He comments acidly on Mackenzie King living at number 96 and uses such phrases as "an awful hot air artist" and "grandstand actor." Interestingly, two years later, during the 1911 campaign, King rented number 117 from Mrs. Wilhelmina Hoffman (her husband died in 1910). At no time as an adult did King ever own a home in Berlin/Kitchener or even live there for any length of time. Apart from the brief Zuber and Hoffman rentals, his only other local place of residence was a suite at the Walper Hotel during the 1908 election.

41 "Will Reside in Berlin," *Berlin Daily Telegraph*, June 3, 1909. Also see "Nominations Were Tame," *Berlin News Record*, June 22, 1909.

42 "Hitch Has Occurred," *Berlin News Record*, July 6, 1909.

43 "A Message of Peace … The Entire World," *Berlin Daily Telegraph*, July 12, 1909.

44 The First World War period in Berlin has spawned several books, many studies and theses, a play, and innumerable theories. For specific Victoria Park links and details on toppling the Kaiser's bust, burning the pavilion and dunking aldermen, see mills, *Victoria Park:100 Years*, 18–24 and 40–44. For the general Berlin scene, including the 1915–16 name-change controversy, see English and McLaughlin, *Kitchener: An Illustrated History*, 107–30.

45 "Labor Day Celebration Was a Great Success," *Berlin News Record*, September 7, 1909.

46 Ibid.

47 "Labor Day Celebration an Unqualified Success" and "Significance of Labor Day," *Berlin Daily Telegraph*, September 7, 1909.

48 This was probably due more to Reid's position with the Berlin Public School Board than to any Mackenzie King influence.

49 See various overlapping articles, *Berlin News Record* and *Berlin Daily Telegraph*, May 29 and 30, 1911. Post-unveiling events were fouled up. The governor general was to have addressed the Canadian Club in the Victoria Park pavilion. No seating arrangements had been made, so Grey spoke longer to the crowd at the unveiling.

50 John Carter, "The Reciprocity Election of 1911," *Waterloo Historical Society Annual Volume* 62 (1975), 77–91. Also see Annamaria Tessaro, "Mackenzie King in Waterloo," *Waterloo Historical Society Annual Volume* 66 (1979), 18–40. This pair of detailed studies concerning Mackenzie King is representative of the many that have been done in secondary and university level history courses in his hometown.

51 "Cityhood Celebration a Magnificent Success," *Berlin Daily Telegraph*, July 18, 1912; "Many Towns … Congratulating Berlin," *Berlin News Record*, July 18, 1912.

52 "Kitchener Honors Son at Thronged Reception," *Kitchener Daily Record*, September 13, 1922.

53 Ibid.

54 Laurier did not publicly promise to make King a cabinet member or the minister of labor. In

his Victoria Park speech of September 24, 1908, he simply said that he would suggest to his colleagues to have the Department of Labor under a separate minister. Weichel certainly wasn't alone in having faulty memory: ex–*Daily Telegraph* editor D. Alex Bean, in 1948, put the same words in Laurier's mouth. He also had King speaking *after* Laurier that day. See "A Victory and A Defeat," *Hamilton Spectator*, July 10, 1948. This is part of a series of articles by Reginald Hardy that contains several interesting (though memory-flawed) first-hand interviews with local associates of King. A set is in the Mackenzie King vertical file at the Kitchener Public Library's Grace Schmidt Room. These articles are quite different from what Hardy later published in book form: *Mackenzie King of Canada* (Toronto: Oxford University Press, 1949).

55 "City's Distinguished Son ... Victoria Park," *Kitchener Daily Record*, September 14, 1922.

56 King's two speeches on September 13 overlapped in many areas and must be read together to gain a full understanding of his message. Coverage likewise overlapped in the *Daily Record* and must be followed carefully. "Kitchener Honors Son at Thronged Reception," Kitchener Daily Record, September 13, 1922. Also see "Billy King Banquetted By Kitchener Board of Trade," *Kitchener Daily Record*, September 14, 1922; and "City's Distinguished Son ... Victoria Park," *Kitchener Daily Record*, September 14, 1922.

57 "Liberal Chief Asks Rejection of Isms," *Kitchener Daily Record*, September 8, 1947.

58 "New Bandstand Opened Here By Mayor Leavine," *Kitchener-Waterloo Record*, July 24, 1950.

4. Hayes: Mackenzie King and Waterloo County

1 William Lyon Mackenzie King Diary Transcripts, microform (Toronto: University of Toronto Press, 1973), September 8, 1947.

2 See Geoffrey Hayes, "From Berlin to the Trek of the Conestoga: A Revisionist Approach to Waterloo County's German Identity," *Ontario History* 91(2) (Autumn 1999), 131–49.

3 On the King family see Charlotte Gray's excellent *Mrs. King: The Life and Times of Isabel Mackenzie King* (Toronto: Viking, 1997).

4 Herbert Kalbfleisch noted that through McDougall's connections the *Canadier* press "received the bulk of the local municipal printing contracts, much to the dismay of [another Berlin German-language newspaper] the *Journal*. In 1861 he received a gold watch in recognition of his services to the Liberal party. The *Journal* viewed the gift as open bribery. When in December 1863, McDougall was proposed as Registrar of Waterloo County, the *Journal* countered with the suggestion that an honest man in the person of A.J. Peterson be appointed." Herbert Kalbfleisch, "Among the Editors of Ontario German Newspapers, 1835–1818," *Canadian-German Folklore* 1 (1961), 79, 80.

5 Kitchener Public Library, Grace Schmidt Room of Local History, "Report of the Inspector of Registry Offices In the Matter of the Official Inquiry into Certain Charges Preferred Against the Late Registrar for the County of Waterloo and also the Reports of the Executive Council on the Same, 1891," 7, 15.

6 Ibid., 13, 16.

7 Ibid., 22. The Kitchener Public Library holds but a few personal accounts for Dougall McDougall, suggesting that he at least kept close watch on his grocery bill. See KPL, Manuscript Collection 29.

8 King Diaries (Transcripts), August 28, 1894.

9 Ibid., August 29, 1894.

10 An excellent study of King's electoral success in North Waterloo is by Annamaria Tessario, "Mackenzie King in North Waterloo," *Waterloo Historical Society* 66 (1978), 18–40.

11 Wilfrid Laurier University Archives (WLU), William Lyon Mackenzie King Collection, file 1.3.1, King to C. Mortimer Bezeau, September 25, 1911.

12 King Diaries (transcripts), September 24, 1911.

13 On King's psychoanalysis see Paul Roazen, *Canada's King: An Essay in Political Psychology* (Oakville, ON: Mosaic Press, 1998).

14 Jonathan Vance, *Death So Noble: Memory, Meaning and the First World War* (Vancouver: University of British Columbia Press, 1997), 125.

15 See Hayes, "From Berlin to the Trek of the Conestoga."

16 Mabel Dunham, *The Trek of the Conestoga* (Toronto: Macmillan, 1924), "Foreword."

17 WLU, King Collection, file 1.3.23, King to C. Mortimer Bezeau, November 3, 1931.

18 Ibid., file 1.3.24, King to Bezeau, June 11, 1932.

19 See Gerald Noonan, *Redefining Canada: Homer Watson's Spiritual Landscape: A Biography* (Waterloo: MLR Editions, 1997).

20 King Diaries (Transcripts), September 8, 1947.

21 Ibid.

22 The Walper Hotel was built in 1893, during the latter part of Queen Victoria's reign. It was bought and refurbished by Joseph Zuber in 1908, during Edward VII's rule: Karen English, "The History of The Walper Hotel," http://www.walper.com/html/history.html, accessed December 27, 2001.

23 Ibid.

24 Ibid., September 9, 1947.

25 Ibid.

26 Ibid.

27 Ibid.

28 Roazen, *Canada's King*, 150.

5. Waiser: King and Chaos: The Liberals and the 1935 Regina Riot

1 Quoted in the Ottawa *Journal*, June 14, 1935.

2 Ibid.

3 See Bill Waiser, *Saskatchewan's Playground: A History of Prince Albert National Park* (Saskatoon: Fifth House, 1989), ch. 3.

4 National Archives of Canada, Manuscript Division, W.L.M. King papers, vol. 205, W.L.M. King to J.G. Gardiner, June 21, 1935.

5 Ibid., June 25, 1935.

6 Ibid., King Diaries, June 26, 1935.

7 Bill Waiser, *All Hell Can't Stop Us: The 1935 On-to-Ottawa Trek and Regina Riot* (Calgary: Fifth House, 2003), forthcoming.

8 King Diaries, July 2, 1935.

9 Ibid.

10 Ibid., July 3, 1935.

11 Ibid., July 5, 1935.

12 King Papers, vol. 205, July 26, 1935.

13 During subsequent federal election campaigns Gardiner cited the Regina Riot as an example of Conservative problem solving. See N. Ward and D.E. Smith, *Jimmy Gardiner: Relentless Liberal* (Toronto: University of Toronto Press, 1990), 187.

14 King Papers, vol. 205, July 26, 1935.

6. Wardhaugh: Considering Both Sides of the Ledger: J.W. Dafoe and Mackenzie King

1 Michael Bliss, *Right Honourable Men: The Descent of Canadian Politics from Macdonald to Mulroney* (Toronto: HarperCollins, 1994), 123.

2 Ramsay Cook, *The Politics of John W. Dafoe and the Free Press* (Toronto: University of Toronto Press, 1963), 27–28.

3 Cook, *The Politics*, 33.

4 Ibid., 29, 48.

5 Murray Donnelly, *Dafoe of the Free Press* (Toronto: Macmillan, 1968), 78.

6 University of Manitoba Archives, J.W. Dafoe Papers, box 1, file 4, Dafoe to A. Bridle, June 14, 1921. Although Dafoe could not accept the Liberal Party, he could also not fully support a regionally based party. Instead he became an advocate of an eventual union of moderates from both groups.

7 Dafoe was critical of King's absence from Canada during the war but was also critical of Fielding's negative reaction to Borden's wish to have Canada sign the Versailles Treaty in her own right: Donnelly, *Dafoe* (Toronto: Macmillan, 1968), 106.

8 As quoted in Cook, *The Politics*, 87.

9 Dafoe Papers, box 4, file 4, Dafoe to C. Sifton, July 21, 1919.

10 King's career had given him a reputation as a reformer. He was the grandson of the 1837 rebel, William Lyon Mackenzie, and his university training had focused on social problems. His book *Industry and Humanity* dealt with post-war reconstruction. His years in Laurier's cabinet were spent in the new Department of Labour.

11 Dafoe Papers, box 4, file 4, Dafoe to Sifton, February 14, 1921.

12 Ibid., November 10, 1920.

13 Ibid., box 1, file 2, Dafoe to A. Bridle, June 14, 1921; Cook, *The Politics*, 113, 114.

14 Dafoe Papers, box 1, file 7, Dafoe to A.K. Cameron, May 23, 1941.

15 Ibid., box 4, file 4, Dafoe to Sifton, December 19, 1921.

16 Ibid., box 1, file 4, Dafoe to W.A. Buchanan, November 30, 1923.

17 For a full discussion of King's early perceptions and sympathies toward the Prairie West

see R.A. Wardhaugh, "The 'Impartial Umpire' Views the West: Mackenzie King and the Search for the New Jerusalem," *Manitoba History* (Spring 1995), 11–12.

18 Dafoe Papers, box 4, file 4, Dafoe to Sifton, July 11, 1922.

19 Ibid., box 1, file 4, Dafoe to W.A. Buchanan, November 30, 1923.

20 Ibid., box 4, file 4, Dafoe to Sifton, December 27, 1923.

21 Ramsay Cook, "J.W. Dafoe at the Imperial Conference, 1923," *Canadian Historical Review* 51(1) (March 1960), 20, 21.

22 Dafoe Papers, box 1, file 4, Dafoe to W.A. Buchanan, November 30, 1923.

23 Ibid., box 5, file 1, Dafoe to J.A. Stevenson, January 28, 1924.

24 Ibid., box 4, file 4, Dafoe to Sifton, February 13, 1924.

25 Ibid., April 3, 1925.

26 Ibid., June 30, 1925.

27 J.W. Dafoe, T.A. Crerar, A.B. Hudson, Frank O. Fowler, Edgar Tarr, and H.J. Symington were the main members of this group.

28 Dafoe Papers, box 4, file 4, Dafoe to Sifton, June 30, 1925.

29 Ibid., box 2, file 5, Dafoe to R. Forke, November 16, 1925.

30 Ibid., box 4, file 4, Dafoe to Sifton, November 20, 1925.

31 Ibid., April 3, 1925.

32 Ibid., February 19, 1926.

33 National Archives of Canada, William Lyon Mackenzie King Papers, J1 Primary Correspondence Series, reel 2289, vol. 154, 112619-21, Hudson to King, September 18, 1926.

34 "Dafoe was much closer to King in 1926 than he had ever been before … after a decade of wondering he was back in the Liberal party, and somewhat uneasy about it": Cook, *The Politics*, 168–69.

35 Dafoe Papers, box 5, file 5, Dafoe to J. Willison, September 17, 1926.

36 Dafoe was unimpressed by Dunning's work as minister of railways and his decision to move the port terminal of the Hudson Bay Railway from Nelson to Churchill: "There is a great big question mark in my mind against the said Mr. Dunning. I am beginning to wonder if there was not something in the recom-mendation, left-handed, given him by a leading Saskatchewan Liberal when he told King that in getting Dunning he was getting the biggest double-crosser in the business": ibid., box 2, file 2, Dafoe to G. Dexter, August 4, 1927.

37 A debate over school lands in the natural resource transfer negotiations between the Alberta provincial government and Ottawa conjured up Dafoe's suspicions that King was still too weak and under the influence of Quebec. Any move by the federal government to advance the interests of Catholic schools in Alberta would force the editor to "revert to my earlier opinion about him [King]": ibid., box 2, file 5, Dafoe to Forke, May 25, 1926.

38 Ibid., file 8, Dafoe to W.D. Gregory, September 17, 1926.

39 Ibid., box 3, file 7, Dafoe to D.A. McArthur, October 7, 1930.

40 Ibid., box 2, file 2, Dafoe to Dexter, August 8, 1930.

41 Ibid., November 3, 1930.

42 Ibid., box 3, file 3, Dafoe to J.M. MacDonell, December 31, 1930.

43 Dafoe's disdain for Bennett was remarkably vicious, but he had no doubt the criticism of the *Free Press* would be "thoroughly vindicated"; "Bennett has been sent to us as a scourge and the stiffer the application the swifter the cure," he noted in January 1931. Dexter was informed to tell the prime minister that paper was "at the sword's point with him on practically every policy to which he is devoted"; "He is undoubtedly a madman," Dafoe claimed. "I do not use that term as meaning that he is mentally disordered, but in the sense that so many of the great figures in history have been essentially mad, that is, that they have pursued their objects with a total disregard of the amenities of life and of the consequences. Mr. Bennett … is not a great man … [he is] a little man with a big manner. It is perhaps fortunate that his talents are limited because with his delusions of grandeur and his various obsessions he would certainly wreck this country if his abilities matched his ambitions": ibid., box 2, file 2, Dafoe to Dexter, January 20, 1931; October 19, 1932.

44 Ibid., November 20, 1931. Mackenzie King

spent the latter half of 1931 attempting to clear himself and the party of the Beauharnois Scandal, in which the King government had been accused of exchanging political favours for corporate gifts and donations. The scandal involved disclosures of close connections between the Liberal government and the Beauharnois syndicate, which had been given the contract for a diversion to the St Lawrence River. See T.D. Regehr, *The Beauharnois Scandal: A Story of Canadian Enrepreneurship and Politics* (Toronto, 1990)."

45 Ibid., box 4, file 2, Dafoe to N.W. Rowell, July 28, 1931.
46 Ibid., box 5, file 4, Dafoe to F. Underhill, October 7, 1932.
47 Ibid., box 3, file 9, Dafoe to Vincent Massey, December 7, 1931.
48 Cook, *The Politics*, 202–03.
49 Dafoe Papers, box 3, file 9, Dafoe to Vincent Massey, December 7, 1931.
50 Ibid., file 3, Dafoe to King, August 8, 1933.
51 Cook, *The Politics*, 202–03.
52 Dafoe Papers, box 1, file 7, Dafoe to A.K. Cameron, May 23, 1934.
53 Ibid., box 4, file 8, Dafoe to H. Sifton, March 20, 1933.
54 Ibid., box 2, file 1, Dafoe to Wallace Dafoe, November 26, 1935.
55 Donnelly goes so far as to argue that King's weak support for the League was the "primary" reason Dafoe had refused to enter the cabinet in 1935: Donnelly, *Dafoe*, 153.
56 Dafoe Papers, box 4, file 2, Dafoe to Escott Reid, November 10, 1936.
57 Ibid., box 2, file 8, Dafoe to Viscount Greenwood, May 21, 1937.
58 Dafoe and King shared the same position on the role of the commission and in its findings.
59 Dafoe Papers, box 5, file 1, Dafoe to J.A. Stevenson, February 12, 1942.
60 Ibid., box 1, file 6, Dafoe to Crerar, May 5, 1941.
61 Ibid., box 2, file 3, Dafoe to Dexter, April 4, 1941.
62 Ibid., box 1, file 4, Dafoe to E.K. Brown, January 12, 1943.
63 Ibid., box 3, file 3, Dafoe to King, November 10, 1943.
64 Ibid., December 20, 1943.
65 Ibid., box 5, file 5, Dafoe to Frederick Whyte, February 17, 1943.

66 Donnelly, *Dafoe*, 168, 178.
67 "Dafoe's transformation had been gradual, but in the inter-war period he had grown a great deal in stature; grown from a party journalist in the strictest sense to a man with breadth of view. He had come better to understand his country, to see that its uniqueness rested in the fact that it was an experiment in cultural relations and that its very existence depended on the success of that experiment": Cook, *The Politics*, 268.
68 Ibid., 272.
69 This is the argument of G.V. Ferguson, *John W. Dafoe* (Toronto: Ryerson, 1948), 17–18.
70 As quoted in J.E. Rea, "'Clay from Feet to Forehead': The Mackenzie King Controversy," *Beaver* 73/2 (1993), 32.

7. Bangarth: Mackenzie King and Japanese Canadians

1 Note that the use of the word "internment" here does not suggest an equating of experiences with the Jewish internment/concentration camps that were established in Europe at this time by the Germans. In fact, only about seven hundred Japanese Canadians and Japanese nationals were actually interned (in the *exact* sense of the word) at a camp near Angler, Ontario. Nevertheless, I do not use the word "evacuation" here, as some researchers do, because it does not accurately describe what was experienced by more than 22,000 Canadians of Japanese descent.
2 The term "Oriental," now antiquated, referred to people who were of Chinese, Japanese, and South Asian background.
3 The term "Oriental question" was used variously by Mackenzie King and other Canadian politicians to refer to issues of, for example, Asian immigration, disfranchisement, and economic competition.
4 There were also specific issues present immediately before and at the outset of the Second World War that affected the decision for internment. These too will be explored in this essay, but the focus will largely be on the period 1907–38, an important and interesting thirty-one years that is missed by simply concentrating on 1942. Part of this discussion will necessarily deal with the concepts of "race"

and racism, but these will be used in a context that is specific to their time and place. Race and racism, understandably, had very different meanings in Victorian and post-Victorian Canada than they do today, and it is important to recognize this lest historical presentism pervade the final conclusions.

5 C.P. Stacey, *A Very Double Life: The Private World of Mackenzie King* (Toronto: Macmillan, 1976). Another work that tries to probe King's psyche based on his diaries is Joy Esberey's *Knight of the Holy Spirit: A Study of William Lyon Mackenzie King* (Toronto: University of Toronto Press, 1980). Esberey generally fixates on the maudlin, without offering any sharp insights into King's character. More recently, Paul Roazen in *Canada's King: An Essay in Political Psychology* (Oakville: Mosaic Press, 1998) ponders King's 1916 treatment by preeminent American psychiatrist Adolf Meyer. King was convinced that other people were influencing him via electrical currents. Roazen's contribution to the historiography on King is a thoughtful, historical-psychological account that does not succumb to the "weird Willie" industry. For an intellectualist background of King's spiritual beliefs see Ramsay Cook, "Spiritualism, Science of the Earthly Paradise," *Canadian Historical Review* 65(1) (March 1984), 4–27.

6 Norman Hillmer and J.L. Granatstein, "Historians Rank the Best and Worst Canadian Prime Ministers" *Maclean's*, April 21, 1997.

7 H.S. Ferns and B. Ostry, *The Age of Mackenzie King: The Rise of the Leader* (London: Heinemann, 1955).

8 John English and J.O. Stubbs, eds., *Mackenzie King: Widening the Debate* (Toronto: Macmillan, 1978).

9 Michael Bliss, *Right Honourable Men: The Descent of Canadian Politics from Macdonald to Mulroney* (Toronto: HarperCollins, 1994).

10 Ferns and Ostry, *The Age of Mackenzie King*, 78–91, 214.

11 The foremost of these include: Ken Adachi, *The Enemy That Never Was: A History of the Japanese Canadians* (Toronto: McClelland & Stewart, 1991); Roger Daniels, *Concentration Camps North America: Japanese in the United States and Canada During World War II*

(Malabar, FL: Robert Kreiger, 1981); Patricia Roy et al., *Mutual Hostages: Canadians and Japanese in the Second World War* (Toronto: University of Toronto Press, 1990); Ann Gomer Sunahara, *The Politics of Racism* (Toronto: Lorimer, 1981); and W. Peter Ward, "British Columbia and the Japanese Evacuation," *Canadian Historical Review* 57 (September 1976), 289–309.

12 See, for example, James Walker, "The Fall and Rise of Africville," *Literary Review of Canada* 2 (July 1993), 3–5.

13 Keibo Oiwa, "The Structure of Dispersal: The Japanese Canadian Community of Montreal, 1942–1952," *Canadian Ethnic Studies* 18(2) (1986), 20–37; Audrey Kobayashi, "The Japanese Canadian Redress Settlement and Its Implications for Race Relations," *Canadian Ethnic Studies* 24(1) (1992), 1–19; Peter Nunoda, *A Community in Transition and Conflict: The Japanese-Canadians, 1935–1951* (Ph.D. thesis, University of Manitoba, 1990).

14 King's great friend, business leader John D. Rockefeller, for example, spent a large amount of money in the construction of Riverside Church in New York, in which the portals held carvings of the images of Darwin and Einstein. The church endures as a monument to the paradox and confusion of the times. R. Bothwell et al., *Canada 1900–1945* (Toronto: University of Toronto Press, 1987), 200–01.

15 Mariana Valverde, *The Age of Light, Soap and Water: Moral Reform in English Canada, 1885–1925* (Toronto: McClelland & Stewart, 1993), 109–111. See also Roger Daniels, *The Politics of Prejudice* (Gloucester, MA: Peter Smith, 1966).

16 The Chevalier de Lamarck (1744–1829) was a French naturalist whose theory of organic evolution held that acquired characteristics can be inherited. In the late nineteenth century, Max Nordau published *Degeneration,* 3rd. ed. (London: Heinemann, 1895), in which he extended the concept even further by claiming that emotional, melancholic, and feminized artists and writers were as much to blame for race degeneration as criminals, prostitutes, and anarchists. Nordau also claimed, among other things, that Impressionist painting practices were due to a disease of the retina, which

caused painters to see the world as a collection of coloured blotches. Nordau's plan for regeneration consisted of the purification and the masculinization of "the race": Valverde, *The Age of Light, Soap and Water*, 109, 189.

17 King Diary, January 11, 1909, King Papers, MG26, J13.

18 William Lyon Mackenzie King, *Industry and Humanity: A Study in the Principles Underlying Industrial Reconstruction* (Toronto: Thomas Allen, 1918), 323.

19 W.L. Mackenzie King, "Crowded Housing, Its Evil Effects," *Daily Mail and Empire*, September 18, 1897; Ferns and Ostry, *The Age of Mackenzie King*, 80; Murray Nicolson, *Woodside and the Victorian Family of John King* (Ottawa: Minister of Supply and Services Canada, 1984); R. Bothwell et al., *Canada 1900–1945* (Toronto: University of Toronto Press, 1987), 16.

20 Nicolson, *Woodside and the Victorian Family of John King*, 23.

21 I jump from King's childhood and early adulthood to his early political career as a public servant out of necessity because there is very little source material, either primary or secondary, to sustain any kind of lengthy discussion of this transitional period.

22 For more information on the Vancouver Riots see Howard Sugimoto, *Japanese Immigration, the Vancouver Riots, and Canadian Diplomacy* (New York: Arno Press, 1978).

23 King Diary, February 17, 1938, King Papers, MG26, J13; W. Peter Ward, *White Canada Forever: Popular Attitudes and Public Policy Toward Orientals in British Columbia* (Montreal: McGill-Queen's University Press, 1978), 70–74.

24 The Chinese, who sustained more damage, were later given approximately $26,990. *Report of W. L. Mackenzie King, C. M. G., Commissioner, Appointed to Inquire into the Losses and Damages Sustained by the Japanese Population in the City of Vancouver in the Province of British Columbia, on the Occasion of Riots in that City in September, 1907* (Ottawa: King's Printer, 1908); Canada, Royal Commission to Investigate Losses Sustained by the Chinese Population of Vancouver, *Report*, 1908; King Diary, February 17, 1938, King Papers, MG26, J13; Ward, *White Canada Forever*, 67–74.

25 W.L. Mackenzie King, *Report of the Department of Labour for the Fiscal Year 1907–1908* (Ottawa: King's Printer, 1908), 104; Sessional Paper No. 36.

26 King, *Report of the Department of Labour*, 11; King Papers, Notes & Memoranda, MG26, J4, C33925; King, *Industry and Humanity*, 75–76.

27 King, *Report of the Department of Labour*; Sessional Paper No. 36, 102.

28 W.L. Mackenzie King, *Report on the Need for the Suppression of the Opium Traffic in Canada* (Ottawa: King's Printer, 1908); Statutes of Canada, 1908, c. 50.

29 Canada, *House of Commons Debates*, January 26, 1911, pp. 2518–53; Statutes of Canada, 1911, c. 17.

30 King, *Report ... into the Losses and Damages sustained by the Japanese ... 1907*.

31 W.L. Mackenzie King, *Report of W.L. Mackenzie King, C.M.G., Commissioner Appointed to Enquire into the Methods by Which Oriental Laborers Have Been Induced to Come to Canada* (Ottawa: King's Printer, 1908), 53–54, 76–80; King, Draft Memorandum re: Mission to India and China, n.d. (approx. 1909), King Papers, MG26, J4, vol. 22, C15394–5; King, *Report of the Deputy Minister of Labour*, 11; Ward, *White Canada Forever*, 74–75.

32 King, *Report of W. L. Mackenzie King, C. M. G., Commissioner Appointed to Enquire into the Methods by Which Oriental Laborers Have Been Induced to Come to Canada*, 53–54, 76–80; King, Draft memorandum re: Mission to India and China, n.d. (approx. 1909), King Papers, MG26, J4, vol. 22, C15394; King Diary, March 17, 1908, King Papers, MG26, J13.

33 King Diary, March 17, 19, 20, 1908; January 26, 1909, King Papers, MG26, J13; King, *Report of W. L. Mackenzie King, C.M.G., on the Subject of Immigration to Canada from the Orient and Immigration from India in Particular* (Ottawa: King's Printer, 1908).

34 P.C.1908-1225.

35 P.C. 1908-27.

36 King Diary, March 26, 1909, King Papers, MG26, J13.

37 King, *Industry and Humanity*, 53. For a more detailed discussion of this principle see pages 53–61.

38 Canada, House of Commons, *Debates*, May 8, 1922, 1555.

39 King Diary, January 11, 1909, January 16, 1909, March 18, 1909, King Papers, MG26, J13; Canada, House of Commons, *Debates*, May 8, 1922, 1555.

40 Statutes of Canada, 1923, c. 38.

41 Interview between King and the Japanese Consul, April 2, 1925, King Papers, MG 26, J4, vol. 80, file 634, C61268–70.

42 The practice of "picture brides" was a system of arranged marriage through photographs exchanged between the would-be groom in Canada and the prospective woman in Japan. If the would-be groom liked what he saw in the photo, he would write to his relatives and the "marriage" would be registered in Japan. Memo: Japanese Immigration, March 31, 1925. King Papers: Notes & Memoranda, MG 26, J4, C2694, vol. 80, C61264–5; Canada, House of Commons, *Debates*, January 31, 1928, 60–62, June 8, 1928, 3980.

43 Vancouver *Province*, February 17, 1938.

44 J. Marshall, "The Japanese Invasion of Canada," *Collier's*, October 14, 1939; C.L. Shaw, "The Rising Sun's Dark Shadow Over Canada," *Liberty Magazine*, November 11, 1939, in Ken Adachi, *The Enemy That Never Was: A History of the Japanese Canadians*, 2nd ed. (Toronto: McClelland & Stewart, 1991), 188.

45 Premier Patullo to King, January 26, 1938, King Papers, MG 26, J1, vol. 256, 218388–89; Ian Mackenzie to King, February 26, 1938, ibid., vol. 253, 216060; King to Mackenzie, March 1, 1938, ibid., 216062–63A; Canada, House of Commons, *Debates*, February 17, 1938, 567–75.

46 King Diary, MG26, J13, January 19, 1946; Blair Neatby, *William Lyon Mackenzie King, 1924–1932* (Toronto: University of Toronto Press, 1963), 332, 358. Ian Mackenzie's belief that his anti-Asian stance played an important part in maintaining his seat and thwarting CCF success was expressed in the House of Commons in 1945. See Canada, House of Commons, *Debates*, December 17, 1945, 3704.

47 Canada, House of Commons, *Debates*, February 25, 1941, 1019.

48 Ward, *White Canada Forever*, 107.

49 Patricia Roy has very succinctly classified these stereotypes as the following: the challenge to morality, overwhelming numbers, the Japa-nese military threat, unfair economic competition, and inassimilability. These are not mutually exclusive, however, as the arguments were seldom based on logic and blurred due to repetition and intensity. Patricia Roy, "British Columbia's Fear of Asians, 1900–1950," *Histoire Sociale/Social History* 13(25) (May 1980), 163, 165–71.

50 King Diary, March 3, 1928, King Papers, MG26, J13.

51 Interview with acting president of Waiwupu, Mr. Liang Tun-Yen, March 9, 1909, King Papers, MG26, J4, vol. 42, file 222, C15481; King Diary, March 9, 1909, King Papers, MG26, J13.

52 See J.L. Granatstein, *Conscription in the Second World War, 1939–1945* (Toronto: Ryerson, 1969).

53 Declaration of the Existence of a State of War Between Canada and Japan, December 8, 1941, King Papers, MG26, J5, D58190–94; Ward, *White Canada Forever*, 148–149.

54 King Diary, February 19, 24, 1942, King Papers, MG26, J13; Bothwell, et al. *Canada, 1900–1945*, 385.

55 Ward, *White Canada Forever*, 149.

56 *The Globe and Mail*, February 26, 1941.

57 July 26, 1940; February 24, September 23, November 18, 1941; July 24, 1944, War Committee Minutes, Privy Council Office, King Papers, MG26, J4. While the Japanese *did* shell Estevan Point on Vancouver Island, no other military attacks were made against Canada's West Coast. There were, however, balloon attacks on the West Coast of North America. Under the auspices of a project named FUGO, unmanned bomb-carrying balloons were launched from Japan and fewer than one hundred bombs landed on Canada during the Second World War. The balloon offensive, however, did not succeed, as no forest fires were set and no epidemics of disease broke out. Still, it is believed that FUGO bombs may still exist undetected in many parts of North America. "Telegram from R. W. Mayhew, MP, Victoria to King," February 7, 1945; letter to King from Premier Hart, B.C., February 10, 1945; and enclosed letter from B. R. Mullaly, Lt. Col., Secretary of the Joint Services Committee, Pacific Coast, to Premier Hart, January 24, 1945; "Top Secret Memo," March 6, 1945, War Committee Minutes, Privy Council Office, King Papers, MG26, J4; Sandra Bell, "Bombs from Balloons,"

National Library News 30(7–8) (July–August 1998), 16–17.

58 King Diary, February 20, 23, and 24, 1942, King Papers, MG26, J13.

59 Ibid., Jan. 8, 1941; War Committee Minutes, Sept. 26, 1940, King Papers, MG26, J4; House of Commons, *Debates*, November 12, 1940.

60 King Diary, February 19, 1942, King Papers, MG26, J13.

61 King Diary, February 23, 1942, King Papers, MG26, J13; Canada, War Cabinet Committee, *Minutes*, February 26, 1942.

62 N.A. Robertson to Mackenzie King, December 10, 1941, King Papers, MG26, J4, vol. 361, C249381.

63 Order in Council P.C. 1486, February 24, 1942; *Commons Debates*, February 27, 1942, pp. 917–920; King Diary, February 24, 1942, King Papers, MG26, J13.

64 See Daniels, *Concentration Camps North America*. For the Mexican American cases see Michi Weglyn, *Years of Infamy: The Untold Story of America's Concentration Camps* (New York: Morrow, 1976).

65 See, for example, Sunahara, *The Politics of Racism*, 13–14.

66 I would not go so far as the authors of *Mutual Hostages* in saying that the Japanese Canadians "effectively became hostages for Canadians in Japanese hands." This, I believe, would imply a link between cause and effect that cannot, with all the available documents, be convincingly proven. Roy et al., *Mutual Hostages*, 101.

8. Perras: No Need to Send an Army Across the Pacific: Mackenzie King and the Pacific Conflict, 1939-45

1 Diary, January 5, 1944, W.L.M. King Papers, Diaries, National Archives of Canada (NAC).

2 C.P. Stacey, *Canada and the Age of Conflict: A History of Canadian External Relations. Volume 2: 1921–1948* (Toronto: University of Toronto Press, 1981), 275. See also Roger Sarty, *The Maritime Defence of Canada* (Toronto: Canadian Institute of Strategic Studies, 1996); and Galen Roger Perras, *Franklin Roosevelt and the Origins of the Canadian-American Security Alliance, 1933–1945: Necessary But Not Necessary Enough* (Westport: Praeger, 1998).

3 Diary, April 8, 1908; October 19, 1909; and December 3, 1919, King Papers, NAC; "Report of the Admiral of the Fleet Viscount Jellicoe of Scapa on Naval Mission to the Dominion of Canada," December 31, 1919, Department of National Defence (DND) Records, RG24, vol. 11900, file AE4–3–51, NAC; and Roger Sarty, "The Ghosts of Jellicoe and Fisher: The Royal Canadian Navy and the Quebec Conferences," in David B. Woolner, ed., *The Second Quebec Conference Revisited* (New York: St. Martin's Press, 1998), 144.

4 9th meeting minutes of the Imperial Conference, 1923, Imperial Conference Records, CAB32/9, Public Record Office (PRO); and Correlli Barnett, *The Collapse of British Power* (Gloucester: Allan Sutton, 1972), 194.

5 Diary, October 29, 1936, King Papers, NAC. In July 1936 Roosevelt had told King that some American senators favoured occupying British Columbia if America and Japan were at war. He also asked King for a highway across Canadian soil so that American forces could move quickly to Alaska in a crisis. Finally, after visiting Alaska and British Columbia in late 1937 and dismayed by the poor state of Canadian defences, Roosevelt arranged for senior Canadian commanders to meet their American counterparts in January 1938. The Americans stunned the Canadians by suggesting that they might want air bases in British Columbia and that Canada's West Coast should be incorporated into the American military command system; diary, July 31, 1936, King Papers, NAC; Norman Armour memorandum, November 9, 1937, State Department Post Records, Canada, RG84, Entry 2195A, file 800 1937 Political Affairs Defense and Foreign Policy, National Archives and Records Administration (NARA). In 1921 Canadian militia officer and journalist C.F. Hamilton had contended that America might become "an uncommonly ugly neighbour" if Canada could not safeguard its neutrality against Japan, a notion repeated by historian A.R.M. Lower in 1938. Most importantly, fears of American intervention convinced Canada's military to produce Defence Scheme No. 2 to ensure Canadian neutrality in a war between Japan and the United States; C.F. Hamilton memorandum, March 1921, C.F. Hamilton Papers, vol. 3, file

12; A.R.M. Lower, "The Defence of the West Coast," *Canadian Defence Quarterly* 16 (October 1938), 32–35; and "Defence Scheme No. 2 Plan for the Maintenance of Canadian Neutrality In the Event of a War Between the United States and Japan," April 11, 1938, Directorate of History and Heritage, Department of National Defence (DHH), file 322.016 (D12).

6 O.D. Skelton, "Canadian War Policy," August 24, 1939, King Papers, Memoranda and Notes, vol. 228, NAC; and no. 1166, Skelton to C.G. Power, June 22, 1940, in David R. Murray, ed., *Documents on Canadian External Relations (DCER), Volume 8: 1939–1941. Part II* (Ottawa: Department of External Affairs, 1976), 1272.

7 H.D.G. Crerar to J.L. Ralston, July 23, 1940, RG24, vol. 2925, file HQS 3496 vol. 3, NAC; "Joint Canadian–United States Basic Defense Plan No. 2 (Short Title ABC–22)," July 28, 1941, in Murray, *DCER, Volume 8*, 249–61; Commanding Officer Pacific Command to United States Liaison Officer Seattle, "Naval Vessels Available – Pacific Command," November 10, 1941, RG24, vol. 11778, file COPC 8375–102/2 vol. 1; and Air Vice-Marshal L.S. Breadner to Power, "West Coast Situation," October 28, 1941, C.G. Power Papers, box 59, file D1030, Queen's University Archives (QUA).

8 Diary, September 7 and August 15, 1940, King Papers, NAC; no. 20, Gerald Campbell to Dominions Office, August 16, 1940, Dominions Office Records, DO 114/113, PRO; King to Skelton, "Singapore Conference," King Papers, Correspondence, vol. 284, file C-IJ Campbell 1940; and Skelton to King, "Singapore Conference," October 11, 1940, ibid.

9 No. 1000, Crerar to W.K. Campbell, April 11, 1942, Royal Commission on Hong Kong Records, RG33/20, vol. 3, NAC; Crerar to C.P. Stacey, October 23, 1953, H.D.G. Crerar Papers, vol. 21, file 958C.009 (D329), NAC; Paul Dickson, "Crerar and the Decision to Garrison Hong Kong," *Canadian Military History*, 3 (Spring 1994), 102; and COS (41) 308th meeting, September 3, 1941, Chiefs of Staff Committee Records, Minutes, CAB 79/14, PRO.

10 Crerar to Napier Moore, July 27, 1941, Crerar Papers, vol. 19, file 958C.009 (D333); Grant Dexter, "Talk with Maj. Gen. Crerar," Grant Dexter Papers, box 2, file 20, QUA; and "War

Problems Affecting Canada," Toronto *Globe and Mail*, June 21–July 18, 1941. Australia's Parliament had discussed Canadian army inactivity while Australia had suffered heavy losses in Greece and the Middle East; E.B. Rogers to King, August 29, 1941, Department of External Affairs Records, RG25, vol. 2560, file 3939–L–40, NAC.

11 King dressed down Sumner Welles in November 1941 about Canada's exclusion from the Japanese talks; Sumner Welles memorandum of discussion with Hume Wrong, November 25, 1941, Sumner Welles Papers, Franklin Delano Roosevelt Library (FDRL), box 161, file Canada.

12 Senator Norman Lambert reported that King's rage upon learning of the Newfoundland meeting had been "unbounded"; Dexter memorandum, September 16, 1941, Dexter Papers, box 2, file 20, QUA; no. 1367, Ralston to King, September 2, 1941, King Papers, Memoranda and Notes, vol. 428, file 2, NAC; Cabinet War Committee (CWC) minutes, September 10, 1941, Privy Council, Cabinet War Committee Records, RG2 7c, NAC; and no. 162, Secretary of State for Dominion Affairs to Secretary of State for External Affairs, September 19, 1941, RG33/20, vol. 2, file 5, NAC.

13 CWC minutes, September 24 and October 2, 1941, RG2 7c, NAC.

14 Dexter memorandum, Dexter Papers, box 2, file 20, QUA; and diary, December 9 and 11, 1941, King Papers, NAC.

15 COS appreciation, December 10, 1941, RG2 7c, NAC; and CWC minutes, December 10, 1941, ibid.

16 "Canada's Staff Plan Doesn't Make Sense," and "Who Is the Prime Minister?" Vancouver *Sun*, February 24 and 25, 1942; Dexter memorandum, February 28, 1942, Dexter Papers, box 3, file 21, QUA; COS to the Ministers, March 10, 1942, RG2 7c, NAC; Stuart to the CWC, March 17, 1942, ibid.; CWC minutes, March 18, 1942, ibid.; and C.P. Stacey, *Arms, Men and Governments: The War Policies of Canada 1939–1945* (Ottawa: Department of National Defence, 1970), 47n.

17 Kim Richard Nossal, "Chunking Prism: Cognitive Process and Intelligence Failure," *Inter-*

national Journal, 32 (Summer 1977), 559–76; Advisory War Committee minutes, January 12, 1942, Series A5954/46, Item 813/2, National Archives of Australia [NAA]; and Australian Chiefs of Staff, "Australian-Canadian Co-operation in the Pacific – Appreciation of Defence of Australia and Adjacent Areas," January 29, 1942, Series A3300, Item 219, NAA.

18 King to Odlum, January 12, 1942, King Papers, Correspondence, vol. 331, file O'Connell-Purdy, NAC; King to Odlum, January 20, 1942, RG25, vol. 819, file 676; and William Glasgow to External Canberra, January 17, 1942, Series A3095/1, Item 35/9, NAA.

19 CWC minutes, January 14, 1942, RG2 7c, NAC; Stuart, "Australian Request for Military Aid from Canada," January 27, 1942, J.L. Ralston Papers, vol. 38, file Australia Gen (Secret), NAC; CWC minutes, February 12 and 18, 1942, RG2 7c, NAC; and 145th COS meeting minutes, February 24, 1942, RG24, vol. 8081, file NSS 1272–2 (vol. 6), NAC.

20 Australian COS, "Probable Immediate Moves in the Proposed New ANZAC Area," March 5, 1942, Series A2671, Item 143/1942; and H.V. Evatt quoted in Norman Harper, *A Great and Powerful Friend: A Study of Australian American Relations Between 1900 and 1975* (St. Lucia: University of Queensland Press, 1987), 112.

21 CWC minutes, March 26 and April 1, 1942, RG2 7c, NAC; and Pacific War Council minutes for April 1, 1942, Franklin Roosevelt Map Room Files, box 168, FDRL. State Department official John Hickerson revealed that Roosevelt deliberately had singled Canada out "solely with the (political) object of playing up Canada's part in the Council vis-à-vis the members from 'down under'." Welles had said that Roosevelt had noted Australia's inability to comprehend why Canada was continuing "to send troops to England instead of despatching them to Australia": Diary, April 2, 1942, Maurice Pope Papers, vol. 1, NAC; and Leighton McCarthy to N.A. Robertson, March 26, 1942, RG25, vol. 2961, file 35.

22 C.J. Burchell to Skelton, October 28, 1940, RG25, vol. 2736, file 329–40 pt. 1, NAC.

23 Robertson to King, March 23, 1942, RG25, vol. 2168, file 53–MP–40, NAC; diary, March 27 and April 8, 1942, King Papers, NAC; CWC

minutes, April 8, 1942, RG2 7c, NAC; and C.D. Howe to King, April 13, 1942, in John F. Hilliker, ed., *Documents on Canadian External Relations. Volume 9: 1942–1943* (Ottawa: Department of External Affairs, 1980), 1039.

24 CWC minutes, April 9, 1942, RG2 7c, NAC; diary, April 9, 1942, King Papers, NAC; Evatt to John Curtin, April 14, 1942, Series A5954/1, Item 581/17, NAA; diary, April 15, 1942, King Papers, NAC; and King to Evatt, April 28, 1942, King Papers, Memoranda, vol. 348, reel H–1529, p. C240280.

25 Australian–Canadian relations during the war are explored in R.G. Haycock, "The 'Myth' of Imperial Defence: Australian–Canadian Bilateral Military Co-operation, 1942," *War & Society* 2 (May 1984), 65–84; J.F. Hilliker, "Distant Ally: Canadian Relations With Australia During the Second World War," *Journal of Imperial and Commonwealth History* 13 (October 1984), 46–67; and Galen Roger Perras, "She Should Have Thought of Herself First: Canada and the Provision of Military Aid to Australia, 1939–1945," in Margaret Macmillan, Francine McKenzie, and Galen Roger Perras, eds., *Parties Long Estranged: Canada and Australia in the Twentieth Century* (Vancouver: University of British Columbia Press, in press).

26 "Joint Canadian–United States Basic Defense Plan (Second Joint Draft)," September 25, 1940, DHH, file 112.11 (D1A); PJBD "First Report," October 4, 1940, DHH, file 82/196 vol. 1; "Joint Canadian–United States Basic Defense Plan – 1940," October 10, 1940, ibid.; Stuart to Crerar, October 10, 1940, DHH, file 112.11 (D1A); Stuart to Crerar, October 11, 1940, DHH, file 82/196 vol. 1; and "ABC–22," July 28, 1942, in Murray, *DCER Volume 8*.

27 O.M. Biggar to King, April 22, 1941, DHH, file 112.11 (D1A); CWC minutes, April 23, 1941, RG2 7c, NAC; Roosevelt to F.H. LaGuardia, May 16, 1941, Roosevelt Papers, President's Secretary's File, box 25, file Canada: Permanent Joint Board on Defense, FDRL; Jay Pierrepont Moffat, "Notes on Visit to Washington July 10–July 12, 1941," Jay Pierrepont Moffat Papers, MS Am 1407, vol. 47, Houghton Library [HL]; PJBD minutes, May 28–29 1941, DHH, file 82/196; and "Joint Canadian–United States Basic Defense Plan No.

2 (Short Title ABC–22)," July 28, 1941, in Murray, *DCER Volume 8*. Stacey has called the PJBD's debate on May 27–28, 1941 "probably the most strained" in the body's history: *Arms, Men and Governments*, 352.

28 L.T. Gerow to Senior Army Member, June 17, 1941, War Department, War Plans Division Records, RG165, Entry 281, file WPD 4330–21, NARA; Lt. Colonel Nelson M. Walker, "Report of Observation – Alaska – General," December 5, 1941, ibid., file WPD 3512–146; and Gerow to General George C. Marshall, "Defensive Preparations in Western Canada," December 15, 1941, War Department, Operations and Plans Division Records, Executive Files, RG165, Exec file 8, book 1, NARA. See also General Frank McCoy, Hanson W. Baldwin, and Major General George Fielding Eliot, "War Planning," *Council of Foreign Relations Report No. A–B 35*, December 15, 1941.

29 Major General Maurice Pope, "Note on Question of the United States–Canada Unity of Command," December 18, 1941, DHH, file 72/145; Robertson to King, December 22, 1941, RG25, vol. 810, file 614, NAC; Keenleyside, "Recent Trends in United States–Canada Relations," December 27, 1941, RG25, vol. 5758, file 71(s), NAC; and PJBD minutes, January 20, 1942, King Papers, Memoranda, vol. 319, file F3369.

30 Fred Pollock, "Roosevelt, the Ogdensburg Agreement, and the British Fleet: All Done With Mirrors," *Diplomatic History* 5 (1981), 203–19; and Chief of Naval Operations to Marshall, "Unity of command over joint operations," December 1941, RG165, Entry 281, file WPD 2917–35, NARA.

31 Lt. General John DeWitt to General R.O. Alexander, May 29, 1942, RG24, vol. 18823, War Diary of General Staff HQ Pacific Command, NAC.

32 PJBD meeting minutes, April 27, 1942, DHH, file 314.009 (D17); L.F. Stevenson, "Memorandum regarding RCAF reinforcing Alaska in an emergency," May 14, 1942, RG24, vol. 11765, file PC 010–9–20; no. A431X214, Stevenson to Air Force HQ [AFHQ], May 27, 1942, Power Papers, box 69, file D2019, QUA; CWC minutes, May 14, 1942, RG2 7c, NAC; Air Commodore F.V. Heakes to Biggar, May 20, 1942, DHH, file 314.009 (D17); and COS meeting

minutes, May 29, 1942, Power Papers, box 69, file D2019, QUA.

33 No. 402A465, Stevenson to AFHQ, May 30, 1942, Power Papers, box 69, file D2019; "Memorandum of telephone call from Lt. Gen. Stuart, Victoria, at 2340 hours, May 30th, 1942," June 1, 1942, ibid.; Power memorandum for record, May 31, 1942, ibid.

34 Stanley W. Dziuban, *Military Relations Between the United States and Canada* (Washington, DC: Department of the Army, 1959), 253; no. MP40, Pope to Stuart, June 1, 1942, DHH, file 314.009 (D67); diary, June 1, 1942, Pope Papers, vol. 1, NAC; "Report of telephone conversation – Lieut. General Embick, US Army, and Air Commodore H.V. Heakes, RCAF, regarding movement of squadrons to Yakutat and resultant action – 1145 hours 1.6.42," June 1, 1942, Power Papers, box 69, file D2019; and no. A80, Heakes to Embick, June 1, 1942, ibid.

35 W.A.B. Douglas, *The Creation of a National Air Force: The Official History of the Royal Canadian Air Force. Volume II* (Toronto: University of Toronto Press, 1986), 412–14; WDC to US Liaison Officer Victoria, May 18, 1942, RG24, vol. 13823, War Diary Pacific Command HQ, NAC; no. 2304z23, Commodore W.J.R. Beech to Naval Services HQ, May 23, 1942, Privy Council Records, RG2, vol. 32, file D–19–1 (1942); no, X463A476, Stevenson to AFHQ, June 1, 1942, Power Papers, box 69, file D2019; no. MP35, Pope to Stuart, May 28, 1942, DHH, file 314.009 (D67); and diary, May 28, 1942, Pope Papers, vol. 1, NAC.

36 Memorandum of 1st PWC meeting, April 3, 1942, Roosevelt Papers, Map Room Files, box 168, file 3, FDRL; and King memorandum, April 15, 1942, RG25, vol. 2152, file 149, NAC.

37 Robertson to King, March 2, 1942, RG2, vol. 48, file D–19–1, NAC; and Robertson to King, April 6, 1942, RG25, acc. 89–90/029, box 28, file 23–(A)s pt. 1, NAC.

38 King to C. Mortimer Bezeau, April 21, 1942, King Papers, Correspondence, vol. 321, file Babbage to Blackmore, NAC.

39 Canadian General Staff, "Japanese Occupation of the Aleutian Islands," July 15, 1942, Power Papers, box 70, file D2028, QUA; Canadian General Staff, "An Appreciation of the World

Military Situation With Particular Regard to Its Effect in Canada (as of First July 1942)," August 4, 1942, Ralston Papers, vol. 37, file Appreciations Military Gen. (Secret 1940–42), NAC; COS to the CWC, CWC document 252, August 13, 1942, RG2 7c; CWC minutes, August 26, 1942, ibid.; and Privy Council Order PC 7995, September 4, 1942, Minutes and Orders in Council, 1867–1959, RG2 1, vol. 1520, file 2639G. Force D's two corvettes and three auxiliary cruisers guarded Alaskan convoys until October 30, 1942.

40 Forrest C. Pogue, *George C. Marshall: Organizer of Victory, 1943–1945* (New York: Viking, 1973), 154–55; 58th Joint Chiefs of Staff (JCS) meeting minutes, January 22, 1943, Joint Chiefs of Staff Decimal File 1942–1945, RG218, file CCS 334 Joint Chiefs of Staff (1–14–43), NARA; and Combined Chiefs of Staff, CC170/1, "Report to the President and Prime Minister," January 23, 1943, *Wartime Conferences of the Combined Chiefs of Staff: Arcadia, Casablanca, Trident. Volumes 1 + 2 (Dec 1941–May 1943)*, reel 1, Scholarly Resources Inc. (SRI). Planners had suggested a 15–18 division effort, supplemented by Soviet forces, to retake Kiska, invade the Kuriles, and use Siberian bases to bomb Japan; Joint Planning Staff, JCS 182 Enclosure B, "Campaign Against Japan via the Northern Route," January 1, 1943, Joint Chiefs of Staff Records, Geographic File 1942–1945, RG218, file CCS 381 Japan (8–25–42), NARA.

41 "Western Defense Command" memorandum, May 1, 1943, RG165, OPD, Exec file 6, item 13, NARA; "General Staff Report on Greenlight Force Period From Inception to Despatch to Adak," July 1943, RG24, vol. 2921, file HQS 9055–1, NAC; and no. PCO2616, George Pearkes to Stuart, April 20, 1943, DHH, file 322.009 (D490). General Bernard Montgomery had judged Pearkes a "gallant soldier" who "would fight his Division bravely till the last man was killed: but he has no brains and the last man would be killed all too soon"; Bernard Montgomery to Crerar, April 25 and May 13, 1942, Crerar Papers, vol. 2, file 958C.009 (D182), NAC.

42 No. CAW305, Pope to Stuart, May 10, 1943, RG24, vol. 2919, file HQS 9055(1), NAC; and Hickerson to Embick, May 11, 1943, State Department Records, Permanent Joint Board on Defense, RG59, box 10, file Correspondence of PJBD April-June, NARA; no. PCO2020, Pearkes to Stuart, May 25, 1943, file 322.009 (D490), DHH; and Stuart to Ralston, May 26, 1943, RG24, vol. 2919, file HQS 9055(1), NAC.

43 Diary, May 26, 1943, King Papers, NAC; and Robertson to King, May 27, 1943, King Papers, Memoranda, vol. 348, file 3770 WWII Aleutians 1942–43; and CWC minutes, May 27, 1943, RG2 7c, NAC.

44 Diary, May 28, 1943, Pope Papers, vol. 1, NAC; no. CAW353, Pope to Stuart, May 28, 1943, file 314.009 (D49), DHH; and Henry Stimson to Ralston, May 29, 1943, ibid. Chief USN planner Admiral C.M. Cooke had objected to including the Canadians, but Admiral Ernest King, though agreeing that adding the Canadians would lead to needless administrative and logistical complications, had no objection to allowing Canadian participation if the War Department insisted; C.M. Cooke to E. King, May 15, 1943, Strategic Plans Division Records, Series XII, box 175, file Alaska-Misc, Naval Historical Center (NHC); and E. King to Marshall, May 19, 1943, RG165, OPD, file OPD 336 Security, NARA.

45 PWC 31st meeting minutes, May 20, 1943, Roosevelt Papers, Map Room Files, box 168, file 3, FDRL.

46 Diary, May 27, 28, and 30, 1943, King Papers, NAC.

47 Stuart to Ralston, May 31, 1943, RG24, vol. 2919, file HQS 9055(1), NAC; Ralston to Stimson, June 3, 1943, ibid.; supplementary minutes of 91st JCS meeting, June 8, 1943, RG218, JCS Decimal File 1942–1945, file CCS 334 Joint Chiefs of Staff (5–21–43), NARA; Captain Forrest B. Royal to Pope, June 25, 1943, RG218, JCS Geographic File 1942–1945, file CCS 381 North Pacific (6–13–42), NARA; and no. CAW446, Pope to Stuart, June 28, 1943, file 314.009 (D49), DHH.

48 Diary, June 1, 1943, Pope Papers, vol. 1, NAC.

49 Military members minutes, June 7, 1943, George Pearkes Papers, box 11, file 11.14, University of Victoria Archives; no. PCA280, Pearkes to General H.F.G Letson, June 11, 1943, file 322.009 (D481), DHH; and no.

GS710, Stuart to Pearkes, June 25, 1943, RG24, vol. 2919, file HQS 9055(1), NAC.

50 Brigadier W.H. Macklin, "Administrative Report on Greenlight Force Covering Period from Inception of Project to Despatch of Force to Adak," July 22, 1943, RG24, vol. 13381, file July 1943, NAC; War Diary of Le Régiment de Hull, June 1943, RG24, vol. 15182, NAC; and Galen Roger Perras, *Stepping Stones to Nowhere? The United States, Canada, and the Aleutian Islands Campaign, 1942–1943* (doctoral dissertation, University of Waterloo, 1995), 280–82.

51 Galen Roger Perras, "Canada as a Military Partner: Alliance Politics and the Campaign to Recapture the Island of Kiska," *The Journal of Military History* 56 (July 1992), 444–45.

52 Diary, June 10, 1944, Pope Papers, vol. 1, NAC; and R.H. Roy, *For Most Conspicuous Bravery: A Biography of Major-General George R. Pearkes, VC, Through Two World Wars* (Vancouver: University of British Columbia Press, 1977), 189.

53 C.P. Stacey, *Official History of the Canadian Army in the Second World War. Volume One. Six Years of War: The Army in Canada, Britain and the Pacific* (Ottawa: Department of National Defence, 1955), 500–05. J.W. Pickersgill had advised King to say nothing because Canadians "might experience a sense of keen disappointment" when they realized there had been no battle; King, "Memorandum re participation of Canadian forces in operations in Alaskan and Aleutian areas," August 21, 1943, King Papers, Memoranda, vol. 361, file 3853, NAC; transcript of "Broadcast by the Prime Minister the Rt. Hon. W.L. Mackenzie King on participation of Canadian forces in Alaska and the Aleutians," August 21, 1943, King Papers, Memoranda, vol. 361, file 3853, NAC.

54 Brigadier P. Earnshaw memorandum, May 31, 1943, file 112.3M2 (D459), DHH.

55 Notes of DeWitt-Pearkes meeting, July 5, 1943, RG24, War Diary of Greenlight, vol. 13831; no. CGS787, Murchie to Pearkes, July 12, 1943, file 322.009 (D483), DHH; G.S. Currie to Ralston, July 19, 1943, Ralston Papers, vol. 43, file Currie, Col. G.S. 1943–44; and Pearkes to Major General A.E. Potts, July 13, 1943, file 322.009 (D486), DHH.

56 Pearkes to Stuart, August 13, 1943, file 322.009 (D482), DHH; and Pearkes to Stuart, August 26, 1943, file 322.009 (D533), DHH. See also Galen Roger Perras, "We Have Opened the Door to Tokyo: United States Plans to Seize the Kurile Islands, 1943–1945," *The Journal of Military History* 61 (January 1997), 65–91.

57 Stuart, "Reduction in Operational Troops in Canada," August 30, 1943, RG2 7c, NAC.

58 Odlum to King, 27 July 1943, Victor Odlum Papers, vol. 138, file WWII China and Indochina 1943–45, NAC; T.C. Davis to Robertson, August 24, 1943, RG25, vol. 2453, file 250–1943, NAC; 34th PWC meeting minutes, August 11, 1943, RG2, vol. 14, file W–29–1, NAC; and Lieutenant Commander Geoffrey Todd, "Appreciation of RCN Ship Requirements for the War Against Japan and for the Post-War Navy," July 29, 1943, RG24, vol. 3844, file NSS 1017–10–34 pt. 1, NAC.

59 Shelagh D. Grant, "Northern Nationalists: Visions of 'A New North', 1940–1950," in Kenneth S. Coates and William R. Morrison, eds., *For Purposes of Dominion: Essays in Honour of Morris Zaslow* (North York: Captus Press, 1989), 47–48; Hugh L. Keenleyside, *Memoirs of Hugh L. Keenleyside. Volume 2: On the Bridge of Time* (Toronto: McClelland and Stewart, 1989), 72; and Keenleyside to King, "Canadian–American Relations in the Northwest," July 29, 1943, King Papers, Correspondence, vol. 337.

60 CWC minutes, September 8 and October 12, 1943, RG2 7c, NAC.

61 Diary, December 1, 1943, King Papers, NAC.

62 Lewis Clark to Hickerson, February 25, 1944, RG165, OPD, file OPD 336.4 Canada (Section 1–A), NARA; R.B. Gibson to CGS, February 3, 1944, DHH, file 112.21009 (D197); Pearkes to Secretary DND, January 25, 1944, DHH, file 322.009 (D488); Pearkes to Secretary DND, January 17, 1944, DHH, file 322.009 (D50); and Gibson to Pearkes, January 29, 1944, ibid.; and Murchie to Pearkes, March 28, 1944, DHH, file 112.1 (D7).

63 Diary, February 19, 1944, King Papers, NAC; and Power aide-memoire, February 10, 1944, RG2, vol. 32, file D–19–1 (Asia) 1943–44).

64 Diary, May 15, 1944, King Papers, NAC; "Improvements in the Machinery for Empire Co-

operation Desired by the Australian Government," May 15, 1945, Series A5954/1, Item 289/10, NAA; and PMM (44) 14th meeting minutes, ibid. British Minister of Production Oliver Lyttleton wanted to concentrate on domestic reconstruction, while Secretary of State for Air Archibald Sinclair worried about the impression Britain would make if it did not attack Japan "with all the resources at our disposal": Oliver Lyttleton, "Man-Power for the Japanese War," War Cabinet Memoranda, CAB 66/48, WM (44) 173, PRO; and WM (44) 48th conclusions, April 13, 1944, War Cabinet Minutes, CAB 65/42, PRO.

65 CWC minutes, May 24, 1944, RG2 7c, NAC.

66 289th COS meeting minutes, June 7, 1944, file 193.009 (D32), DHH; and Stuart to Murchie, June 3, 1944, Crerar Papers, vol. 5, file 5–5–4, NAC.

67 Pope to J.H. Jenkins, February 9, 1944, Pope Papers, vol. 1; Pope to Jenkins, April 4, 1944, RG25, vol. 5749, file 52–C(s) pt. 1; and Jenkins, "Appreciation of Canadian Participation in the Pacific Theatre of War," April 24, 1944, file 193.009 (D32), DHH.

68 "Memorandum to the Cabinet War Committee: re: Canadian participation in the war against Japan," June 14, 1944, RG2 7c, NAC; CWC minutes, June 14, 1944, ibid.; King to Dominions Secretary, June 27, 1944, in John F. Hilliker, ed., *Documents on Canadian External Relations. Volume 10, 1944–1945. Part I* (Ottawa: Department of External Affairs, 1987), 380–81.

69 JP (44) 176 (Final), "Employment of Canadian Forces After the Defeat of Germany," July 24, 1944, file 82/1125, DHH; 297th COS meeting minutes, August 17, 1944, file 193.009 (D34), DHH; and Gibson to Ralston, August 19, 1944, Ralston Papers, vol. 49, file Japan 1944.

70 Heeney to King, "Canadian participation in the war against Japan," August 22, 1944, in Hilliker, *DCER Volume 10*, 393–96; King to defence ministers, August 30, 1944, Ralston Papers, vol. 49, file Japan 1944; and CWC minutes, August 31, 1944, RG2 7c, NAC.

71 COS to the Ministers, "Canadian participation in the Pacific war," September 6, 1944, RG24, vol. 2921, file HQS 9131, NAC; Howe to King, August 31, 1944, RG25, vol. 5758, file 68–C(s);

diary, September 6, 1944, King Papers, NAC; and Cabinet conclusions, September 6, 1944, in Hilliker, *DCER Volume 10*, 410–11.

72 Sarty, "The Ghosts of Jellicoe and Fisher," 146.

73 Nelles, "Aide Memoire for the First Sea Lord on the employment of Canadian naval forces after the defeat of Germany," August 31, 1944, file 1650–1, DHH; diary, September 6 and 13, 1944, Angus Macdonald Papers, vol. 1503, folder 392, Public Archives of Nova Scotia (PANS); diary, September 13, 1944, King Papers, NAC; and CWC minutes, September 13, 1944, RG2 7c, NAC.

74 WM (44) 96th and 102nd conclusions, July 26 and August 4, 1944, CAB 65/43, PRO; WP (44) 380, COS, "Man-Power one year after the defeat of Germany," CAB 66/52, PRO; diary, September 14, 1944, King Papers, NAC; CWC minutes, September 14, 1944, RG2 7c, NAC; Robertson, "War against Japan; participation by Canadian forces," RG25, vol. 5758, file 68–C(s); Pope memorandum, September 17, 1944, file 82/1125, DHH; and CCS minutes, September 16, 1944, in *Foreign Relations of the United States: The Conference at Quebec 1944* (Washington, DC: Government Printing Office, 1972), 379.

75 Diary, September 22 and October 5 and 11, 1944, Macdonald Papers, vol. 1503, folder 392, PANS; CWC minutes, September 22 and October 5 and 11, 1944, RG2 7c, NAC; and Cabinet conclusion, November 14, 1944, RG2, Cabinet Conclusions, vol. 2936, reel T–2364. Almost 25,000 RCAF personnel had signed up for Tiger Force in 1945, but only 335 badly needed engineers had joined from a pool of 6,600 candidates. More than 39,000 men had volunteered for the CAPF by July 1945; but C.P. Stacey has noted that a shortage of trained infantry might have emerged in combat as it had in Europe in 1944. The RNC suffered the worst embarrassment when HMCS *Uganda* sailors voted to leave Okinawa to return home because they had not volunteered to fight in the Pacific; Brereton Greenhous, Stephen J. Harris, William C. Johnston, and William G.P. Rawling, *The Crucible of War 1939–1945: The Official History of the Royal Canadian Air Force. Volume III* (Toronto: University of Toronto Press, 1994), 123–24; Stacey, *Six Years*

of War, 517; and Bill Rawling, "A Lonely Ambassador: HMCS *Uganda* and the War in the Pacific," *The Northern Mariner* 8 (January 1998), 39–63.

76 Fleet Admiral William D. Leahy to Letson, December 21, 1944, RG24, vol. 11960, file TS4–18, NAC; no. W73669, Marshall to Douglas MacArthur, April 28, 1945, General Headquarters United States Army Forces Pacific Records, RG4, box 16, reel 594, General Douglas MacArthur Foundation; and MacArthur to Marshall, April 28, 1945, ibid. Admiral King had opposed operations in the Philippines in favour of attacks against the Kuriles, Formosa, and along the Chinese coast; Grace Person Hayes, *The History of the Joint Chiefs of Staff in World War II: The War Against Japan* (Annapolis: Naval Institute Press, 1982), Chapter 27. At one point in March 1945 the increasingly frustrated Canadian services had briefly considered fielding a tri-service contingent in the Kuriles; COS minutes, March 20, 1945, RG24, vol. 8082, file 1272–2 vol. 7, NAC.

77 Diary, March 29, 1945, King Papers, NAC; JP (45) 185 (Final), JPS, "Participation on Coronet – information for the Dominions," DO 35/1725, file WG 773/15/39, PRO; Clement Attlee to King, August 4, 1945, RG2, vol. 33, file D–19–1 (Asia), NAC; Gibson to Minister of National Defence McNaughton, "Employment Canadian Army Pacific Force," August 6, 1945, RG24, vol. 2924, file HQS 9131, NAC; Attlee to King, August 13, 1945, ibid., file HQS 9131–33; and Cabinet conclusion, August 14, 1945, RG2, vol. 2636, reel T–2364.

78 F.L.C. Floud to Sir Harry Batterbee, May 24, 1938, DO 35/586, file G88/55, PRO.

79 Basil H. Liddell Hart, *History of the Second World War* (London: Cassell, 1970), 219; George F.G. Stanley, *Canada's Soldiers: The Military History of an Unmilitary People* (Toronto: Macmillan, 1954), 380–81; Carl Vincent, *No Reason Why: The Canadian Hong Kong Tragedy – An Examination* (Stittsville: Canada's Wings, 1981); and Galen Roger Perras, "'Our Position in the Far East Would be Stronger Without this Unsatisfactory Commitment': Britain and the Reinforcement of Hong Kong, 1941," *Canadian Journal of History* 30 (August 1995), 231–59.

80 Rogers to King, October 13, 1942, in Hilliker, *DCER*, 376; and John Curtin press briefing, February 2, 1943, in Clem Lloyd and Richard Hall, eds., *Backroom Briefings: John Curtin's War* (Canberra: National Library of Australia, 1997), 133.

81 Diary, October 6, 1939, King Papers, NAC.

82 Stephen J. Harris, *Canadian Brass: The Making of a Professional Army* (Toronto: University of Toronto Press, 1988), 5.

83 Stacey, *Arms, Men and Governments*, 115; and Samuel P. Huntington, *The Soldier and the State: The Theory and Politics of Civil-Military Relations* (Cambridge, MA: Belknap, 1957), 72.

84 Diary, September 14, 1944, King Papers, NAC.

85 "WIB Survey Number 53," December 30, 1944, King Papers, Memoranda, vol. 427, file PCO War Committee Memoranda October–December 1944; and J.L. Granatstein, *Canada's War: The Politics of the Mackenzie King Government 1939–1945* (Toronto: Oxford University Press, 1975), 412.

9. Lackenbauer: Right and Honourable: Mackenzie King, Canadian–American Bilateral Relations, and Canadian Sovereignty in the Northwest, 1943-48

1 On this "mass of contradictions" see C.P. Stacey, *Mackenzie King and the Atlantic Triangle* (Toronto: Macmillan, 1976), 61–68.

2 *The Forked Road: Canada 1939–1957* (Toronto: McClelland and Stewart, 1976), 73.

3 J.L. Granatstein critiqued this "plot folk" school in his 1988 Joanne Goodman lecture, *How Britain's Weakness Forced Canada into the Arms of the United States* (Toronto: University of Toronto Press, 1989), 4–7. See also Norman Hillmer's introduction to *Partners Nevertheless: Canadian–American Relations in the Twentieth Century* (Toronto: Copp Clark Pitman, 1989). King's "forked road" comment has played an enduring role in the works of those who wish to cast him as a "sell-out." C.P. Stacey wisely noted that this passing phrase should not be taken too seriously, having been put into King's mouth by his trusted adviser O.D. Skelton. Stacey, *Mackenzie King and the Atlantic Triangle*, 63.

4 Shelagh Grant, *Sovereignty or Security? Government Policy in the Canadian North, 1936–*

1950 (Vancouver: University of British Columbia Press, 1988), 20, 70–71.

5   Elizabeth Brebner incorporated Shelagh Grant in this school, although I would strongly suggest that her overall tone of an American "conspiracy" against Canadian sovereignty, and her reserved judgments on the King government's ability to withstand pressures, place her more soundly in the "sell-out" school, albeit in a more moderate sense. "Sovereignty and the North: Canadian–American Co-operation 1939–45" in Bob Hesketh, ed., *Three Northern Projects* (Edmonton: Canadian Circumpolar Institute and Edmonton & District Historical Society, 1996).

6   Granatstein, *How Britain's Weakness Forced Canada into the Arms of the United States.*

7   C.P. Stacey, *Arms, Men and Governments* (Ottawa: Queen's Printer, 1970), 379–88. Stacey has even less to say in *Canada and the Age of Conflict. Vol. 2: 1921–1948: The Mackenzie King Era* (Toronto: University of Toronto Press, 1981), 361–63.

8   *Canada and the United States: Ambivalent Allies* (Montreal and Kingston: McGill-Queen's University Press, 1994), 169.

9   J.L. Granatstein and Norman Hillmer are more positive of the big picture. They praise the federal government for recognizing its lax position at the beginning of the war ("in its too-easy turning over to the Americans of the keys to the national attic") and acting after 1943 "with toughness and skill to protect the national interest." Purchasing back permanent military installations in the North at war's end "on terms that fully protected Canadian sovereignty" showed the King Government's astuteness. Unfortunately, no comment is made of how this issue carried over into the postwar period: *For Better or For Worse: Canada and the United States to the 1990s* (Toronto: Copp Clark Pitman, 1991), 156. Granatstein offers a similar, albeit more reserved, judgment in *Canada's War: The Politics of the Mackenzie King Government, 1939–1945* (Toronto: University of Toronto Press, 1975), 323.

10   Gordon Smith, "Territorial Sovereignty in the Canadian North: A Historical Outline of the Problem" (Ottawa, Department of Northern Affairs and National Resources, 1963); Memorandum, Department of National Defence to Cabinet Defence Committee, "Sovereignty in the Canadian Arctic in Relation to Joint Defence Undertakings," n.d., *Documents on Canadian External Relations* (DCER) 12 (1946), 1556; Grant, *Sovereignty or Security?* 3–48; David J. Bercuson, "Continental Defense and Arctic Sovereignty, 1945–50: Solving the Canadian Dilemma," in Keith Neilson and Ronald G. Haycock, eds., *The Cold War and Defense* (New York: Praeger, 1990), 154.

11   Edwin R. Carr, "Great Falls to Nome: the Inland Air Route to Alaska, 1940–45," (Ph.D. dissertation, University of Minnesota, 1946); Kenneth Charles Eyre, "Custos Borealis: The Military in the Canadian North" (Ph.D. thesis, King's College, University of London, 1981), 82–95.

12   Richard Diubaldo, "The Canol Project in Canadian–American Relations," Canadian Historical Association *Historical Papers* 1977, 179–95; Stanley W. Dziuban, *Military Relations Between the United States and Canada, 1939–1945* (Washington: Office of the Chief of Military History, Department of the Army, 1959), 228–35.

13   "Duff" Pattullo, the British Columbia premier, also pushed strongly for the highway project to ease the strains of the Great Depression.

14   Thompson and Randall, *Ambivalent Allies*, 168–69; Dziuban, *Military Relations*, 217–28; Stacey, *Arms, Men and Governments*, 382–83. C.P. Stacey deemed the highway insufficient and with little military utility (apart from its connection with the air route).

15   See the chapters by Kenneth Coates, Julie Cruikshank, and Richard Stuart in K.S. Coates, ed., *The Alaska Highway: Papers of the 40th Anniversary Symposium* (Vancouver: University of British Columbia Press, 1985); K.S. Coates and W.R. Morrison, *The Alaska Highway in World War II: The U.S. Army of Occupation in Canada's Northwest* (Toronto: University of Toronto Press, 1992); Coates, *North to Alaska* (Toronto: McClelland and Stewart, 1992); Grant, *Sovereignty or Security?*

16   Granatstein, *Canada's War*, 323.

17   J.W. Pickersgill and D.F. Forster, *The Mackenzie King Record* (Toronto: University of Toronto Press, 1960) (hereafter MKR), I, 436.

18   Ibid.; William Lyon Mackenzie King (hereafter

WLMK) Diary, microfiche (Toronto: University of Toronto Press, 1980), 21 March 1942.

19 Vincent Massey, *What's Past Is Prologue* (Toronto: Macmillan, 1963), 371; Clyde Sanger, *Malcolm MacDonald: Bringing an End to Empire* (Montreal and Kingston: McGill-Queen's University Press, 1995), 237–39; WLMK Diary, March 29, 1943. The full text of MacDonald's memorandum is reprinted in Coates, *The Alaska Highway*, 95–101.

20 Grant, *Sovereignty or Security?* 56–57. On the "would-be-architects of a 'new north'" see Grant, "Northern Nationalists: Visions of a 'New North,' 1940–1950," in Kenneth S. Coates and William R. Morrison, eds., *For Purposes of Dominion: Essays in Honour of Morris Zaslow* (North York, ON: Captus Press, 1989).

21 Brebner, "Sovereignty and the North," 55; Sanger, *Malcolm MacDonald*, 241; Granatstein, *Canada's War*, 322; Dziuban, *Military Relations*, 210–11; John W. Holmes, *The Shaping of Peace: Canada and the Search for World Order* (Toronto: University of Toronto Press, 1979), 174–77. On the prolonged negotiations over the disposal of the Canol project, see DCER 11 (1944–45), Part II, Chapter 8, Section C: Canol Project, 1450–92; Richard Diubaldo, "The Canol Project," and Dziuban, *Military Relations*, 331–34.

22 Stacey, *Arms, Men and Governments*, 386–87; Dziuban, *Military Relations*, 137–41.

23 Brebner, "Sovereignty and the North," 53.

24 See Stacey, *Arms, Men and Governments*, 387.

25 The obvious exception was the government's absolute disregard for Aboriginal rights in the north, a subject worthy of additional research. See Coates and Morrison, *The Alaska Highway in World War II*, chap. 3, "The Native People and the Environment."

26 On this perspective see Donald Barry, "Continuity and Change in Canadian Foreign Policy: From the Pre-War to the Post-War Experience, 1935–1957" (Ph.D. dissertation, Johns Hopkins University, 1977).

27 Robert Bothwell, "The Cold War and the Curate's Egg," *International Journal* (Summer 1998), 407–18.

28 MKR, IV, 6.

29 See "Final Report of the Advisory Committee on Post-Hostility Problems," January/February 1945, DCER 11 (1944–45), Part II, 1567–73; and Group Captain W.W. Bean, RCAF, Secretary, Chiefs of Staff Committee, "An Appreciation of the Requirements for Canada–U.S. Security," November 8, 1946, NAC, PCO Records, vol. 74, File D-19-2 (Sept.–Dec. 1946). The north was no longer a strategic barrier – "neither the United States nor Canada looked on the North as a *place* to be protected because of some intrinsic value," Kenneth Eyre has suggested; "it was seen as a *direction*, an exposed flank." Eyre, "Forty Years of Military Activity in the Canadian North, 1947–87," *Arctic* 40(4) (December 1987), 294.

30 Bercuson, "Continental Defense and Arctic Sovereignty," 154.

31 Barry, *"Continuity and Change"; Final Report of the Advisory Committee on Post-Hostilities Problems,* January/February 1945, and Extract of Minutes of Cabinet War Committee, DCER 11 (1944–45), Part II, 1567–74; Granatstein, *Canada's War*, 323; Bercuson, "Continental Defense and Arctic Sovereignty," 155; Bercuson, *True Patriot: The Life of Brooke Claxton, 1898–1960* (Toronto: University of Toronto Press, 1993), 154–55.

32 See Joseph Jockel, *No Boundaries Upstairs: Canada, the United States, and the Origins of North American Air Defence, 1945–1958* (Vancouver: University of British Columbia Press, 1987), chap. 2, "Joint Planning for Defence Cooperation, 1945–47."

33 American officials recognized Canadian insecurities about sovereignty in the north, but the concept of "defence against help" was not part of their worldview. The State Department knew it had to respect and attempt to allay Canadian sensitivities, but anticipated generally friendly and informal relations with their northern neighbour, even in the realm of security and defence issues. This was the type of arrangement they could expect, if the opinions of prominent Canadians like Blair Fraser could be believed. Fraser, speaking with Department of State officials in July 1945, said "that the Americans need have no fear of the willingness of Canadians to collaborate with the United States Armed Forces after the war. He said that the general staffs in Ottawa, particularly the Air Staff, were 'fed up' with the

British and criticized them more bitterly than the most outspoken American." Fraser also mentioned that he expected Canada's relations with Russia to deteriorate: Memorandum of Conversation, "Integration of Canadian and American Armed Forces," July 26, 1945, National Archives (Washington), RG 59 (State Department Records), Decimal File 1945–49.

34 See Robert A. Spencer, *Canada in World Affairs: From UN to NATO 1946–1949* (Toronto: Oxford University Press, 1959), 284–324.

35 Ibid.

36 Jockel, *No Boundaries Upstairs*, 9, 11.

37 May 9, 1946, *MKR*, III, 219–20; WLMK Diary, fiche 229, May 9, 1946; Bercuson, "Continental Defense and Arctic Sovereignty," 155–56. See also WLMK Diary, Fiche 231, July 9, 1946; Grant, *Sovereignty or Security?* 173.

38 *MKR*, III, 265–66. On the British perspective, see, for example, Top Secret Memorandum, "United States Bases in Canada," n.d. (November 1946), NAC, MG 26 J4, vol. 380, file Defence 1946–47, and Public Records Office (PRO), CAB 131/5, Defence Committee Minutes, January 2, 1947, 3–4.

39 A *Financial Post* article in late June 1946, suggesting that US members of the PJBD had issued Canada a virtual ultimatum on northern defence and offered to build, equip, and operate series of Arctic bases, tweaked King's political antennae and evoked a warranted corrective from the prime minister himself in the House of Commons. See "Canada 'Another Belgium' in U.S. Base Proposal?" *Financial Post*, June 29, 1946, 1–2; "Mr. King's Denial," ibid., July 6, 1946, 1; Jockel, *No Boundaries Upstairs*, 24; Grant, *Sovereignty or Security?* 177; Bercuson, "Continental Defense and Arctic Sovereignty," 158–59. The State Department indicated it would be willing to issue a joint denial in appreciation of Canadian concerns, but the Canadian government declined the offer. "Memorandum for the Prime Minister," June 27, 1946, NAC, RG 25 G2 Acc. 84–85/226 vol. 11, File 9061–40.

40 Bercuson, "Continental Defense and Arctic Sovereignty," 160; WLMK diary, fiche 236, November 14, 1946; MKR, III, 367.

41 Ron Purver, "The Arctic in Canadian Security Policy, 1945 to Present," in D.B. Dewitt and D.

Leyton-Brown, eds., *Canada's International Security Policy* (Scarborough, ON: Prentice Hall, 1995), 82–84; James Eayrs, *In Defence of Canada, vol. 3: Peacemaking and Deterrence* (Toronto: University of Toronto Press), 343–44; Bercuson, "Continental Defense and Arctic Sovereignty," 161. Joseph Jockel had pointed out, however, that Canadian officials (including King), and historians later, failed to grasp the spirit of senior thinking in the United States. Acheson, when he spoke with the president before the meeting, wanted President Truman to have King make "a basic decision" about the Canadian–American defence relationship. In fact, Truman and Acheson themselves were not aware of the details King claimed to have "converted" them on. The president and secretary of state did not discuss any details and the Americans thus had no specific agenda; therefore the diplomatic officials could be flexible to Canadian concerns and needs. Second, the MCC itself transferred mixed signals. Canada was not of overwhelming military importance to the United States, and the Americans did not wish to erect a Maginot Line across the far reaches of the continent. Senior Canadian defence and political decision-makers were, by contrast, extremely interested in American military decisions and mistakenly assumed the United States was equally interested in Canada. Senior American officials assumed that a close, informal, and friendly working relationship had been establish with a faithful ally to the north, and thus the left the management of this relationship to less senior officials. See Jockel, "The Canada–United States Military Co-operation Committee and Continental Air Defence, 1946," *Canadian Historical Review* 64(3) (September 1983), 352–77. If senior American officials can be criticized, it is not for having sinister strategic designs for Canada, but perhaps for not devoting enough specific attention to Canada. The plan that King saw as so threatening merely faded away without any real backing in the Pentagon.

42 Top secret memorandum, J. Graham Parsons, State Department Member, PJBD, to Secretary of State, January 24, 1947, National Archives (Washington), RG 59, PJBD, File: 36th Rec-

ommendation: General Principles. Parsons also noted that Canadian approval for the revised recommendation, "having regard for Canada's historic ties with the United Kingdom, is regarded by the Canadian Government as a momentous decision in that it will increasingly orient Canada's forces towards the United States."

43 Gordon Smith defined the sector principle as "Each state with a continental Arctic coastline automatically falls heir to all islands lying between this coastline and the North Pole, which are enclosed by longitudinal lines drawn from the eastern and western extremities of the same coastline to the Pole": "Sovereignty in the North: The Canadian Aspect of an International Problem," in R.St.J. Macdonald, ed., *The Arctic Frontier* (Toronto: University of Toronto Press, 1966).

44 WLMK diary, November 22, 1946, MKR, III, 370; February 12, 1947, IV, 24–25; House of Commons, *Debates*, February 12, 1947, 359–61; Bercuson, "Continental Defense and Arctic Sovereignty," 155. For the full text of the press release see *Foreign Relations of the United States 1947*, vol. 3, 104–05.

45 Memorandum, May 1, 1946, NAC, RG 25, vol. 3347, file 9061-A-40 pt.1; G.W. Smith, *Canada's Arctic Archipelago: 100 Years of Canadian Jurisdiction* (Ottawa: DIAND, 1980).

46 Memorandum from DEA to Cabinet Defence Committee, May 30, 1946, DCER 12 (1946), 1561–64.

47 C.D. Howe, March 4, 1947, House of Commons, *Debates*, 990; N.D. Bankes, "Forty Years of Canadian Sovereignty Assertion in the Arctic, 1947–87," *Arctic* 40/4 (December 1987), 287.

48 See Robert A. Spencer, *Canada in World Affairs: From UN to NATO 1946–1949* (Toronto: Oxford University Press, 1959), 310; "British Press Praises New Canada–U.S. Pact," *Montreal Star*, February 14, 1947, 21; "Canada–U.S. Defence: French-Canadian Press Applauds Arrangement," ibid., February 20, 1947, 12; "Our Defence Can't Wait," ibid., February 14, 1947, 12; Ansel E. Talbert, "US–Canadian 'Electronic Front' is 2000 Miles North of Border," *Washington Post*, April 6, 1947, 3B.

49 See, for example, Minutes of the Cabinet De-

fence Committee Meeting, August 16, 1947, DCER 13 (1947), 1505, 1510. President Truman himself appeared before the House in June and assured parliament that participation in bilateral defence was "on the basis of equality, and the sovereignty of each is carefully respected." House of Commons, *Debates*, June 11, 1947, 4063.

50 Bercuson, "Continental Defense and Arctic Sovereignty," 163–66.

51 For example, Shelagh Grant purported to have evidence of U.S. intentions to undertake northern Canadian security unilaterally (by right of the Monroe Doctrine), and thus undermine Canadian sovereignty, if Canada did not comply with its designs. A planning document created by a USAAF intelligence official in October 1946 is used as an indication of this serious contingency plan. Further reading and contextualizing of the report, however, undermines the idea that it represented a serious potential threat to Canadian sovereignty. By all appearances the report was only a minor planning document, by no means a statement of policy. It explicitly advocated that the United States instead take steps to overcome "Canada's pronounced national sensitivity regarding her territorial integrity and independence." Even if the report was taken at face value, it proposed a course that placed a clear premium on co-operation with the Canadians, not violation of their sovereignty: Office of PC/S Intelligence, USAAF, "USAAF Study on Problems of Joint Defence in the Arctic," October 29, 1946, as cited by Grant, *Sovereignty or Security?* 159, and the full text of the report, appendix G, 302–09. David Bercuson observed that she misrepresented or misunderstood "internally generated 'think' pieces, discussing hypothetical situations," that did not constitute official U.S. policy – "in fact, there is not a shred of evidence that any top-level US policy body ever disputed Canada's claims to the Arctic Archipelago": David Bercuson, review of Grant, *Sovereignty or Security?* in *Canadian Historical Review* (1989), 587–88.

52 Memorandum on "United States Activities and Official Personnel in Canada," Minutes of Second Meeting of Advisory Council on

Northern Development, June 1, 1948, DCER 14 (1948), 1526–27. Lester B. Pearson was extremely positive about the Americans after the meetings in December 1946. See PRO, CAB 131/3, Cabinet Defence Committee minutes, Annex I, 1–2.

53 I would be remiss to suggest that there were no voices in the United States administration that were cause for Canadian alarm during the war. Perhaps foremost among them was Adolf A. Berle, assistant to the secretary of state and economic adviser to Roosevelt, who envisioned a "new American Empire" (predicated on British defeat) that would see a reorganization of the economic life of the western hemisphere into "one continent and one economy" (in the words of Hugh Keenleyside). Grant suggested that he later expanded this vision to the Arctic by stating that American (rather than Canadian) control over Greenland represented the first triumphant military implementation of the Monroe Doctrine on a frontier. She then ties this mindset to the U.S. War Department's rejection of Ottawa's request to establish a Canadian military mission in Washington in 1941. Grant, *Sovereignty or Security?* 58, 63–64, and quote from Berle Diary, February 13, 1941, in Grant, 63. There is no indication that Berle's vision was prevalent or pervasive in official circles, and to characterize American policy on such a basis neglects the American bureaucratic politics at play during the war. Even Malcolm MacDonald conceded in early 1943 that most American control over the northwest projects had been locally directed (and not from Washington), and that the War Department largely ignored the State Department during the period. Furthermore, the high commissioner himself recognized that there could be no question as to "the good faith of the American Administration in supporting the agreements which they have made with the Canadian Government." Memo to WLMK, April 6, 1943, reprinted in Grant, *Sovereignty or Security?* appendix D, 271–72. Certainly the administration's co-operation and accommodation with the Canadian government over the northwest projects prevailed over any ill-conceived plans among local American authorities for post-war domination over the region. The array of competing American interests did not allow men such as Berle or local officials to implement their "pipe dreams" as the state-sanctioned, strategic policy assumed by the more conspiracy-minded historians.

54 Jockel, *No Boundaries Upstairs*, 20.

55 Grant, *Sovereignty or Security?* 156.

56 Stacey makes this same comment in *Mackenzie King and the Atlantic Triangle*, 67.

10. Struthers: Unequal Citizenship: The Residualist Legacy in the Canadian Welfare State

1 According to a study of economic well-being within fourteen OECD nations covered by the Luxembourg Income Study, the United States in 1997 (the most recent year for which comparative data are available) had the highest overall poverty rate (18 percent) and the highest rate of income inequality (a Gini coefficient of after-tax household income of 0.3869). Canada ranked in the second tier of OECD nations with a poverty rate of 12.4 percent and a Gini coefficient of 0.3019. In contrast, Sweden's poverty rate was 8.65 percent; its Gini coefficient was 0.2530. See Lars Orsberg and Andrew Sharpe, "International Comparisons of Trends in Economic Well-being," paper presented to the annual meeting of the American Economic Association, January 7–9, 2000; revised February 28, 2000, 23, 28, and Table 4. Available at http://www.csls.ca. See also Bruce Little, "Canada in the Middle of Income Ranking," *The Globe and Mail*, "Amazing Facts," May 12, 2000.

2 *Saturday Night*, February 1993, 41, as cited in "Introduction" to David Thomas, ed., *Canada and the United States: Differences That Count* (Peterborough: Broadview Press, 1993), 18.

3 Antonia Maioni, "The Canadian Welfare State at Century's End," *International Journal of Canadian Studies* 16 (Fall 1997), 177; Keith Banting, "Visions of the Welfare State," in Shirley B. Steward, ed., *The Future of Social Welfare Systems in Canada and the United Kingdom* (Halifax: Institute for Research on Public Policy, 1986), 151; Raymond B. Blake, Penny E. Bryden, and J. Frank Strain, eds., "Preface" to *The Welfare State in Canada: Past, Present, and Future* (Concord, ON: Irwin, 1997), vii.

4 Pat and Hugh Armstrong with Claudia Fegan, *Universal Healthcare: What the United States Can Learn From the Canadian Experience* (New York: New Press, 1998), 1; Robert Evans, "Less is More: Contrasting Styles in Health Care," in Thomas, ed., *Canada and the United States*, 21.

5 Maoini, "The Canadian Welfare State at Century's End," Table 1, 75; Julia S. O'Connor, "Social Justice, Social Citizenship, and the Welfare State, 1965–1995: Canada in Comparative Context," in Rick Helmes-Hayes and James Curtis, eds., *The Vertical Mosaic Revisited* (Toronto: University of Toronto Press, 1998), Table 1, 189; Keith Banting, "The Welfare State and Inequality in the 1980s," *Canadian Review of Sociology and Anthropology* 24(3) (1987); John Myles, "When Markets Fail: Social Welfare in Canada and the United States," in Gosta Esping-Andersen, ed., *Welfare States in Transition: National Adaptations in Global Economies* (London: Sage Publications, 1996); Mel Hurtig, *Pay the Rent or Feed the Kids: the Tragedy and Disgrace of Poverty in Canada* (Toronto: McClelland and Stewart, 1999), Figure 5, 17; Orsberg and Sharpe, "International Comparisons of Trends in Economic Well-Being," Table 4. Between 1994 and 1998, income inequality in Canada began to widen once again. By 1998 Canada's Gini coefficient for after-tax household income had risen to 0.3150, "its highest level in the 28 years Statscan has been making these calculations": Bruce Little, "Here's How the Rich–Poor Gap Grew," *The Globe and Mail*, "Amazing Facts" June 19, 2000.

6 As cited in Hurtig, *Pay the Rent*, Table 5, 17; Figure 41, 182. See also O'Connor, "Social Justice, Social Citizenship and the Welfare State," 191; Gosta Esping-Andersen, *The Three Worlds of Welfare Capitalism* (Princeton: Princeton University Press, 1990), 54; Gregg M. Olsen, "Locating the Canadian Welfare State: Family Policy and Health Care in Canada, Sweden, and the United States," *Canadian Journal of Sociology* 19(1) (1994), 1–20.

7 Michael J. Prince, "From Health and Welfare to Stealth and Farewell: Federal Social Policy, 1980–2000," in Leslie A. Pal, ed., *How Ottawa Spends 1999–2000, Shape Shifting: Canadian Governance Toward the 21st Century* (Don Mills, ON: Oxford University Press, 1999), 180–81.

8 James Struthers, *No Fault of Their Own: Unemployment and the Canadian Welfare State, 1914–1941* (Toronto: University of Toronto Press, 1983), 200–07. For the gendered dimensions of the residualist origins of unemployment insurance in Canada see Ruth Roach Pierson, "Gender and the Unemployment Insurance Debates in Canada, 1934–1940," *Labour/le Travail* 25 (Spring 1990), 77–103.

9 On the influence of Keynesianism within the federal civil service between 1938 and 1946 see Doug Owram, *The Government Generation: Canadian Intellectuals and the State, 1900–1945* (Toronto: University of Toronto Press, 1986), and Robert Bryce, *Maturing in Hard Times: Canada's Department of Finance through the Great Depression* (Montreal/Kingston: McGill-Queen's University Press, 1986), 232. For a different perspective see Robert Malcolm Campbell, *Grand Illusions: The Politics of the Keynesian Experience in Canada, 1945–1975* (Peterborough: Broadview Press, 1987).

10 Ibid., 120–24.

11 Ibid., 177–82; Alvin Finkel, "Paradise Postponed: A Re-examination of the Green Book Proposals of 1945," *Journal of the Canadian Historical Association* 4 (1993), 122–23, 126, 130, 140.

12 W.L.M. King, *Industry and Humanity* (1918; Toronto: University of Toronto Press, 1973), 222.

13 Struthers, *No Fault*, 199.

14 Ibid., 179.

15 On the origins of the 1956 Unemployment Assistance Act see James Struthers, "Shadows From the Thirties: The Federal Government and Unemployment Assistance, 1941–1956" in Jacqueline S. Ismael, ed., *The Canadian Welfare State: Evolution and Transition* (Edmonton: University of Alberta Press, 1987), 3–32; on seasonal benefits within unemployment insurance see L. Richard Lund, "Fishing for Stamps: The Origins and Development of Unemployment Insurance for Canada's Commercial Fisheries, 1941–71," *Journal of the Canadian Historical Association* 6 (1995), 179–208.

16 On the history of Canada's first old age pension scheme and the movement for universality in pensions see James Snell, *The Citizen's Wage: the State and the Elderly in Canada, 1900–1951* (Toronto: University of Toronto Press, 1996), and James Struthers, "Building a Culture of Retirement: Class, Politics, and Pensions in Post World War II Ontario," *Journal of the Canadian Historical Association* 8 (1997), 259–70.

17 As Reg Whitaker has argued persuasively, by the late 1940s "it is difficult … to avoid the conclusion that the Liberal party had indeed become the Government party to the extent that the question of whether, for example, the bureaucrats were Liberals or whether, conversely, the Liberals had themselves become bureaucrats, is rather problematic": *The Government Party: Organizing and Financing the Liberal Party of Canada, 1930–58* (Toronto: University of Toronto Press, 1977), 167. An excellent illustration of this point can be found in the close collaboration between George Davidson, deputy minister of health and welfare, and Paul Martin, minister of national health and welfare, in shaping Ottawa's decision to embrace a flat-rate, minimalist universal pension between 1949 and 1951. See, for example, National Archives of Canada (NA), RG 29, vol. 2376, file 275-4-2 (2), George Davidson to Paul Martin, "Why we should proceed with old age pensions," September 21, 1950.

18 John S. Morgan, "Social Security: One Step at a Time," *The Canadian Forum* 31 (December 1951), 198–99; NA, RG 29, vol. 2376, file 275-4-1 (1), "Findings" of Parliamentary Committee on Old Age Security, June 1950; James Struthers, "Family Allowances, Old Age Security, and the Construction of Entitlement in the Canadian Welfare State, 1943–1951," in Peter Neary and J.L. Granatstein, eds., *The Veterans Charter and Post–World War II Canada* (Montreal/Kingston: McGill-Queen's University Press, 1998), 189–98.

19 Struthers, "Building a Culture of Retirement," 270; P.E. Bryden, *Planners and Politicians: Liberal Politics and Social Policy, 1957–1968* (Montreal/Kingston: McGill-Queen's University Press, 1997), 17–20.

20 Bryden, *Planners and Politicians*, chap. 3, 54–77.

21 For middle-income Canadian workers with a lifetime of average earnings in manufacturing, the income replacement rate of public pensions within Canada in 1980 was ".34 and .49 for single workers and one-earner couples respectively. The corresponding figures in the United States were .44 and .66": John Myles and Les Teichroew, "The Politics of Dualism: Pension Policy in Canada," in Jill Quadagno and John Myles, eds., *States, Labor Markets, and the Future of Old Age Policy* (Philadelphia: Temple University Press, 1991), 101. By 1990, however, public pension replacement rates in the two countries had converged, and for low-income retirees were markedly higher within Canada. See Myles, "When Markets Fail," Table 5.5, 125. However, Canadian public pension provisions are still low in relation to most OECD nations. Out of sixteen leading industrial nations, Canada ranked twelfth in its percentage of average wage replacement through public pensions; see *The Economist*, November 30–December 6, 1996; Richard Deaton, *The Political Economy of Pensions: Power, Politics, and Social Change in Canada, Britain, and the United States* (Vancouver: University of British Columbia Press, 1989), 165–66; Bryden, *Planners and Politicians*, 93.

22 Struthers, "Building a Culture of Retirement" 271–76; Bryden, *Planners and Politicians*, 92–99.

23 Myles and Teichroew, "The Politics of Dualism," 93; Canada, Special Senate Committee on Retirement Age Policies, *Retirement Without Tears* (Ottawa: Queen's Printer, 1979); Canada, Task Force on Retirement Income Policy, *The Retirement Income System in Canada: Problems and Alternative Policies for Reform* (Hull: Task Force on Retirement Income Policy, 1980); Keith Banting, "Institutional Conservatism: Federalism and Pension Reform," in Jacqueline S. Ismael, ed., *Canadian Social Welfare Policy: Federal and Provincial Dimensions* (Montreal and Kingston: McGill-Queen's University Press, 1985).

24 Rodney Haddow, *Poverty Reform in Canada: 1958–1978: State and Class Influences on Policy-Making* (Montreal and Kingston: McGill-Queen's University Press, 1993), 99–100; 108–09.

25 Kenneth Bryden, *Old Age Pensions and Policy-Making in Canada* (Montreal and Kingston: McGill-Queen's University Press, 1974), 130–33; http://www.hrdc-drhc.gc.ca/isp/oas/ispb184.shtml, 16/12/99; Myles, "When Markets Fail," 123.

26 Prince, "From Health and Welfare to Stealth and Farewell," 170–74. In his federal budget, which revealed an unexpectedly large fiscal surplus, Finance Minister Paul Martin restored full indexing to OAS, acknowledging the political force of the senior citizens' lobby on this issue.

27 Margaret Little, *"No Car, No Radio, No Liquor Permit": The Moral Regulation of Mothers' Allowances in Ontario, 1920–1997* (Don Mills, ON: Oxford University Press, 1998); James Struthers, *The Limits of Affluence: Welfare in Ontario, 1920–1970* (Toronto: University of Toronto Press, 1994), chap. 1, 19–49; Nancy Christie, *Engendering the State: Family, Work, and Welfare in Canada* (Toronto: University of Toronto Press, 2000), chaps. 3 and 4, 94–159.

28 J.W. Pickersgill and Donald Forster, eds., *The Mackenzie King Record: Vol. 2, 1944/1945*, 35, excerpt from King Diary, June 29, 1944.

29 Struthers, "Family Allowances, Old Age Security, and the Construction of Entitlement," 179.

30 Ibid., 185.

31 Ibid., 186–87.

32 Laurel Sefton Macdowell, "The Formation of the Canadian Industrial Relations System During World War II," *Labour/Le travail* 3 (1978), 175–96; Dominique Jean, "Family Allowances and Family Autonomy: Quebec Families Encounter the Welfare State, 1945–1955," in Bettina Bradbury, ed., *Canadian Family History: Selected Readings* (Toronto: Copp Clark Pitman, 1992); Bob Russell, "The Politics of Labour Force Reproduction: Funding Canada's Social Wage, 1917–1946," *Studies in Political Economy* 14 (Summer 1984); Doug Owram, *The Government Generation: Canadian Intellectuals and the State* (Toronto: University of Toronto Press, 1986), 311–14; Struthers, "Family Allowances, Old Age Security, and the Construction of Entitlement," 179–89.

33 For a recent and differing interpretation see Christie, *Engendering the State*, chap. 7, 249–309.

34 Haddow, *Poverty Reform in Canada*, 92–101.

35 Prince, "From Health and Welfare to Stealth and Farewell," 172–74.

36 Douglas Durst, "Phoenix or Fizzle?: Background to Canada's New National Child Benefit," in Douglas Durst, ed., *Canada's National Child Benefit: Phoenix or Fizzle?* (Halifax: Fernwood, 1999), 11–14; Ken Battle, "The National Child Benefit: Best Thing Since Medicare or New Poor Law?" in ibid., 40–41; for a well-documented study of extent and depth of child poverty in Canada see Mel Hurtig, *Pay the Rent or Feed the Kids: The Tragedy and Disgrace of Poverty in Canada* (Toronto: McClelland and Stewart, 1999). For low income working families a maximum $1,293 annual NCBS payment is stacked on top of the $1,151 basic annual CCTB available for the first child. For a second child the NCBS adds $1,087 to this amount. Monthly NCBS cash payments, however, are not available in most provinces to children of families on social assistance. http://www.nationalchildbenefit.ca/ncb/govtofcan4.shtml

37 http://www.campaign2000.ca/rc/unsccMAY02/un3.html

38 Battle, "The National Child Benefit," 39, 56–57. The combined total of federal spending on these three programs (in 1998 dollars) was $6.9 billion in 1984, compared with $6 billion in 1998. http://www.nationalchildbenefit.ca/ncb/NCB-2002/3.html

39 Jane Pulkingham and Gordon Ternowetsky, "Child Poverty and the CCTB/NCB: Why Most Poor Children Gain Nothing," in Durst, *Canada's National Child Benefit*, 103–14; Pete Hudson, "So There You Go!" in ibid., 116–17.

11. Westhues: Sociology for a New Century: Mackenzie King's First Career

1 See Seymour Martin Lipset, "The Sorry State of American Sociology," *Sociological Forum* 9(2) (1994), 199–200; Irving L. Horowitz, *The Decomposition of Sociology* (New York: Oxford, 1993); Larry T. Reynolds, "Two Deadly Diseases and One Nearly Fatal Cure: The Sorry State of American Sociology," *American Sociologist* 29 (Spring 1998), 20–37; Joe R. Feagin, "Soul-Searching in Sociology: Is the Discipline in Crisis," *Chronicle of Higher Education*, October 15, 1999, p. B4ff; and many others.

2 See William V. D'Antonio, "Recruiting Sociologists in a Time of Changing Opportunities," in T.C. Halliday and M. Janowitz, eds., *Sociology and Its Publics* (Chicago: University of Chicago Press,1992), 99–136.

3 See Richard Hofstadter, *Social Darwinism in American Thought* (Boston: Beacon Press, 1944).

4 William Buxton and Stephen P. Turner, "From Education to Expertise: Sociology as a 'Profession,'" in T.C. Halliday and M. Janowitz, eds., *Sociology and Its Publics* (Chicago: University of Chicago Press, 1992), 373–408.

5 See I. McKay, "Changing the Subject(s) of the 'History of Canadian Sociology': The Case of Colin McKay and Spencerian Marxism, 1890–1914," *Canadian Journal of Sociology* 23 (Spring 1998), 389–412.

6 Herbert Brown Ames was also linked to Kitchener in a tangential fashion. In 1921 the Ames-Holden Tire Factory was established in Kitchener.

7 Herbert Brown Ames, *The City below the Hill* (1897; Toronto: University of Toronto Press, 1972), 6.

8 For details of this period see R. MacGregor Dawson, *William Lyon Mackenzie King: A Political Biography, 1874–1923* (Toronto: University of Toronto Press, 1958).

9 See John English and Kenneth McLaughlin, *Kitchener: An Illustrated History* (Waterloo: Wilfrid Laurier University Press, 1983).

10 See Caroline W. Montgomery, "Settlements," in W. Bliss, ed., *The New Encyclopedia of Social Reform* (New York: Funk and Wagnalls, 1910), 1106–07; reprinted in Kenneth Westhues et al., *The Working Centre: Experiment in Social Change* (Kitchener: Working Centre, 1995).

11 See Mary Jo Deegan, *Jane Addams and the Men of the Chicago School, 1892–1918* (New Brunswick, NJ: Transaction, 1988).

12 Quoted in Deegan, *Jane Addams*, 1988.

13 Ibid., 84.

14 Ibid., 89.

15 Ibid., 200.

16 See W. L. Mackenzie King, "Trade-Union Organization in the United States," *Journal of Political Economy* (March 1897), 210–15.

17 See Sally Zerker, "Printers, Technology, and Unionism," in K. Lundy and B. Warme, eds., *Work in the Canadian Context* (Toronto: Butterworths, 1986), 122–30.

18 W.L. Mackenzie King, "The International Typographical Union," *Journal of Political Economy* (September 1897), 458–84 at 460.

19 Quoted in Dawson, *William Lyon Mackenzie King*, 80.

20 See also Charlotte Gray, *Mrs. King: The Life and Times of Isabel Mackenzie King* (Toronto: Viking Penguin, 1997).

21 John Kenneth Galbraith, *Age of Uncertainty* (Boston: Houghton Mifflin, 1977), 61.

22 Quoted in John Robert Colombo, *Colombo's Canadian Quotations* (Edmonton: Hurtig, 1974), 529.

23 See Robert C. Bannister, *Sociology and Scientism, The American Quest for Objectivity, 1880–1940* (Chapel Hill: University of North Carolina Press, 1987).

24 See Russell Jacoby, *The Last Intellectuals: American Culture in the Age of Academe* (New York: Basic Books, 1987).

25 Deegan, *Jane Addams*, 19.

26 See Allen F. Davis and Mary Lynn McCree, eds., *Eighty Years at Hull-House* (Chicago: Quadrangle Books, 1969).

27 See *Good Work News* (Kitchener: Working Centre Quarterly Newsletter, 1982); Kenneth Westhues et al., *The Working Centre: Experiment in Social Change* (Kitchener: Working Centre, 1995).

28 W. L. Mackenzie King, *Industry and Humanity* (Toronto: Thomas Allen, 1918), 480.

Further Reading

Prepared by P. Whitney Lackenbauer

Bibliographies

Grant, Madeline. "William Lyon Mackenzie King: A Bibliography," in *Mackenzie King: Widening the Debate*, eds. English, John and J.O. Stubbs. Toronto, Macmillan Press, 1978. 221-53.

Henderson, George F., comp. *W.L. Mackenzie King: A Bibliography and Research Guide*. Toronto, University of Toronto Press, 1998.

Owram, Doug, ed. *Canadian History: A Reader's Guide, vol. 2: Confederation to Present.* Toronto, University of Toronto Press, 1994.

Books

Adachi, Ken. *The Enemy That Never Was: A History of the Japanese Canadians.* Toronto, McClelland and Stewart, 1991.

Beck, J. Murray. *Pendulum of Power: Canada's Federal Elections.* Scarborough, Prentice-Hall of Canada, 1968.

Bercuson, David J. *True Patriot: The Life of Brooke Claxton, 1898-1960.* Toronto, University of Toronto Press, 1993.

Bertrand, Luc. *L'énigmatique Mackenzie King.* Vanier, Éditions L'Interligne, 2000.

Betcherman, Lita-Rose. *Ernest Lapointe: Mackenzie King's Great Quebec Lieutenant.* Toronto, University of Toronto Press, 2002.

Bliss, Michael. *Right Honourable Men: The Descent of Canadian Politics from Macdonald to Mulroney.* Toronto, HarperCollins, 1994.

Bothwell, Robert, Ian Drummond, and John English. *Canada 1900-1945*, rev. ed. Toronto, University of Toronto Press, 1990.

Bothwell, Robert, Ian Drummond, and John English. *Canada Since 1945: Power, Politics, and Provincialism*, 2nd ed. Toronto, University of Toronto Press, 1989.

Brennan, Patrick H. *Reporting the Nation's Business: Press-Government Relations During the Liberal Years, 1935-1957.* Toronto, University of Toronto Press, 1994.

Brown, Robert Craig and Ramsay Cook. *Canada 1896-1921: A Nation Transformed.* Toronto, McClelland and Stewart, 1974.

Cook, Ramsay. *The Politics of John W. Dafoe and the Free Press.* Toronto, University of Toronto Press, 1963.

Cook, Ramsay. *The Regenerators: Social Criticism in Late Victorian Canada.* Toronto, University of Toronto Press, 1985.

Craven, Paul. *'An Impartial Umpire': Industrial Relations and the Canadian State, 1900-1911.* Toronto, University of Toronto Press, 1980.

Creighton, Donald. *The Forked Road: Canada 1939-1957.* Toronto, McClelland and Stewart, 1976.

Dawson, R. McGregor. *The Conscription Crisis of 1944.* Toronto, University of Toronto Press, 1961.

Dawson, R. McGregor. *William Lyon Mackenzie King: A Political Biography, vol. 1: 1874-1923.* Toronto, University of Toronto Press, 1958.

Dziuban, Stanley W. *Military Relations Between the United States and Canada, 1939-1945.* Washington, Office of the Chief of Military History, Department of the Army, 1959.

Eayrs, James. *In Defence of Canada: From the Great War to the Great Depression, vol. 1.* Toronto, University of Toronto Press, 1964.

Eayrs, James. *In Defence of Canada: Appeasement and Rearmament, vol. 2.* Toronto, University of Toronto Press, 1965.

Eayrs, James. *In Defence of Canada: Growing Up Allied, vol. 3.* Toronto, University of Toronto Press, 1980.

English, John. *The Decline of Politics: The Conservatives and the Party System, 1901-20.* Toronto, University of Toronto Press, 1977.

English, John and Kenneth McLaughlin. *Kitchener: An Illustrated History.* Waterloo, Wilfrid Laurier University Press, 1983.

English, John and J.O. Stubbs, eds. *Mackenzie King: Widening the Debate.* Toronto, Macmillan Press, 1978.

Esberey, Joy. *Knight of the Holy Spirit: A Study of William Lyon Mackenzie King.* Toronto, University of Toronto Press, 1980.

Ferns, H.S. & Ostry, B. *The Age of Mackenzie King: The Rise of the Leader.* London, William Heinemann, 1955.

Graham, Roger. *Arthur Meighen: A Biography.* 3 vols. Toronto, Clarke, Irwin, 1960-1965.

Graham, Roger, ed. *The King-Byng Affair, 1926: A Question of Responsible Government.* Toronto, Copp Clark, 1967.

Granatstein, J.L. *Canada's War: The Politics of the Mackenzie King Government, 1939-1945,* 2nd ed. Toronto, University of Toronto Press, 1990.

Granatstein, J.L. *Conscription in the Second World War, 1939-1945.* Toronto, Ryerson Press, 1969.

Granatstein, J.L. *How Britain's Weakness Forced Canada into the Arms of the United States.* Toronto, University of Toronto Press, 1989.

Granatstein, J.L. *Mackenzie King: His Life and World.* Scarborough, McGraw-Hill Ryerson, 1977.

Granatstein, J.L. and J.M. Hitsman. *Broken Promises: A History of Conscription in Canada.* Toronto, Oxford University Press, 1977.

Grant, Shelagh D. *Sovereignty or Security? Government Policy in the Canadian North, 1936-1950.* Vancouver, University of British Columbia Press, 1988.

Gray, Charlotte. *Mrs. King: The Life and Times of Isabel Mackenzie King.* Toronto, Viking, 1997.

Hardy, Reginald. *Mackenzie King of Canada: A Biography.* Toronto, Oxford University Press, 1949.

Haydon, Andrew. *Mackenzie King and the Liberal Party*. Toronto, Allen, 1930.

Hayes, Geoffrey. *Waterloo County: An Illustrated History*. Kitchener, Waterloo Historical Society, 1997.

Hutchison, Bruce. *The Incredible Canadian: A Candid Portrait of Mackenzie King: His Work, His Times, and His Nation*. Toronto, Longmans Green, 1953.

LeSueur, William D. *William Lyon Mackenzie: A Reinterpretation*, edited and with an introduction by A.B. McKillop. Toronto, Macmillan, 1979.

Lewis, John. *Mackenzie King, The Man: His Achievements*. Toronto, Morang, 1925.

Ludwig, Emil. *Mackenzie King: A Portrait Sketch*. Toronto, Macmillan, 1944.

King, William Lyon Mackenzie. *Industry and Humanity: A Study in the Principles Underlying industrial Reconstruction*. Toronto, Thomas Allen, 1918. Reprinted with an introduction by David Jay Bercuson, Toronto, University of Toronto Press, 1973.

MacFarlane, John. *Ernest Lapointe and Quebec's Influence on Mackenzie King's Foreign Policy*. Toronto, University of Toronto Press, 1999.

Mackenzie King: A Personal View. Waterloo, Association for Canadian Studies, 1977.

Martin, Paul. *A Very Public Life*. 2 vols. Ottawa, Deneau, 1983-85.

McGregor, Fred A. *The Fall and Rise of Mackenzie King, 1911-1919*. Toronto, Macmillan, 1962.

McLaughlin, Kenneth. *Waterloo: An Illustrated History*. Burlington, Ont., Windsor Publications, 1990.

mills, rych. *Victoria Park: 100 Years of a Park and Its People*. Kitchener, Victoria Park Historical Committee, 1996.

mills, rych. *Kitchener 1880-1960*. Portsmouth, NH, Arcadia Publishing, 2003.

Morton, W. L. *The Progressive Party in Canada*. Toronto, University of Toronto Press, 1950.

Neatby, Blair. *The Politics of Chaos: Canada in the Thirties*. Toronto, Macmillan, 1972.

Neatby, Blair. *William Lyon Mackenzie King: The Lonely Heights, vol.2: 1924-1932*. Toronto, University of Toronto Press, 1970.

Neatby, Blair. *William Lyon Mackenzie King: The Prism of Unity, vol.3: 1933-1939*. Toronto, University of Toronto Press, 1975.

Nicolson, Murray. *Woodside and the Victorian Family of John King*. Studies in Archeology, Architecture and History. Ottawa, National Historic Parks and Sites Branch of Parks/Environment Canada, 1984.

Owram, Doug. *The Government Generation: Canadian Intellectuals and the State, 1900-1945*. Toronto, University of Toronto Press, 1986.

Pickersgill, J.W. *The Liberal Party*. Toronto, McClelland and Stewart, 1962.

Pickersgill, J.W. *Seeing Canada Whole: A Memoir*. Toronto, Fitzhenry and Whiteside, 1994.

Pickersgill, J.W. and Donald Forster, eds. *The Mackenzie King Record, vols. 1-4*. Toronto, University of Toronto Press, 1960-70.

Regehr, T. D. *The Beauharnois Scandal: A Story of Canadian Entrepreneurship and Politics*. Toronto, University of Toronto Press, 1990.

Roazen, Paul. *Canada's King: An Essay in Political Psychology*. Oakville, Mosaic Press, 1998.

Rogers, Norman. *Mackenzie King*. Toronto, G.N. Morang, 1935

Roy, Patricia, et al. *Mutual Hostages: Canadians and Japanese in the Second World War*. Toronto, University of Toronto Press, 1990.

Saint-Aubin, Bernard. *King et son époque*. Montreal, La Presse, 1982.

Smith, David E., *Regional Decline of a National Party: Liberals on the Prairies* (Toronto, University of Toronto Press, 1981)

Stacey, C.P. *Arms, Men and Governments: The War Policies of Canada, 1939-1945*. Ottawa: Queen's Printer, 1970.

Stacey, C.P. *Canada and the Age of Conflict: A History of Canadian External Relations. Vol.2: 1921-1948, The Mackenzie King Era*. Toronto, University of Toronto Press, 1981.

Stacey, C.P. *Mackenzie King and the Atlantic Triangle*. Toronto, Macmillan, 1977.

Stacey, C.P. *A Very Double Life: The Private World of Mackenzie King*. Toronto, Macmillan, 1976.

Struthers, James. *No Fault of Their Own: Unemployment and the Canadian Welfare State, 1914-1941*. Toronto, University of Toronto Press, 1983

Sunahara, Ann Gomer. *The Politics of Racism: The Uprooting of Japanese Canadians during the Second World War*. Toronto, James Lorimer, 1981.

Teatero, W.R. *Mackenzie King: A Man of Vision*. Don Mills, Nelson and Sons, 1978.

Thompson, John Herd with Allen Seager. *Canada, 1922-1939: Decades of Discord*. Toronto, McClelland and Stewart, 1985.

Valverde, Mariana. *The Age of Light, Soap and Water: Moral Reform in English Canada, 1885-1925*. Toronto, McClelland and Stewart, 1993.

Veatch, Richard. *Canada and the League of Nations*. Toronto, University of Toronto Press, 1975.

Von Baeyer, Edwinna. *Garden of Dreams: Kingsmere and Mackenzie King*. Toronto, Dundurn Press, 1990.

Ward, Norman, ed. *A Party Politician: The Memoirs of Chubby Power*. Toronto, Macmillan, 1966.

Ward, N. and Smith, D.E. *Jimmy Gardiner: Relentless Liberal*. Toronto, University of Toronto Press, 1990.

Ward, W. Peter. *White Canada Forever: Popular Attitudes and Public Policy Toward Orientals in British Columbia*, 3rd ed. Montreal, McGill-Queen's University Press, 2002.

Wardhaugh, Robert A. *Mackenzie King and the Prairie West*. Toronto, University of Toronto Press, 2000.

Whitaker, Reg. *The Government Party: Organizing and Financing the Liberal Party of Canada, 1930-1958*. Toronto, University of Toronto Press, 1977.

Articles and Chapters*

Baker, William M. "The Miners And The Mediator: The 1906 Lethbridge Strike and Mackenzie King." *Labour* 11 (1983). 89-117.

Baker, William M. "The Personal Touch: Mackenzie King, Harriett Reid, and the Springhill Strike, 1909-1911," *Labour* 13 (1984). 159-176.

Blackburn, Robert H. "Mackenzie King, William Mulock, James Mavor, and the University of Toronto Students' Revolt of 1895," *Canadian Historical Review* 69/4 (1988). 490-503.

* This section focuses on the period since the mid-1970s. For listings of earlier primary and secondary articles, see Madeline Grant, "William Lyon Mackenzie King: A Bibliography," in *Mackenzie King: Widening the Debate*, eds. John English and J.O. Stubbs (Toronto, Macmillan Press, 1978), 221-53 and George F. Henderson, comp., *W.L. Mackenzie King: A Bibliography and Research Guide* (Toronto, University of Toronto Press, 1998).

Byers, Daniel. "Mobilizing Canada: The National Resources Mobilization Act, the Department of National Defence, and Compulsory Military Service in Canada, 1940-1945," *Journal of the Canadian Historical Association* 7 (1996). 175-203.

Carter, John. "The Reciprocity Election of 1911: Waterloo North, A Case Study," *Waterloo Historical Society* 62 (1974). 77-87.

Cooper, Barry. "On Reading Industry and Humanity: A Study in the Rhetoric Underlying Liberal Management," *Journal of Canadian Studies* 13/4 (1978-79). 28-39.

Courtney, John C. "Mackenzie King and Prince Albert Constituency: The 1933 Redistribution," *Saskatchewan History* 29/1 (1976). 1-13.

Courtney, John C. "Prime Ministerial Character: An Examination of Mackenzie King's Political Leadership," *Canadian Journal of Political Science* 9/1 (1976). 77-100.

Craven, Paul. "King and Context: A Reply to Whitaker," *Labour* 4 (1979). 165-186.

Crowley, Terence A. "Mackenzie King and the 1911 Election," *Ontario History* 61/4 (1969). 181-196.

Dryden, Jean E. "The Mackenzie King Papers: An Archival Odyssey," *Archivaria* 6 (1978). 40-69.

Esberey, Joy E. "Personality and Politics: A New Look at the King-Byng Dispute," *Canadian Journal of Political Science* 6/1 (1973). 37-55.

Esberey, Joy E. "Prime Ministerial Character: An Alternative View," *Canadian Journal of Political Science* 9/1 (1976). 101-06.

Ferns, H. S. "Mackenzie King On Television," *British Journal of Canadian Studies* 3/2 (1988). 308-312.

Flanagan, Thomas. "Problems of Psychobiography," *Queen's Quarterly* 89/3 (1982). 596-610.

Fleming, R. B. "Hostess to a Nation." *Beaver* 77/4 (1997). 7-14.

Granatstein, J.L. and Robert Bothwell. "A Self-Evident National Duty, 1935-39," *Journal of Imperial and Commonwealth History* 3/2 (1975). 212-33.

Harbour, Frances V. "Conscription and Socialization: Four Canadian Ministers," *Armed Forces & Society* 15/2 (1989). 227-247.

Hayes, Geoffrey. "From Berlin to the Trek of the Conestoga: A Revisionist Approach to Waterloo County's German Identity," *Ontario History*, 91/2 (1999). 131-149.

Hillmer, Norman and Granatstein, J. L. "Historians Rank the Best and Worst Canadian Prime Ministers," *Maclean's*, April 21, 1997.

Hoogenraad, Maureen. "Mackenzie King in Berlin." *Archivist* 20/3 (1994). 19-21.

How, Douglas. "One Man's Mackenzie King," *Beaver* 78/5 (1998). 31, 33-37.

Humphries, Charles W. "Mackenzie King Looks at Two 1911 Elections," *Ontario History* 56/3 (1964). 203-206.

Keyserlingk, Robert H. "Mackenzie King's Spiritualism and His View of Hitler in 1939," *Journal of Canadian Studies* 20/4 (1985-86). 26-44.

Kurial, Richard. "Odd Man Out: Mackenzie King and the First Quebec Conference August 1943," *Journal of Unconventional History* 5/1 (1993). 60-87.

MacFarlane, John. "Double Vision: Ernest Lapointe, Mackenzie King and the Quebec Voice in Canadian Foreign Policy, 1935-1939," *Journal of Canadian Studies* 34/1 (1999). 93-111.

MacFarlane, John. "Mr. Lapointe, Mr. King, Quebec and Conscription," *Beaver* 75/2 (1995). 26-31.

Maitland, Leslie. "At Home with the Prime Ministers: National Historic Sites." *Archivist* 20/
3 (1994). 6-8.

Mallory, J. R. "Mackenzie King and the Origins of the Cabinet Secretariat," *Canadian Public
Administration* 19/2 (1976). 254-266.

Martin, Ged. "Mackenzie King, the Medium and the Messages," *British Journal of Canadian
Studies* 4/1 (1989). 109-135.

Martin, Joe. "William Lyon Mackenzie King: Canada's First Management Consultant?,"
Business Quarterly 56/1 (1991). 31-36.

Neatby, H. Blair. "Mackenzie King and the Depression: The Reluctant Reformer," *Canadian
Issues* 3 (1987). 39-49.

Neatby, H. Blair. "Mackenzie King and French Canada," *Journal of Canadian Studies* 11/1
(1976). 3-13.

Neatby, H. Blair. "Mackenzie King and the National Identity," *Transactions of the Historical
and Scientific Society of Manitoba* 24 (1967/68). 77-87.

Neatby, H. Blair. "The Political Ideas of William Lyon Mackenzie King," in *Les idées politique
des premiers ministres du Canada / The Political Ideas of the Prime Ministers of Canada*
ed. Marcel Hamelin. Ottawa: L'université d'Ottawa, 1969. 121-137.

Pennanen, Gary. "Battle of the Titans: Mitchell Hepburn, Mackenzie King, Franklin
Roosevelt, and the St. Lawrence Seaway," *Ontario History* 89/1 ((1997). 1-21.

Pollock, Fred E. "Roosevelt, the Ogdensburg Agreement, and the British Fleet: All Done
with Mirrors," *Diplomatic History* 5/3 (1981). 203-220.

Prang, Margaret. "Mackenzie King Woos Ontario, 1919-1921," *Ontario History* 58/1 (1966).
1-20.

Rea, J. E. "Clay from Feet to Forehead": The Mackenzie King Controversy." *Beaver* 73/2
(1993). 27-34.

Rea, J. E. "The Conscription Crisis: What Really Happened?" *Beaver* 74/2 (1994). 10-19.

Read, Colin and Donald Forster. "'Opera Bouffe': Mackenzie King, Mitch Hepburn, the
Appointment of the Lieutenant Governor and the Closing of Government House, Toronto, 1937." *Ontario History* 69/4 (1977). 239-256.

Salaff, Stephen. "The Diary and the Cenotaph: Racial and Atomic Fever," *Canadian Dimension* 13/3 (1978). 8-11.

Sauer, Angelika. "Goodwill and Profit: Mackenzie King and Canadian Appeasement," in *A
Country of Limitations: Canada and the World in 1939 / Un pays dans la gene: le Canada
et le Monde en 1939* ed. Norman Hillmer et. al. Ottawa, Canadian Committee for the
History of the Second World War, 1996.

Senese, Donald. "Willie and Felix: Ill-Matched Acquaintances," *Ontario History* 84/2 (1992).
141-148.

Sharp, Mitchell. "Decision-Making in the Federal Cabinet," *Canadian Public Administration* 19/1 (1976). 1-7.

Spaulding, William B. "Why Rockefeller Supported Medical Education In Canada: The William
Lyon Mackenzie King Connection," *Canadian Bulletin of Medical History* 10/1 (1993). 67-76.

Stacey, C.P. "The Divine Mission: Mackenzie King and Hitler", *Canadian Historical Review*
61/4 (1980). 502-512.

Stacey, C. P. "'A Dream of My Youth': Mackenzie King in North York," *Ontario History* 76/3
(1984). 273-286.

Stacey, C.P. " Mackenzie King Diaries, 1891-1931 ", *Canadian Historical Review* 58/2 (1977). 234-36.

Staebler, H. L."Mackenzie King," *Waterloo Historical Society* 38 (1951). 10-13.

Swainson, Donald. "Neurosis and Causality in Canadian History," *Queen's Quarterly* 89/3 (1982). 611-616.

Tessaro, Annamaria. "Mackenzie King in North Waterloo," *Waterloo Historical Society* 66 (1978). 18-40.

Waite, P. B. "Debauching the Archangels." *Beaver* 74/6 (1994-95). 17-28.

Waite, P. B. "Late Harvest: Mackenzie King and the Italian Lady," *Beaver* 75/6 (1995-96). 4-10.

Waite, P. B. "Mr. King and Lady Byng," *Beaver* 77/2 (1997). 24-30.

Ward, W. Peter. "British Columbia and the Japanese Evacuation," *Canadian Historical Review* 57/3 (1976). 289-309.

Wardhaugh, Robert. "Awaiting the Return of Commonsense: Mackenzie King and Alberta," *National History* 1/3 (1997).

Wardhaugh, Robert A. "A Marriage of Convenience? Mackenzie King and Prince Albert Constituency." *Prairie Forum* 21/2 (1996). 177-199.

Wardhaugh, Robert. "The 'Impartial Umpire' Views the West: Mackenzie King and the Search for the New Jerusalem." *Manitoba History* 29 (1995). 11-22.

Whitaker, Reginald. "The Liberal Corporatist Ideas Of Mackenzie King," *Labour* 2 (1977). 137-169.

Whitaker, Reginald. "Political Thought and Political Action in Mackenzie King," *Journal of Canadian Studies* 13/4 (1978-79). 40-60.

Wilbur, Richard. "Canada as Interpreted by W.L.M. King and Others," *Acadiensis* 7/1 (1977). 136-141.

The King Diaries

The Mackenzie King diaries are available to researchers on 492 microfiches (Toronto, University of Toronto Press, 1973-1980), and will soon to be available online through the National Archives of Canada website. A more accessible source for the post-1939 period is J.W. Pickersgill and Donald Forster, eds. *The Mackenzie King Record, vols. 1-4* (Toronto, University of Toronto Press, 1960-70), which provides an edited version of the diaries where the official biography stopped. These four volumes cover the main political issues revealed by King to his diary, but do not delve into King's personal peculiarities.

Index

The Life and Times of Confederation 1864-1867: Politics, Newspapers and the Union of British North America

P.B.Waite

Peter Waite's book on the events leading to the 1867 Confederation of British North American colonies is one of the best, and
liveliest, on the subject. This attractive new edition with pictures
of the places and people will appeal to all with an interest in
Canadian history and this seminal period in the country's
national life.

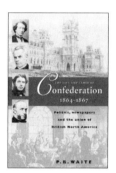

468 pages • 6 x 9 inches • approx 45 photos, 2 maps • endnotes, bibliography,
index • ISBN 1-896941-23-0 • paperback • Canada $24.95, U.S.A. $19.95

The Incredible War of 1812: A Military History

by J.M. Hitsman, updated by Donald E. Graves

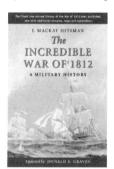

Widely regarded as the best one-volume history of the War of
1812, this book is available in a handsome paperback edition
with additional maps and illustrations and extensive new appendices and notes.

"A good book, lavishly illustrated, and its author is pleasantly unimpressed by conventional wisdom." *The Times Literary Supplement* on the 1st edition.

432 pages • 6 x 9 inches • about 60 pictures and maps • ISBN 1-896941-13-3 •
paperback • Canada $22.95, U.S.A. $18.95

Guns Across the River: The Battle of the Windmill, 1838

Donald E. Graves

In 1838, seeing political turbulence in Canada as an opportunity, a clandestine American organization, the Patriot Hunters, launched a series of attacks across the border.
The most ambitious took place in 1838 when a force occupied a windmill near Prescott,
Ontario. British regulars and Canadian militia captured
this "Alamo of the North" and the surviving invaders were
executed or deported to an Australian penal colony.
Donald E. Graves brings a fresh approach to an event often
regarded simply as an episode in the Canadian rebellions;
the American invaders, he maintains, hoped to emulate the
feats of Davy Crockett, Jim Bowie and the "Go Ahead Men"
who seized a large part of Mexico.

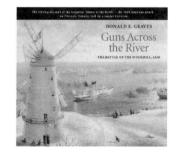

264 pages • 9 x 8 inches • about 100 pictures and maps •
ISBN 1-896941-21-4 • paperback • Canada $24.95, U.S.A. $19.95

Prices shown are Canadian and American prices at the time of publication. Different prices may apply in other markets.

Forgotten Patriots: Canadian Rebels on Australia's Convict Shores

Jack Cahill

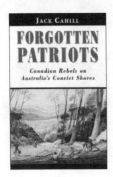

After the rebellions in Upper and Lower Canada in 1837-38 were suppressed, some of the rebels and their American supporters were hanged and some had their sentences commuted to "transportation for life." Based in part on journals written by the prisoners, this book tells of the scurvy and death on the crowded ships that carried them to Australia and of the hard life in the convict colonies, their attempted escapes, and the eventual return of many to Canada and the U.S.

288 pages • 5.5 x 8.5 inches • about 40 pictures and maps • ISBN 1-896941-07-9 • paperback • Canada $18.95, U.S.A. $16.95

Quebec, 1759: The Siege and the Battle

by C.P. Stacey, updated and edited by Donald E. Graves

Return of a classic by a superb military historian.

The fall of Quebec to British forces in 1759 led to the ultimate defeat of the French empire in North America. The dramatic battle on the Plains of Abraham which secured final victory for Major General James Wolfe not only set the course for the future of Canada – it opened the door to the independence of the American colonies some twenty years later.

In this handsome new edition, Stacey's text appears in its entirety. Editor Donald E. Graves has added picture essays and maps, appendices containing important new information, and updated references and bibliography, making this the most complete and authoritative book on the military operation that changed the course of history.

272 pages • 9 x 8 inches landscape • approx 150 pictures and maps • endnotes, appendices, bibliography, index • ISBN 1-896941-26-5 • paperback • Canada $27.95, U.S.A. $21.95

Robin Brass Studio Inc.

10 Blantyre Avenue

Toronto, ON M1N 2R4

Canada

For a complete description of all our books, visit www.rbstudiobooks.com